SAHARA

THE UNTOLD STORY

TAMAL BANDYOPADHYAY

JAICO PUBLISHING HOUSE

Ahmedabad Bangalore Bhopal Bhubaneswar Chennai
Delhi Hyderabad Kolkata Lucknow Mumbai

Published by Jaico Publishing House
A-2 Jash Chambers, 7-A Sir Phirozshah Mehta Road
Fort, Mumbai - 400 001
jaicopub@jaicobooks.com
www.jaicobooks.com

SAHARA: THE UNTOLD STORY
ISBN 978-81-8495-546-0

First Jaico Impression: 2014

Printed by
Rashmi Graphics
#3, Amrutwel CHS Ltd., C.S. #50/74
Ganesh Galli, Lalbaug, Mumbai - 400 012
E-mail: tiwarijp@vsnl.net

SAHARA INDIA PARIWAR DISCLAIMER

The book *Sahara: The Untold Story*, written by Shri Tamal Bandyopadhyay, is based on a particular notion, wrong perceptions supported by limited and skewed information. Hence, it does not reflect the true and complete picture.

The book portrays Sahara in bad light by attributing unfound facts and incidents to which we have objections.

The book also overlooks, or at the best just glances over, the contributions made by Sahara India Pariwar by financially including the poor and rural India, and inculcating in them the habit of saving, thus paving the road of progress on the one hand and safeguarding them from the clutches of money lenders and loans on the other.

This book on Sahara does not explain the fact of how Sahara in its journey of 37 years has become one of the biggest conglomerates of the country just because of the stout business ethics, quality business practices and years of relentless services to its customers and depositors, which has generated faith among crores of our depositors, investors and customers across the country.

The book also forgets to address this core constituent of the story of Sahara India Pariwar, about whom everyone talks but does not venture to know – the very poor depositors who have faith in us and whose hard-earned earnings Sahara is a faithful custodian of, for so many years.

The book at best can be treated as a perspective of the author with all its defamatory content, insinuation and other objections, which prompted us to exercise our right to approach the court of law in order to save the interest of the organization and its crores of depositors and 12 lakhs workers.

By getting the opportunity to put forward our objections and reservation in the form of a disclaimer in this book, in the best tradition of Sahara and our respect for a journalist's freedom, we are allowing the author to publish the book and withdrawing the case we had filed against the publication of the book.

We are sure that the readers are intelligent enough to see through the maze of plots and appreciate the values that we stand for and the activities we undertake for nation building.

We also wish the author success, though we don't agree with many of the things and the way they were presented in the book.

To Sir, the late Beetashok Bhattacharya,
the window to life and literature
during my college and university days

CONTENTS

PART III

PART IV

PREFACE

"All characters appearing in this work are fictitious. Any resemblance to real persons, living or dead, is purely coincidental."

This is a typical disclaimer that any work of fiction carries. But this book is different. None of the charters – living or dead – and incidents mentioned here are fictional. They all belong to the real world. *Sahara: The Untold Story* is not a creative work. It's a journalistic work – a result of painstaking research to demystify India's most secretive and largely unlisted conglomerate, the Sahara India Pariwar, which has excelled in raising money from people over decades and courted endless controversies.

I have sifted through thousands of pages of legal papers: affidavits, petitions, judgments of high courts and India's apex court; directives and notifications of regulators, both banking and markets; minutes of closed door meetings; and media reports. Besides, I have interviewed several people across India who have been associated with the group in one way or another – regulators, chartered accountants, legal experts and journalists who track the group.

I have also bought a packet of Davidoff cigarettes (though I am not a smoker) and a bottle of Grey Goose (and I'm not a vodka drinker either) to appreciate the finer taste of Subrata Roy, the Sahara India Pariwar boss.

I mention all this to explain my approach to a subject that is extremely complex – if not anything else, just for the mystery that shrouds it.

This book could well have been called "The Death of a Four-Letter Word". When I started the project, my objective was to understand the financial intermediary called residuary non-banking companies (RNBCs), named so for the lack of a better word, when two finance ministry bureaucrats were busy classifying all non-banks in the 1960s.

At the fag end of the day, they were tired but they could not leave their job unfinished as a cabinet note had to be prepared that night for presentation the next day. So, for want of a better word, a bunch of non-banks that were into neither home loans and car loans nor hire purchase and lease were called residuary non-banking companies, as they were residues in the list of non-banks.

Indeed, the RNBCs were subjected to directed lending norms, tightened in phases over the years, and capital adequacy ratio but the Reserve Bank of India (RBI) struggled to supervize them. There were month-long inspections of books by RBI inspectors every year, but the regulator was still not happy. It tightened the noose when YV Reddy became governor of the Indian central bank. I wanted to chronicle the growth and demise of RNBCs.

Sahara India Finance Corp. Ltd is the biggest among them, followed by the Peerless General Finance & Investment Co. Ltd. Peerless was born four-and-a-half decades before Sahara, in Bangladesh, when the world was in the grip of the biggest Depression. It grew by leaps and bounds in the 1970s and 1980s, even becoming the lender of last resort for some state governments. Peerless was able to challenge the RBI's authority at various courts, until a Supreme Court judgment dealt a blow to it in January 1996.

Its story is interesting but very different from that of Sahara's with all its mystery, secrecy, glitz and glamour. This is because of Sahara's promoter Roy's proximity to filmdom and sports and politicians of every hue. There are other differences as well: while Peerless went to court challenging the regulator, Sahara published advertisements in national newspapers congratulating the banking regulator for tightening the RNBC norms in 1987.

Roy, the guardian angel of the group, whose feet are touched by everybody in the Pariwar, is an entrepreneur who wants to reach out to a million lives and who feels claustrophobic in regulations. So, the clash with the regulators is inevitable. But when one regulator slams the door, Roy opens another. This play has been on since 1978 – when Sahara was set up.

Roy soaks in the glamour of cricket and the film world, and exudes patriotism, with a statue of Bharat Mata (the presiding deity of the group, on a chariot driven by four fierce-looking lions, representing four religious communities in India) adorning his headquarters in Lucknow. The other India, the millions of illiterate, poor depositors in northern and central

India, stands in awe of him. Roy is the Robin Hood of a country where only 35% of the adult population has access to formal banking services. But does he also exploit them? Do these poor people actually keep money with him or are they a front for others?

Sahara: The Untold Story is this story. The first chapter sets out the context; the second chapter is devoted to Peerless. Chapter three, four and five dwell on Sahara's fight with the RBI, a phase that is over. Chapter six and seven deal with its fight with India's capital market regulator, a phase not over as yet. Chapter eight portrays a few key people who are involved in the Sahara saga. Chapter nine is an attempt to demystify the Roy persona. And chapter ten is a crystal ball gazing into what lies ahead for the group.

The annexures that follow outline the history and growth of shadow banking; carry some of the communications between Sahara, RBI and others which are not in the public domain; and the timelines of the Peerless and the Sahara sagas.

For me, writing about a group that has 4,799 establishments and businesses under 16 verticals in its fold and is the second-largest employer in the country after the Indian Railways is similar to a blind man trying to describe an elephant. I don't have answers to all the questions, even though I have raised them. But they may help you, dear reader, to appreciate the complexities of the Indian financial system, the role of the regulators and judiciary, and offer you glimpses into the psyche of Roy and his pariwar, which no agency has understood fully as yet.

– Tamal Bandyopadhyay

ACKNOWLEDGEMENTS

At the outset, I profusely thank Subrata Roy of Sahara India Pariwar and SK Roy of the Peerless group who, despite their extremely busy schedules, met me and answered all my questions, including uncomfortable ones, with enormous patience and tolerance.

Subrata Roy also gave me an opportunity to experience, first hand, Sahara Shaher in Lucknow, a character in this book.

A big thanks to Khushboo Narayan who assisted me with the research for this book.

While working on the project, I met many people to understand their perception of Sahara, perspective of the RNBC sector, information and guidance. Most of them spoke to me off the record. That has radically shrunk the list of people whom I can formally thank. They are former RBI deputy governors SS Tarapore and the late SP Talwar, former Hindustan Lever Ltd chairman Sushim Mukul Datta, former State Bank of India (SBI) chairman Dipankar Basu, another former SBI chairman and also a former chairman of the Peerless General Finance & Investment

Co. Ltd DN Ghosh, chartered accountants YH Malegam and TN Manoharan, former RBI chief general manager Tulsidas Bandyopadhyay, additional chief secretary of Kerala Dr KM Abraham, former chairman and managing director of Peerless PC Sen, Association of Mutual Funds in India's chief executive officer HN Sinor, industrialist Parasmal Lodha, and Mani Shankar Mukherjee, better known as Sankar, a popular Bengali novelist.

I thank *Mint* and its editor R Sukumar for sparing me from my daily chores at the office for a few weeks to work on this project.

Feroze Jamal read the manuscript, raised incisive questions and made valuable suggestions.

I thank illustrator Shyamal Banerjee for his contribution to this book.

The author photo credit goes to Hemant Mishra.

Others who have chipped in, in various ways, ranging from making available decades-old reports to giving ideas, connecting with people and reading the manuscript, include RBI's principal chief general manager Alpana Killawala, retired banker GK Mishra, SK Giri of Bandhan Financial Services Pvt Ltd, K Kanagasabapathy, director of EPW Research Foundation, Saisuresh Sivaswamy, Somnath Dasgupta, Aniek Paul, Sunil B, Malvika Joshi, Pramit Bhattacharya and Sapna Agarwal.

Finally, I thank my son Sujan, the first reader of every chapter of this book, for his critical comments; and my wife Rita for tolerating my uninterrupted presence at home for weeks, a rare phenomenon in our married life. She was of great help when I burnt the midnight oil in my race against time to meet the deadline for the project.

Part 1

1

JANA-GANA-MANA

On a sweltering May morning in 2013, some 120,000 people were ferried in hundreds of buses hired by Sahara India Pariwar and herded to a large ground on the outskirts of Lucknow. They were on a mission – not theirs – to fulfill one man's dream of clinching an otiose world record: the largest number of people assembled in one place chorusing a national anthem. In this case, India's Jana Gana Mana.

Pakistan held the record until then, of 42,813 people singing its anthem:

Pāk sarzamīn shād bād

Kishwar-e-hasīn shād bād

Tū nishān-e-`azm-e-`ālīshān

Arz-e-Pākistān!

Markaz-e-yaqīn shād bād

Early that morning, crowds poured into the 51-acre Ramabai Ambedkar Rally Sthal – large enough for 30 football fields –

from the nearby cities of Faizabad, Barabanki and Rae Bareli.

The event began at 10am with Subrata Roy, reverently called Saharasri by his employees, and Subrata Roy Sahara in company handouts, speaking of India's greatness and his philosophy of "materialism with emotionalism" that had strung his group together against all adversities.

Roy is the managing worker and chairman of the Pariwar, a business conglomerate with 4,799 establishments in its fold and at least ₹1.52 trillion in assets, including a land bank of 36,631 acres along with business interests in real estate, finance, infrastructure, media and entertainment, health care and hospitality, retail, consumer products, information technology, cricket, hockey and Formula One racing.

High on nationalism, Roy addressed the congregation telling them how the blessings of Mother India, the group's deity, had helped Sahara weather the odds in its journey of 35 years. Then the chorus – Jana-Gana-Mana.

Enthusiasm, and patience, began to wane soon after and the crowd, perspiration dripping, began to fidget. Some tried heading for the nearest exit to the grounds, but the announcer chided them into staying back. "All those heading for the east exit are to immediately return to their places. Do not leave your spot until you are told to. There are cameras all around. The cameras are on you. Come back," the announcer blared.

Representatives of the *Guinness World Records* went through the crowd scribbling notes on clipboards as they took count. "Don't move. The survey officials are still taking a count. Please stay in your places," said the voice from the loudspeaker. Sahara didn't want even one warm body missing from the record's tally. A few hours later, Guinness gave its stamp of approval.

The Ramabai Ambedkar Rally Sthal was one of many places where the singing of the national anthem was staged on 6th May at 10am. In Delhi, the venue was the Indira Gandhi Stadium, the largest indoor sports arena in India which hosted indoor games during the 1982 Asian Games; in Mumbai, it was the Mumbai Metropolitan Region Development Authority grounds at the Bandra Kurla Complex, a venue for most big events in India's financial capital.

Sahara's event was meticulously planned and elaborately rehearsed to ensure its success. At meeting rooms of various Sahara offices, the lyrics were displayed on giant screens and all employees sang to the music, karaoke style, at least for a week before D-day. They rehearsed for hours on 6th May as well.

A sea of Sahara staff and agents – the men in the corporate uniform of black trousers, white shirt and a black tie with the Sahara logo, and the women in black-and-red bordered sarees – stood still holding miniature paper-made national flags. As they progressed to the last stanza of the anthem, they raised the flags for each refrain of Jaya He.

They sang the anthem standing at attention, head and eyes locked in a fixed posture, heels together, toes apart – the chin up, chest out, shoulders back and stomach in position. Days before the event, Sahara put out open invites in newspapers to all Indian citizens to stand at attention and sing the anthem wherever they might be – in schools, colleges, offices or even at traffic crossings – at 10am on 6th May, a Monday.

It asked readers to capture videos of their family members, friends, schoolmates or colleagues singing the anthem and upload these on YouTube and social media "for the whole world to witness the emotional integration, national integration of us, Indians." The Sahara group called the day Bharat Bhawna Diwas (a day to display Indian emotion).

Guinness World Records recognized the record the same day. It typically takes four to six weeks for Guinness to officially recognize a feat as a world record. But it also offers a fast-track process that guarantees a response to an application within three days, on payment of $700 or £450. And if someone wants an instant, on-site verification of a record attempt, one can invite a Guinness adjudicator.

To entice record-seekers with instant gratification, Guinness spices up its offering on its website:

"The presence of an official adjudicator will super-charge the profile and PR potential of your record attempt. The immediate verification of [a] record attempt not only means you can walk away with a *Guinness World Records* certificate but also allows the media to report the new world record straight away."

Of course, inviting a Guinness judge for instant verification comes at an additional cost. Later that week, the website of Sahara Samay, the group's Hindi news television channel, claimed that Sahara's 1.1 million workers (this is similar to Brussels's population) across 4,512 offices had joined in; as had army regiments in seven Indian states. Double-spread advertisements in national newspapers with photographs of the event in Lucknow, Delhi and Mumbai claimed that more than seven million students and five million people across India had sung the national anthem that day. That puts the total number at 13.1 million.

The group also took a Bharat Bhawna Diwas pledge "to free minds from the confines of religion, caste, section and class... To discard negative mindset that rejoices in criticizing others needlessly for sadistic pleasure."

The entire event was public theatre at its best – a show of strength by a group that many believe is well connected with political parties of all hues. And it was done by a conglomerate that is fighting its toughest, most public and pitched battle with an Indian regulator that has ordered a refund of ₹24,000 crore to 30 million of its depositors.

Roy's Bharat Bhawna Diwas was an attempt to demonstrate that he was a real nationalist being targeted by vindictive regulators for being a Robin Hood to India's vast unbanked poor. Only about 35% of India's adult population is covered under formal banking services according to a World Bank working paper.[1]

Enough is Enough

It wasn't the first time that Sahara had adopted such tactics to draw public attention. In the third week of March 2013, full-page advertisements splashed across national newspapers in India, screaming "Enough is Enough". These carried a

---

[1] "Measuring Financial Inclusion", World Bank policy research working paper April 2012, p51.

picture of Mother India, a saree-clad goddess bearing the national flag and riding a chariot drawn by four fierce lions, with the slogan, "Bharat Ma is our strength as a saviour from all evils."

With this, Sahara challenged the chairman or any senior executive of India's capital market regulator, the Securities and Exchange Board of India (Sebi), to a 60-minute live television debate with Roy. Through the debate – for which Sahara sought a 10-day notice – the group wanted to "expose the regulator" and the "extreme degree of injustice" it had done in maligning Sahara.

Predictably, Sebi chairman, UK Sinha, did not take up the challenge. In fact, Sinha couldn't be bothered to meet Roy when the Sahara chief visited the Sebi headquarters in Mumbai's Bandra Kurla Complex just weeks later in April. Not that Roy visited quietly; he had gone there with three directors of group companies in a convoy of four cars and a small army of bodyguards wielding machine guns. Roy and the three executives had been summoned to present details of their financial holdings and assets in an ongoing dispute related to bond sales to retail investors by two group firms without Sebi's approval. Prashant Saran, a full-time member of Sebi, met them.

After the hour-long meeting, clad in a half-sleeve white shirt, waistcoat and dark trousers, Roy gave an impromptu speech in Hindi outside Sebi headquarters to the media representatives eagerly waiting for sound bytes. The speech was laced with homilies: "*Aaj ek ghanta Sebi ne bithaya humhe. Ummeed thi ki ek pyali chai ke liye poochenge; lekin woh bhi nahi poocha.*" (Today, Sebi made us wait for an hour. We had hoped for a cup of tea; we were not offered even that.) He also said, "*Is duniya mein kisi sahi aadmi ko galat nahi thehraya ja sakta hai, aur kisi galat aadmi ko sahi nahi.*" (Nobody in this world can project an honest person as dishonest or vice-versa.)

Those who were present at the meeting say, Roy was aggressive initially but cooled down when Saran told him that he would have to sign a piece of paper that would record the proceedings of the meeting. Roy and the other directors were asked to list their assets.

Of all the meetings Roy has had with Sebi and the RBI chiefs over the past decade, about his companies accessing public money, whether in the form of deposits or debentures, he would probably best remember his encounter with CB Bhave, Sinha's predecessor at Sebi. Bhave had put his foot down on clearing the draft red herring prospectus of Sahara Prime City Ltd, which contained information on the group's massive money-raising activities and did not conform to the norms of the capital market regulator. This snowballed into the biggest-ever crisis for Roy's empire, which he had built brick by brick over 36 years.

In June 2010, following normal practice, Roy was ushered into a meeting room adjacent to the Sebi chairman's room on the seventh floor of the headquarters, Sebi Bhawan. Their conversation, according to Sebi insiders, went something like this:

Roy: The Reserve Bank has prejudiced Sebi officers. They are taking a negative view on Sahara's (initial public offering) application without justification.

Bhave: What's the issue? They are yet to get the information they had asked for. Where's the bias? Submit the information. We can have another meeting on this...

Roy: We have taken legal opinion and we are not required to send the information to Sebi. Our regulator is the ministry of corporate affairs. Even former presiding officer of SAT (Securities Appellate Tribunal) Mr. C Achuthan had advised me that you cannot have two regulators like a citizen cannot have two *thanas* (police stations). As we don't accept two regulators, we will not give documents. Why don't you take them from the ministry of corporate affairs like you took information on RNBCs from the RBI?

Bhave: Sebi is not concerned about the legal opinion. Sebi has *asked* for the information and it needs to be submitted.

Roy: They are voluminous. It's summer and many of my people have gone on leave. It's difficult to collate all the information.

Bhave: Let the employees come back from their summer holiday. We will wait.

Roy: If you can clear the application meanwhile...

Bhave: No, no. That can't happen. We need to scrutinize...

Roy (suddenly standing up): *Bus, itna hi?* (That's all?)

Bhave: *Maine jitna bola kafi hai... Aur kuch bolu?* (I have said enough. Should I say more?)

Roy didn't utter another word. He stood up, greeted Bhave with folded hands in the gesture of a *namaste*, and left. The meeting lasted about 15 minutes, over a cup of tea.

When Sinha took over from Bhave at Sebi, he too met Roy at the office. Phone calls from many quarters preceded the meeting where Roy, as was his wont, told Sinha how he had been harassed by the RBI and Sebi so far, and that he would like Sinha to see things in their right perspective.

127 Trucks; 31,000 Metal Trunks

Indeed, the records were voluminous. Almost two-and-a-half years and a protracted legal battle with the market regulator later, on 10th September, 2012, a truck with Uttar Pradesh registration (UP-32-CZ-7837) carried aluminium cartons containing documents to the Sebi office at Bandra Kurla Complex. A second truck that accompanied it carried a Maharashtra number plate (MH-04-CP-2147). These were only two of 127 trucks that would ferry the necessary documents in 31,000 cartons – an unprecedented event in Indian corporate history.

Initially, Sebi did not allow the trucks inside its premises and was unwilling to accept the documents beyond office hours or in installments. The Supreme Court deadline set for supplying the data to Sebi had expired on 10th September.

The Supreme Court had, on 31st August 2012, directed two Sahara companies – Sahara India Real Estate Corp. Ltd and Sahara Housing Investment Corp. Ltd – to refund to investors in three months all the money they had collected by selling optionally fully convertible debentures, or OFCDs, decisively ending a three-year tussle between the regulator and Sahara in favour of Sebi.

India's highest court had upheld the order of the market regulator and that of its appellate tribunal directing the two firms to refund the money after accusing them of violating regulatory norms by raising money through the debentures from the public in the guise of private placements.

Sahara in a 12th September statement said the documents had been stored in warehouses in Lucknow, the site of Sahara's headquarters. A few trucks left the city on 7th September carrying the first consignment of papers but they were delayed due to monsoon rains and couldn't reach the Sebi office in Mumbai before the deadline. Typically, monsoon arrives in most parts of India in June every year and lasts till September.

Via National Highway 3, the distance from Lucknow to Mumbai is a little less than 1,400 km and a vehicle could take up to 23 hours to drive down the stretch, depending on the road and traffic conditions. But a truck takes longer as it can cover at best around 250 km a day.

This was not the sole reason for delay. Assuming that each of Sahara's 30 million investors (that's equal to the population of Malaysia) had just one A4 size document each to account for their investments in Sahara's debentures, the papers stacked up in a pile would be 3,800 metres tall, or 52 times the height of the Qutub Minar, the tallest minaret in India and a world heritage site.

End-to-end, the documents would form a 6,300-km line, twice the distance between the northern and southern ends of the country. And the weight of these documents would be at least 120 tonnes, equivalent to 40 Indian elephants. Sahara said 500 people had been working in three shifts round the clock at its Lucknow warehouse with 20 photocopying machines. Even then, it would take years to finish making the copies. Sahara also offered the estimate that the exercise would take 275 days if there were 1,500 people and 50 photocopying machines engaged in the work.

Incidentally, 202 nations have populations smaller than the total number of investors in Sahara's optionally fully convertible debentures.

In August 2012, an Internet meme claimed Samsung Corp., upset with losing a patent case to Apple Inc., sent 30 trucks full of 5-cent coins to the iPhone maker to settle a $1 billion fine. Not true, of course. Sahara went several steps ahead and actually sent 127 trucks carrying 31,000 metal trunks of documents to Sebi.

The documents are stored at the office of Stock Holding Corp. of India Ltd House (SHCIL), at Mahape, an industrial area of Navi Mumbai that houses, among others, a huge campus of Reliance Industries Ltd, India's largest private sector company by revenue. Most offices occupy huge swathes of land and SHCIL, a custodian and depository services firm, is no different: it is one massive building spread across five acres, about 1 km away from the Thane creek hazardous waste disposal facility.

The vast storage space at SHCIL was built to store share certificates. It used to buzz with activity until the mid-1990s, when Sebi introduced dematerialization of shares – for holding securities electronically – after a duplicate share scam hit the Indian market.

With 3.2 million cubic feet in storage capacity, spread over four floors, SHCIL has four bays – each about 12.20 metres high, 100 metres long and 15 metres wide. Through the use of robotics, SHCIL is able to locate any document in just three minutes and deliver it at a client's office in Mumbai within hours and outside the city in 24 hours.

The facility provides end-to-end solutions for document

management – starting with the collection of documents from clients' offices, to digitization, scanning and condensation so that they occupy minimal space on the server. It also provides password protection and a search engine. This is followed by physical storage of documents, and even destruction of documents at the client's request.

Each document is stored in a plastic pouch and each pouch is bar-coded and stored in fire-resistant cartons. Air-conditioning increases the shelf life of the papers. Old documents are fumigated before digitization is taken up.

Media reports suggest Sebi had contracted SHCIL for storing, digitizing and scanning investor documents and creating a database, at ₹25.97 crore. Originally, Sebi had floated a tender for the job to choose the lowest bidder, but it was found that the winner was working for the Sahara group. So, Sebi junked the tender and went to SHCIL Projects Ltd, a subsidiary of SCHIL.

SHCIL Projects has about a hundred officers on its rolls and can outsource work for special assignments, like handling the Sahara papers. The area is a high-security zone with biometric systems controlling entry to the place where documents are stored. Even the lifts have different swipe cards to restrict entry.

As one enters the SHCIL office premises from the east gate, the view of the building is backed by hills. The storage unit, at the northern end of the edifice, shares a compound wall with a slum settlement. Four guards man the area 24x7 and a board reminds trespassers that entry is restricted.

Over 100,000 sq ft of storage facility is maintained three floors below ground. For days, at 9:30am, migrant labourers called *dehadis* unloaded the Sahara cartons from the trucks and took them to the ground floor of the storage unit.

The cartons were sent to the underground facility through conveyor belts where robots arranged them neatly. The scanning room is on the second floor of the building. After the documents were scanned, they were kept in labelled metal trunks, each weighing around 30 kg. Twenty labourers worked day and night for eight days to move the Sahara boxes to the ground floor unit.

The arrival of the Sahara data forced SCHIL to beef up security, even adding two security cameras to the previously existing four. "*Danger wala kaam hai. Documents bahut sensitive hai na*" (It is a critical assignment as the documents are very sensitive), one of the guards said when the author tried a recce at the facility.

Very Sensitive Document

SCHIL's task appeared difficult but it was nothing compared with what Sebi had let itself in for. The regulator needed to check whether the documents were genuine, for which it needed to hire experts, consultants and even investigators. The process was painful.

There was, for instance, an investor by the name Kalawati. The document relating to her doesn't list the names of her father or husband. Her address doesn't include a door number, street or locality. The name of her agent is given as Haridwar, which is also the name of a pilgrimage city in Uttaranchal. Kalawati figures 5,984 times in different locations on Sahara's list of investors, according to an *Indian*

Express news report from May 2013.

Incidentally, one Kalawati was present at the Supreme Court with her affidavit.

Brushing aside the "5,984 Kalawatis", Roy said, "we have seen in the past some 13,000 Atal Behari Vajpayees among Sahara investors."

The Supreme Court in its order expressed its bemusement at some of these inexplicable facts. "In India, names of cities do not ever constitute the basis of individual names. One will never find Allahabad, Agra, Bangalore, Chennai or Tirupati as individual names," the court said.

Sahara has an explanation for such addresses and names. According to the group, investors in India can simply be identified by their names; in semi-urban areas one may need a few more details, such as street names, to identify the investors, but only for urban areas is a complete address required.[2]

In one of its letters to Sebi, Sahara wrote, "Once again our humble request to you to take all information from the ministry of corporate affairs... There may be jurisdictional problems among regulators as happened between Sebi and IRDA (Insurance Regulatory Development Authority) recently; still business and industry like us should not be put as party in cross fire (sic), as it is happening with us. Please do not make SIRCEL (a) disobedient company in the eyes of the regulator, i.e., the ministry of corporate affairs."

---

[2] Securities and Exchange Board of India order – WTM/KMA/CFD/392/06/2011, dated 23 June 2011. Page 43.

Sahara offered to assist Sebi identify the investors on its list. In fact, as per the Supreme Court order, Sebi is supposed to contact Sahara if it finds any irregularities regarding investors' identities, but Roy says Sebi never contacted Sahara when it conducted the snap verification in Mumbai. "They are manipulating everything to harm Sahara."

For the record, Sahara has always insisted that it opened OFCDs for those who were already connected with the group through other schemes.

Sebi attempted a snap verification of any four addresses from a randomly selected locality in Mumbai. It took the aid of India Post to find the investors at the addresses given, but could not trace them. It could identify two who had invested in the contentious OFCDs. These investors said they had put money into the OFCD issues on being approached by Sahara agents. The investors had no association with the Sahara group.[3]

That blew the lid off Sahara's argument that its OFCDs were privately placed with group associates and not by way of a public issue. This kicked off the bitter battle that Sahara has since been fighting nonchalantly with Sebi, after conceding defeat in a similar battle with the banking regulator.

---

[3] Securities and Exchange Board of India order – WTM/KMA/CFD/392/06/2011, dated 23 June 2011. Page 87.

2

A PEERLESS STORY

A 30-year-old Subrata Roy set up Sahara in 1978 with a capital of ₹2,000, a peon and a clerk, and his father's Lambretta scooter, in Gorakhpur, eastern Uttar Pradesh. For the three-year diploma holder in mechanical engineering from a Gorakhpur college and a student of Holy Child School in Kolkata and CM Anglo Bengali Intermediate College in Varanasi, this was not the first venture. Before starting the deposit-taking business, he had loaded sacks on a truck; supplied stones to the state irrigation department in Gopulganj, Bihar; devised a test for purity of silver and sold electric fans. The brand name of the fan was Air Sahara, which later became the name of his aviation venture. He had also sold salted snacks, Jaya Products, named after his brother, Joy Broto.

Gorakhpur is close to the India-Nepal border, about 265 km from the state capital, Lucknow. Named after saint Gorakhnath, a Hindu tantrik and ascetic, Gorakhpur is known for Hindi litterateur Munshi Premchand; Gita Press, which publishes the Hindu scriptural texts and discourses of eminent saints; the Makar Sankranti fair at Gorakhnath Temple; and of course, Roy.

After the death of his father, Sudhir Chandra Roy, who was a sugarcane technologist at a sugar mill in Uttar Pradesh, Subrata Roy, the eldest son, experimented with quite a few ventures, some along with his wife, Swapna Roy. All failed, according to a 2003 biography on Roy titled *Bangalir Vitta Sadhana: Saharar Itikatha* (A Bengali's Practice of Finance: The Sahara Story), by popular Bengali novelist Sankar.[1]

His para-banking venture took deposits from investors, sometimes as little as ₹1 a day. By 2008, Sahara India Financial Corp. Ltd (SIFCL) was India's largest residuary non-banking company, or RNBC, with a deposit portfolio of ₹20,000 crore, more than double the deposit base of at least one new private bank, DCB Ltd.

In July that year, Sahara India Financial made public its unaudited financial results for the first time. This happened after the banking regulator imposed a three-year sunset window on Sahara, allowing it to accept fresh deposits maturing in June 2011.

The RBI had been forced to act because of alleged persistent violations of its investment norms by Sahara. The Indian central bank accused Sahara India Financial of not following its rules regarding payment of a prescribed minimum rate of interest to depositors, regarding asset-liability management

---

[1] *Bangalir Vitta Sadhana: Saharar Itikatha*, (A Bengali's Practice of Finance: The Sahara Story), Sankar, Sahityam, 18 B Shyamacharan Dey St, Kolkata – 700 073.

guidelines and the so-called know-your-customer (KYC) norms for opening deposits, as well as for failing to inform investors when their deposits matured.

₹1 Company

Forty-six years before the birth of the Sahara group, another Bengali entrepreneur had set up India's first shadow bank or RNBC – a much-abused vehicle in India's financial system, looked down upon by regulators as a four-letter word. He too was a Roy. Radhashyam Roy was a teacher at BM Union High School and an insurance agent for Prudential Insurance Company and Sunlife Insurance of Canada at Narayanganj in what is now central Bangladesh, 14 km from Dhaka. He was 33 when he set up Peerless Insurance Co. Ltd on 25 October 1932 – during the Great Depression – with a capital of ₹300. He founded this with his friend Kali Kumar Chatterjee. An actuary, AT Pal, joined him in the venture.

Narayanganj, on the banks of river Sitalakhya, a distributary of the Brahmaputra, was called the Dundee of Bangladesh, after Scotland's Dundee city, the world's first industrialized jute-polis. It was a centre of business and industry, known especially for its jute trade and textiles mills.

Long before Sahara, Peerless would collect premiums of as little as ₹1 a day, earning it the nickname '₹1 Company'. In 1935, Peerless shifted its headquarters to Kolkata, then Calcutta, India's business capital under the British Raj, to compete directly with British insurance firms.

In 1956, when India nationalized the insurance industry, an innovative Radhashyam Roy changed the company's profile by floating Peerless Social Welfare Scheme and mopping up savings under monthly, quarterly, half-yearly and yearly schemes. Thousands of agents of defunct life insurance companies joined Peerless and it flourished until the RBI found irregularities in its accounting in the 1980s.

Unlike Sahara, which first fought with the banking regulator and then with the Indian markets watchdog, Peerless fought with only the RBI, but that has been a protracted legal battle in high courts and the Supreme Court. However, like Sahara, Peerless too accepted the RBI's diktat asking it to wind down its deposit-taking business. In its heyday, Peerless had a deposit portfolio of ₹10,000 crore.

The main complaint against Peerless was an accounting issue: it treated first-year deposits not as liability but as income. From the customers' perspective, the lapse and forfeiture of deposits were the most critical issues. The drop in commission in following years meant not all agents would collect deposits after the first couple of years and the depositors were the losers.

On the same day he established Peerless Life Insurance Co. Ltd, 25 October 1932, Radhashyam Roy also incorporated Hollywood Pictures Ltd, a film production company. Those weren't his first ventures though. A few days earlier, Roy had launched the Indian National Bank Ltd. His rush to set up these businesses wasn't born as much from any entrepreneurial drive as it was by a perceived slight. Roy had failed to get a government job despite apparently scoring well in the interview. He vowed not to work for anyone else.

That was essentially Roy from his early years, guided more by his heart than his head. Once, when just 15, he picked ₹15 from his elder brother's wallet, left a note under a pillow, and travelled some 500 km from home to Jairambati village in West Bengal's Bankura district. He had decided to lead a monastic life and went there to meet Ma Sarada, wife of the 19th-century mystic Ramakrishna Paramhansa. Ma sent him back.[2]

The story of the Indian National Bank is rather short. Roy and his friend Kali Kumar Chatterjee, the co-promoter of Peerless, wanted to get it a scheduled bank tag in 1943, but the communal riots ahead of the India-Pakistan partition delayed the plan. A scheduled bank is one that is included in the second schedule of the Reserve Bank of India Act 1934 and fulfils certain criteria laid down in Section 42(6)(A) of the Act, in terms of net worth, meeting all reserve requirements, filing returns, being inspected and supervised by the regulators and other such guidelines.

Also, as a logical extension of the film production company, they built Jayshree Cinema Hall at Baranagar in northern Calcutta. It was slated to open on 16 August 1946, but before that could happen, the cinema theatre was handed over to a creditor of the Indian National Bank as it went into liquidation.

With the bank and the theatre gone, Peerless Life Insurance became the flagship company. Roy shifted its headquarters

---

[2] *Peerless – Beej Theka Mohiruho* (Peerless – From Seeds to a Tree), Leela Deb, daughter of Radhashyam Roy, 1996, p14.

from Narayangung to Calcutta in 1935 and Peerless began competing with British insurance firms.

When India nationalized its insurance industry in January 1956, Peerless (and 244 other insurance companies and provident societies) merged with the state-run Life Insurance Corp. of India. Overall, 154 life insurance companies, 16 foreign insurers and 75 provident companies were merged.

India reopened the life insurance industry in 2000, allowing private entities to enter the sector. The first two private companies to open insurance shops post this event were two large Indian financial groups – HDFC Ltd and ICICI Bank Ltd.

Following the nationalization of its insurance firm, the Peerless group floated another company the same year: Peerless General Insurance and Investment Co. Ltd. The word 'insurance' stayed in the name.

In the world of insurance, forfeiture of deposits plays a critical role in generating income. Peerless thrived on this. It became one of the issues on which Peerless fought with the banking regulator at the Calcutta High Court and the Supreme Court for over two decades, till it lost.[3] The other bone of contention was Peerless treating deposits in the first year of a policy as income and not as liability, an actuarial practice followed in insurance.

Post the 1956 nationalization of the life insurance industry, Peerless General Insurance also began issuing welfare certificates under the Peerless Social Welfare Scheme. It

[3]The non-forfeiture clause in an insurance policy allows for the insured to receive all or a portion of the benefits or a partial refund on the premiums paid if the policy lapses over missed premium payments.

mopped up people's savings – a ₹10 premium – under monthly, quarterly, half-yearly and annual schemes, laced with free accident covers from National Insurance Co. Ltd, an outfit of General Insurance Corp. of India.

"Radhashyam Roy saw significant value in serving the smaller savers. Peerless became a generic term. People used to say they are doing Peerless," says former State Bank of India chairman Dipankar Basu, who joined the board of Peerless in 1997 at the insistence of DN Ghosh, then the company's non-executive chairman.

Incidentally, Peerless in 1956 became the first company in India to offer recurring deposits – a variation of term deposits – that help people with regular incomes to deposit a fixed amount every month. Commercial banks started offering these in 1964 and India Post in 1970.

The company never got into the business of general insurance though it had deposited a licence fee with the Controller of Insurance, headquartered in Simla. On 22 October 1974, the word 'insurance' was finally dropped and replaced by 'finance' in the company's name: Peerless General Insurance and Investment Co. Ltd became Peerless General Finance and Investment Co. Ltd.

The BK Regime

The founder Roy passed away in 1960 and his eldest son Bhudeb Kanti Roy took over the group. A bachelor, known as BK in social circles, he began in the company as director and secretary before being named managing director in 1980. Under his stewardship, the business grew in leaps and bounds.

Sometime in 1975, a team of four senior executives visited the UK, the US and Canada to promote the welfare certificates among non-resident Indians. Ajit Kumar Chatterjee, son of the original co-promoter Kali Kumar Chatterjee, was made Peerless's chief London representative. His father died in September 1980.

At home, Peerless's first office outside Kolkata opened in Siliguri, northern Bengal, on 8 May 1970 and, in 1978, the then industries minister, George Fernandes, inaugurated the Delhi branch at Connaught Place.

To entice savers, Peerless began offering life insurance to depositors, through a tie-up with a state-run company, without any extra cost in 1972. In the same year, it introduced an automatic promotion system for agents that gave a dramatic boost to sales. In this so-called pyramid system, the agents formed the base, but a fast-track promotion policy made them special agents, sub-organizers, organizers and then inspectors in quick succession, depending on how much money they were mopping up.

A year later, the RBI issued a directive saying Peerless could only take deposits up to one-fourth of its share capital and reserves. At that time, Peerless's share capital was ₹300,000 and it could not have continued with the business had Peerless failed to convince the regulator to give it an exemption. The RBI relaxed the norm, but put them under other stringent conditions, including regular inspection by the regulator.

By 1982, when Peerless celebrated its golden jubilee, it had 400,000 agents and field officers and some 17 million customers. Fourteen years later, in 1996, when the RBI forced it to recast its board, Peerless had 40 million depositors.

The central office of the RBI's department of non-banking companies that supervises NBFCs and RNBCs is located in Kolkata. This is because historically, West Bengal had the maximum number of RNBCs. Many of them were inspired by Peerless and wanted to emulate its formula of money raising even as quite a few Peerless agents left the fold and started their own business. The other state that witnessed mushrooming of deposit-taking companies in the 1980s was Kerala.

Awash with Gulf money, the southern state gave birth to hundreds of partnership firms that raised money offering 40% or more interest and gave loans at even higher rates. They earned the sobriquet of 'blade company' as they used to cut both the depositors (as many lost money) and borrowers (because of high rates). One of the main sources of income for these companies was giving loans for film production. Some RNBCs in West Bengal also gave money to film producers.

Complex, Dogged Legal Battle

Unable to contain Peerless's growth, which, the RBI felt, was putting millions of small savers at risk, the central bank continued to tweak its light-touch regulations for RNBCs to tighten the noose around Peerless. But each time RBI did that, Peerless moved the court, challenging the regulator. It was a complex, dogged legal battle that spanned more than two decades, a kind not seen in India's corporate history until then. In terms of drama, however, it pales into insignificance when compared with Sahara's battle with the market regulator.

Representing Peerless were legal luminaries such as Siddhartha Shankar Ray, a Congress politician, former chief minister of West Bengal and a governor of Punjab; Somnath Chatterjee, a Communist Party of India (Marxist) leader who would later become the Speaker of the Lok Sabha, the lower house of India's Parliament; and Ashoke Kumar Sen, law minister in Jawaharlal Nehru's Cabinet.

The RBI was represented by Shanti Bhusan, who was a minister of law and justice in the Morarji Desai ministry and reportedly charged ₹1 lakh per appearance; and Harish Salve, who later became the Solicitor General of India.

Under Peerless's small savings schemes, people paid a fixed sum as subscription yearly, half-yearly, quarterly or monthly for years. On the expiry of the maturity period, the subscriber was paid an endowment amount – the face value of the certificate and certain additional amounts by way of bonus. Could this arrangement be called a deposit? Did the RBI have the authority to regulate this? These were some of the critical questions that Indian courts tried to figure out between 1979 and early 1996 while the Chatterjees and Salves were at their oratory best.

To regulate deposit-taking by non-banks, the Reserve Bank of India Act was amended by inserting Chapter III-B [Section 45 (H) to 45 (Q)] in 1963. This empowered the regulator to call for information from financial institutions and give directions. Following this, the RBI issued three sets of directions to regulate acceptance of deposits by non-banking companies, categorizing them into financial, non-financial and miscellaneous companies.

In 1966, it issued directions for non-banking financial companies engaged in hire-purchase finance, housing finance, investments, loan equipment leasing, mutual benefit business, etc., as well as for non-banking non-financial companies (neither a banking company nor a financial company).

Later, the Miscellaneous Non-Banking Companies (Reserve Banking) Directions, 1973, covered entities engaged in the business of collecting money in one lump sum or otherwise. This covered companies selling units, certificates or other instruments to raise capital and using the money to award a specified number of subscribers by lot, draw, prizes or gifts. Subscribers not lucky enough to win any of these would be refunded the money with or without interest.

Instantly, Peerless, which was raising money through certificates but not giving away prizes through draws to its subscribers, sought exemption from complying with the directions. The RBI granted such exemption while capping the company's money-raising limit at 25% of the paid-up capital and its free reserve fund. In 1977, the RBI went a step further and fixed a ceiling for deposits – 36 months under the Miscellaneous Non-Banking Companies (Reserve Bank) Directions.

Predictably, Peerless sought exemption from these provisions as well, and even before the RBI could react to it, India's Parliament passed the Prize Chits and Money Circulation Schemes (Banning) Act, 1978. Armed with that, the state government on 10 August 1979 banned Peerless immediately from doing fresh business and asked it to wind up its existing business.

That was the beginning of a hard fought legal battle that

lasted till 1996 and ended with the RBI's victory over Peerless. It led to a reconstruction of the company's board and a change in its business model. But while the legal fight was on, such was the might of Peerless that RBI officials were given special security at the hearings in Calcutta High Court.

Round One

Peerless filed a writ petition in the Calcutta High Court on 3 September 1979 claiming the Prize Chits and Money Circulation Schemes (Banning) Act, 1978 did not apply to its business. A division bench of the high court agreed with it and an interim order was passed in favour of Peerless, first for a limited period, and later, till the disposal of the writ petition.

Years later, in 1987, the Supreme Court concurred with the subordinate court. But it allowed the RBI to regulate schemes such as those run by Peerless "to prevent exploitation of ignorant subscribers while taking care of the thousands of employees." That part of the ruling was crucial, but it took ten years for the RBI to get this power and by then Peerless had grown substantially.

"It does not require much imagination to realize the adventurous and precarious character of these businesses. Urgent action appears to be called for to protect the public. While on the one hand these schemes encourage two vices affecting public economy, the desire to make quick and easy money and the habit of excessive and wasteful consumer spending, on the other hand, the investors who generally belong to the gullible and less affluent classes have no security whatsoever. Action appears imperative," the court said.

This encouraged the RBI to issue the Residuary Non-Banking Companies (Reserve Bank) Directions, 1987, which disallowed deposits below one year or above ten years. It also fixed the minimum rate of return for 10-year deposits at 10% per annum.

It further stipulated how the money was to be deployed: at least 10% in fixed deposits with a public sector bank; at least 70% in approved securities; and not more than 20% or 10 times the net-owned funds of the company, whichever was lower, in other investments, with the approval of the board of the company.

Most importantly, the RBI made it clear that from15 May 1987, no RNBC could forfeit any amount deposited by a depositor, or any interest or premium bonus. "Every residuary non-banking company shall disclose as liabilities in its books of accounts and balance sheets, the total amount of deposits received together with interest, bonus, premium or other advantage, accrued or payable to the depositors," RBI said in its directions. Forfeits, former Peerless chairman DN Ghosh said, had become "the mainstay of many RNBCs".

Peerless paid agents a commission of 30% on first-year subscription payments towards a scheme and 5% on payments for subsequent years. Some say it had paid even higher commission in the 1970s and '80s. The high initial commission was a disincentive for collecting payments for subsequent years, resulting in defaults in payments and forfeiture of the money paid earlier.

Even within Peerless, not everyone was happy with the forfeiture clause. Ajit Kumar Chatterjee, who later became the vice chairman of Peerless and who claimed Radhashyam Roy, his father's friend, was his teacher, wrote in his book: "Without forfeited money, the whole organization would collapse," and "Forfeiture is like a cancer to Peerless." Forfeiture was Rule No. 2 in Peerless's rule book.

To BK, it was a legal issue; but to Chatterjee, it was a fundamental question.[4]

India Today, in its 30 April 1983 article "A Peerlees Money Spinner", wrote on the risks to small savers:

"How many people would invest their savings in a private company that offers a lower rate of interest than the banks, pockets a part of the savings deposits for administrative costs and refuses to return the savings under certain circumstances? The answer is 12 million people and their deposits total over ₹300 crore."

BK, by then the managing director of Peerless, defended his company in a letter to the editor of *India Today*:

"Your report mentions about the lapsed certificates but fails to point out that the company offers many incentives for continuation of certificates including the special facilities for reviving a certificate, even without payment of arrears. Finally, the certificate holders' money is absolutely safe, since their funds are invested entirely in government custody. All these are fundamental differences between Peerless and

---

[4] A *Peerless Education*, Ajit Kumar Chatterjee, 1999, p110

other non-banking savings companies."

Round Two

The RBI's 1987 directions provoked another RNBC, Timex General Finance and Investment Co. Ltd, to file a writ petition in the Calcutta High Court challenging the validity of the new regulations. A division bench of the court in 1990 disposed of the case but told the RBI to modify the directions and make them reasonable and workable to safeguard the interests of the depositors and protect the employees. Fishing in troubled waters, Peerless got itself involved as a respondent in the writ petition.

The RBI challenged the high court order in the Supreme Court, paving the path to a second round of the battle with Peerless. The company lost no time in filing a writ petition under Article 32 of Indian Constitution in the Supreme Court, challenging the validity of the directions.

Peerless contended that the RBI was not authorized to frame any directions prescribing the manner of investment of deposits, the method of accountancy to be followed or the manner in which the balance sheets and business of accounts were to be drawn. Peerless, following the actuarial method of insurance companies, treated a percentage of the sums collected under its certificates of deposits as part of its income. It used the money to pay commissions to the agents and for meeting other expenses. So, essentially, Peerless was generating working capital from the first-year payments.

What it was really doing was crediting the first-year installments to its profit and loss account to offset the high commissions paid to the agents. At any point in time, the liability for repayment of the deposits together with interest, as appearing in the balance sheet, was higher than the actuarial valuation of the liability. This discounted the future liability to its present value at the rate of earning (say 12%) while the liability for accrued interest was calculated at the rate of interest paid (say 6%).

The All India Field Officers Association, then claiming to represent 1.4 million field officers engaged by Peerless, said that if the 1987 Directions were upheld, Peerless would face closure and the agents would be thrown out on the streets.

However, the Supreme Court, announcing its judgment in 1992, supported the RBI's view that companies such as Peerless should find and invest their own working capital rather than use the deposits collected.

> "No-one can have fundamental right to do any unregulated business with the subscribers'/depositors' money.... No one would legitimately be expected to get immediate profits or dividend without capital investment.
>
> We are not impressed with the argument of Mr Somnath Chatterjee, learned senior advocate for the Peerless, that after some years Peerless will have to close down its business... The working capital is not needed every year as it can be rotated after having invested once. If the entire amount of the subscribers is deposited or invested in the proportion of 10% in public sector banks, 70% in approved securities and 20% in other investments, such amounts will also start earning interest which can be added and adjusted while depositing or investing the subsequent years of deposits of the subscribers."

YH Malegam, chartered accountant and a member of the RBI's Board for Financial Supervision (BFS), a sub-committee of the central board that oversees the work of the department of banking and non-banking supervision, played a critical role in the RBI's victory in this round.

Former RBI deputy governor SS Tarapore's elder brother, Phiroze Tarapore, was working with the research and development division of Tisco (now Tata Steel Ltd) in Jamshedpur. Malegam, a young article clerk in the chartered accountant firm Billimoria & Co., went to Jamshedpur on work in 1952 and struck up a lifelong friendship with Phiroze. One morning in 1992, Tarapore called Malegam, by then a partner in Billimoria, and sought his help.

Malegam wrote a two-page note for submission in the Supreme Court. His argument was impeccable – the character of a receipt cannot be changed by an accounting treatment; deposits or capital receipts cannot become income even if the present value of the liability is less than what has been projected.

Malegam has served as a director on the RBI board since 1994 (with a less-than-a-month gap in 2012). Only Purushottam Das Thakurdas, an industrialist, was a director at the RBI for a longer period – from 1937 to 1949 – but he was an elected board member whereas Malegam was nominated.

After the Supreme Court decision, Peerless shifted to a commission scheme. Out of a monthly installment of, say, ₹100, ₹70 would be treated as deposit in the first two years of subscription. The balance ₹30 would be charged as processing fees in the first year and as maintenance charges in the second year.

The central bank plugged the loophole on 19 April 1993 by amending the 1987 Directions and inserting Paragraph 4A: "No residuary non-banking company shall take from any depositor/subscriber to any schemes run by the company, with or without his consent, any amounts towards processing or maintenance charges or any such charges, by whatever name called, for meeting its revenue expenditure."

It, however, allowed RNBCs to charge a one-time fee of up to ₹10 from a depositor towards the cost of issuing brochures and application forms and servicing the account. At the same time, it cut the maximum maturity period for deposits from 120 months to 84 months.

Round Three, the Final One

Peerless again filed a writ petition in the Calcutta High Court, this time against this reduced tenure. The court in May 1995 upheld the RBI's action, but did not allow it to lower the commissions. That set the stage for the third and final round of legal battle in the Supreme Court. This time around, the RBI filed an appeal against the high court order.

Salve, representing the RBI in the Supreme Court, said that the central bank was regulating the conditions by which deposits may be accepted by non-banking companies or institutions and preventing malpractices.

Somnath Chatterjee, the Communist Parliamentarian and lawyer, contended that the money Peerless collected from subscribers of its schemes could not be called deposits and thus, were not liabilities on the company. He argued that the RBI's action – fixing a uniform maximum ceiling of ₹10 a month towards operations costs irrespective of the volume of business transacted and the technology adopted for rendering the services – violated the right to equality guaranteed under Article 14 of the Indian Constitution.

RNBCs were being targeted, he argued, while banks were allowed to levy service charges and asset management firms could pay their agents handsome commissions. Finally, he played a politically-sensitive card – the closure of Peerless would render 1.4 million agents without jobs.

Chatterjee, known for his debating skills in Parliament, was precise and at his argumentative best but didn't cut ice with the court. Setting aside the 1995 judgment of the Calcutta High Court and dismissing Peerless's writ petition, the Supreme Court in January 1996 said, "It cannot be denied that residuary non-banking companies, like Peerless, play a useful role in the economy by mobilizing savings by tapping that section of the people which the commercial banks are not able to tap. But at the same time, it cannot be ignored that there should be adequate protection for the funds entrusted to them by depositors and for that purpose it is necessary that the working of these companies should be closely monitored and supervised and adequate provisions should be made for enforcement of regulatory provisions that are made for the protection of the interest of the depositors."

The ₹1,400 Crore Hole in the Balance Sheet

The Supreme Court judgment forced Peerless to stop its

practice of treating the first-year deposits as income or even write it back. That created a ₹1,400 crore hole in its balance sheet. The actual negative net worth was ₹1,177 crore, but it got magnified as under RBI norms, Peerless had to achieve a capital adequacy ratio of 12%, to start with, and push it up to 16% after a few years.

DN Ghosh, the former finance ministry official who was instrumental in coining the term RNBCs, appeared on the scene to drive the rescue operations. Promoter Sunil Kanti Roy, or SK Roy, BK's brother, a commerce graduate from City College in Kolkata who took over as Peerless's managing director in August 1996, called Ghosh to head the company as its non-executive chairman. Ghosh's record possibly prompted Roy to set his eyes on him. He was also well known to state chief minister Jyoti Basu

Ghosh, before accepting the offer, reviewed the case and suggested to Peerless that the rectification programme set out by the RBI was reasonable and it should accept it. The sticking point was that Peerless was not willing to project the correct balance sheet as that would show large losses. The RBI wouldn't agree to formalize the rectification programme unless the balance sheet revealed the true position.

Ghosh met the RBI governor C Rangarajan and Tarapore and said that he would take over as chairman of Peerless only if it accepted the RBI's point on the balance sheet. The then finance minister Manmohan Singh and West Bengal chief minister Jyoti Basu also spoke with him.

In 1977, immediately after the Emergency when Indira

Gandhi lost power and the Left Front dethroned Congress chief minister Siddhartha Shankar Ray in West Bengal, Ghosh, at Basu's insistence, became adviser, institutional finance, attached to state finance minister Ashok Mitra. At the time, KS Krishnaswamy, then RBI deputy governor, had handed over an inspection report on Peerless to Ghosh.

It was sensational – the company was using small capital to raise huge money and there were a lot of irregularities in its operations. The RBI was prepared to liquidate the company. Mitra was of the view that the government should take it over. But by 1981, Gandhi was back in power and all the proposed actions against Peerless were stopped. Peerless accepted Ghosh's conditions and he took over as chairman in August 1996, in the same month that SK Roy became the managing director. After a 10-year stint, Ghosh stepped down in 2006. That was three years after Peerless closed the hole in its balance sheet and achieved a positive net worth. By that time, the auditor of the company had also changed – Mukund M Chitale & Co. replaced Lodha & Co.

So, what did Ghosh do right in the time that he was there? He was instrumental in getting Sushim Mukul Datta, former boss of Hindustan Unilever Ltd (then Hindustan Lever Ltd) and Dipankar Basu, former State Bank of India chairman, to join the board of Peerless. While Datta joined immediately, Basu took about a year as he needed the so-called cooling off period after stepping down as State Bank chairman in 1995. Amal Chandra Chakrabortti, a senior partner at audit firm SR Batliboi & Co. and a managing partner at Ernst & Young, joined a few years later. This quartet, with the help of

Peerless boss SK Roy, scripted the turnaround story. The RBI governor Bimal Jalan stood solidly behind the team. Then regulator was initiatilly keen on the Peerless group selling off its hospital venture to make good the hole in the balance sheet, but Ghosh convinced Jalan that even without selling the hospital business his team would be able to generate enough money to clean up the balance sheet.

None of them was an RBI nominee, but they had the blessings of the central bank. Roy chose Ghosh and Ghosh chose his team. Basu took charge of Peerless's investments; Datta handled its subsidiaries and associate companies; and Chakrabortti headed the audit committee, while Ghosh oversaw recoveries and overall organizational structure.

3,500 Employees Had to Go

"Much to my horror I discovered that Peerless had spawned 27 subsidiaries – hospital, IT, shipping, real estate... you name it," Ghosh told me. By liquidating most of these, he arrested the outflow of funds.

That was the first step towards the turnaround.

The second was to recover the large number of sticky loans in the books of the company, and the third was an active investment policy to generate returns on funds. The drop in interest rates in early 2000 was an opportunity to make money by trading bonds as their prices rose; the Peerless treasury made money with both hands.

The fourth and final step was retrenchment of staff. Peerless had about 5,000 employees on its payroll; a golden handshake was given to 3,500 of them.

This would not have been possible in a Communist-ruled state where trade unionism was rampant without chief minister Jyoti Basu's blessings. At Writers' Buildings, the state secretariat, Ghosh had bluntly told Basu that if the downsizing was not possible, Peerless would have to be liquidated.

The Promoters, Too, Backed Him

"I wanted to bring in professionals from outside but I realized that the best way to get work done was from the people inside. I must say SK Roy was extremely cooperative. The entire organization stood behind the new board and brought about the turnaround," Ghosh said.

Datta, who headed Hindustan Lever between 1990 and 1996, accompanied chief minister Basu to the Prabashi Banga Sammelan (an address to overseas Bengalis) in New York in 1996. Among others, barrister Chatterjee and Harshavardhan Neotia, chairman of The Ambuja Realty Group, were in the entourage.

Datta, in fact, had been the original choice for chairman. When PC Sen – BK's successor as the chairman and managing director of Peerless until January 1996 – had to step down following Peerless's defeat in the Supreme Court, he asked Datta to join the board of Peerless as its non-executive chairman, but Datta had declined.

A few months later, when SK Roy took over as managing director of Peerless, after being joint managing director under Sen, he offered the top job to Ghosh.

Ghosh called Datta: "I have been asked to become chairman of Peerless. I told them I won't join unless you join me. I have asked (Dipankar) Basu but he has a cooling-off period." Basu had stepped down as State Bank of India chairman in 1995. Typically, a public sector bank chief has a two-year cooling period before being allowed to take up a new assignment.

The RBI governor Rangarajan also encouraged Datta to join Peerless. "We want people like you. This company foolishly fought with the RBI in the Supreme Court. It is systemically important; there are some 40 million depositors. We want sincere people to guide Peerless," he told Datta.

In his chamber in the assembly house, chief minister Basu told Datta that he should join Peerless or the board would lack credibility. Before making up his mind, Datta also sought the advice of Manmohan Singh.

"I told Mr Ghosh I will join. The two of us met the RBI governor (Rangarajan) and it was decided that we will have overriding powers on all matters," Datta told me.

Datta was not innocent of finance. He was the chairman of the India advisory board of Barclays Plc., was on the advisory committee of the erstwhile Industrial Development Bank of India, and had been the non-executive chairman of Times Bank Ltd since its inception in 1995. At Times Bank, the focus was on liabilities as it was a new outfit, but at Peerless, his task was to shutter the subsidiaries and oversee marketing and sales. It wasn't easy. In his words:

"There was resistance from within as each of the subsidiaries was like a child to them. My first job was to convince them that we were doing the right thing. The RBI sword was always hanging there. (But) there were not too many hard battles. Roy and his deputy Lahiri (Bhargab Lahiri, director, operations) were keen to collaborate with us... The minor arguments were on formulation of new schemes, their monitoring and commission for agents. We made them swallow bitter pills.

We were given only seven years to generate surplus – so we cut cost, cut agents' commission. We needed to work together for the purpose. We used to brief the CM (Basu) at every stage and keep Pranab Mukherjee informed. We never considered the option of failure."

Mukherjee, a Congress legislator, was the general secretary of the party in 1998–99 and subsequently, president of West Bengal Congress. He would eventually become India's President.

By the time Dipankar Basu joined Peerless, a year after Ghosh and Datta, the company had 150 branches and 1,500 employees and the trade unions had filed a writ in the Calcutta High Court seeking a directive for fresh permission from the RBI to gather deposits.

Peerless's problem, according to Dipankar Basu, was unfocussed diversification and not having enough professional managers to run the show.

After BK's death, PC Sen, an engineer, a senior railway officer and chairman and managing director of Burn Standard Co. Ltd, a public sector company and a subsidiary of Bharat Bhari Udyog Nigam Ltd, took over as the chairman and managing director of Peerless in 1986. He was the son-in-law of HK Sen, the immediate past chairman of Peerless, the first Indian actuary, and a former senior executive of Life Insurance Corp. of India. He was also a close friend of BK.

Apparently though, PC Sen had been picked from the market following an ad issued on 10 July 1986 in *The Statesman* in Calcutta (now Kolkata), *The Times of India* in Bombay (now Mumbai), *The Hindu* in Madras (now Chennai) and *The Hindustan Times* in New Delhi:

> "An Excellent Remuneration
>
> A major growth-oriented limited company dealing in finance, having branches in all major cities, wishes to recruit a chief executive... Candidates should have at least 15 years' senior level experience in industry or with financial services organization, banking, merchant banking or lease financing. Preferred age is 45–50 but senior managers who have retired recently may also apply...
>
> An attractive salary and perquisite package including company housing and car will be offered and remuneration will not be a constraint for the appropriate candidate..."

PC Sen, one of the four shortlisted candidates from over 20 applicants, was not the first choice. The company first approached Jahar Sengupa, then chairman of Chloride

(India) Ltd (now Exide Industries Ltd), but he was not willing to join immediately.

Sen had to go in 1996 after the Supreme Court ruling went against Peerless. His wife Krishna, who was heading the Peerless Hospitex Hospital and Research Centre Ltd, also resigned. At least two of his relations were in senior positions in group companies at that time.

Sen's decade-long tenure in Peerless has been the most eventful time for the company, both in terms of aggressive expansion as well as controversies. His father-in-law, HK Sen, died of a heart attack at 79 in his residence in July 1986. PC Sen's wife and daughters were not happy with his decision to join the company as they thought the assignment would be stressful. The "attractive package" enticed him (at Burn Standard he used to get ₹3,500 a month). Besides he was 54 then, four years from retirement. In private sector, there was no retirement age.

"SK Roy came home to convince me to take up the job. He had two conditions – that I would bring a few senior officers from Burn Standard to manage the company and that I would find a buyer for Roy's stake," Sen told me in the drawing room of his Lake Road residence in Kolkata, full of books on subjects as varied as physics and Christianity.

Within days of his joining, the field agents of Peerless camping outside the headquarters on Esplanade East, to press their demands for better terms and conditions of their employment, roughed him up and he had to be hospitalized.

Sen brought Parasmal Lodha, a businessman into trading,

real estates and mining and brother-in-law to JP Chowdhary, chairman of Titagarh Wagons Ltd, to buy a substantial portion of Roy's stake. But that deal became mired in controversy as the power in Delhi was not comfortable with Lodha holding the majority stake in a company that dealt with public money.

"I was politically misunderstood," Lodha told me. Sen approached him, Lodha claimed, as Peerless seemed unable to run its business with the RBI tightening RNBC regulations, and was about to be closed.

Sen made a commitment to Delhi to reverse the deal, and Lodha sold back a large chunk of his stake to Roy with, what he and Sen say, an implicit understanding that Roy would give it back once the political equations changed. However, both Sen and Lodha claim, that has not happened and Lodha has been fighting a legal case against Roy on this. That's a sensational story, fraught with secrecy and political intrigues: extremely interesting but not strictly relevant for this book.

Ajit Kumar Chatterjee's book, *A Peerless Education*, offers few glimpses of the intrigues. He has written how, in London, he received a phone call from SK Roy expressing frustration over the chaotic conditions among office and field workers, and that it was going to be impossible to save the company. A few days after this, he received another call from PC Sen saying, "the board of directors of Peerless just agreed to sell the shares."

"A couple of days later Sunil (SK Roy) telephoned me to talk about the purchaser of Peerless... I could hear him sobbing at the other end. He said that no one came forward to help him run the vast company..."

Two years after the sale, the Peerless shares were reverted to one of the founding families.[5]

SK Roy, the current boss, denies all this. An email sent on his behalf by a senior company executive said, "The statement made by Mr PC Sen and Mr Parasmal Lodha are hereby denied. You are aware that the transfer of shares are presently subjudice and therefore, we are unable to comment on the same."

Sen had a checkered career as the Peerless boss. The day he took over (in August 1986), he said that Roy received a fax from the RBI asking Peerless to stop taking deposits, and he had to move the Calcutta High Court seeking a stay on the RBI direction. However, this could not be confirmed by the RBI

Sen did everything from forging an equity and technology alliance with a Norwegian shipping firm to float Peerless Shipping Ltd for repairing offshore platforms, to being arrested and spending a night in Alipore Central Jail in Kolkata for the alleged violation of India's Foreign Exchange Regulation Act or FERA.

Delaying the Inevitable

Throughout his tenure, Sen fought the RBI, delaying

---

[5] A *Peerless Education*, Ajit Kumar Chatterjee, 1999, pp510-18.

the inevitable. While doing so, he also wanted to create an alternative empire as he knew the Roys would not be able to defend the RNBC business model for long. So, he began setting up subsidiaries in hospitality, healthcare, shipping, software, real estate and every conceivable space – one in every quarter, on an average, in the last few years of his tenure.

He also started giving money to state governments. The first borrower was the West Bengal government. On a bandh day, the then state finance minister Asim Dasgupta called him to his residence in Salt Lake. A police jeep was sent to fetch him as public transport was off the road. Sen gave ₹400 crore to the West Bengal Industrial Development Corp., a state undertaking, at 15%, after hard bargaining.

Assam, Orissa, Andhra Pradesh, Tamil Nadu, Karnataka, Chandigarh and quite a few other states borrowed from Peerless during Sen's regime to meet emergency needs. All such loans made good money for the company as they were priced more than the government bond yields those days. They were routed through state government undertakings.

When the RBI won the final round in the Supreme Court, SK Roy apparently told Sen that it was time for him to retreat. He took a severance package of ₹25 lakh and resigned. By the time the chief minister Jyoti Basu called him to his secretariat to get the lowdown on what was happening in Peerless (this was January 1996), Sen had already resigned. Anil Biswas, then the secretary of CPI(M)'s state unit, called Sen to the party office on Alimuddin Street and asked him to withdraw his resignation, but Sen did not change his mind. In an industry-starved state, Peerless was one company expanding and generating employment and that might have prompted Biswas to tell the aggressive Peerless boss Sen to stick around.

When Ghosh's quartet took over at Peerless, they found signs of indiscriminate lending. For the new board, it was difficult to recover all the loans. It had to write off some of it.

"The RBI norm said a non-banking finance company for registration must have a ₹25 lakh net worth by January 2003. We were running negative net worth, but we managed to turn positive by a very handsome margin and meet the deadline," Dipankar Basu told me at the Peerless office in Mittal Towers, Nariman Point, Mumbai's business district. After Ghosh left the company in 2006, Basu was made the chairman and Datta continues there as a director.

After a massive clean-up drive, 20 of 27 Peerless subsidiaries and associates were closed. The remaining ones were in the hotel, hospital, securities, financial products distribution, financial services (lending) and asset management segments. The seventh was in the form of a joint venture with the West Bengal government for developing real estate.

Today, Peerless General Finance & Investment—the holding company of the group – does not have a lot of business of its own; most of the businesses is carried out by its subsidiaries. There are two possibilities before the group: one, the holding company remains in its current form, continuing to channel the group's businesses through the subsidiaries and affiliates; and two, one successful subsidiary (maybe the lending arm) could be merged with the holding company.

As a sign of good health, the auditor's notes in Peerless's annual report, which used to run on for pages, have been shrinking, with fewer and fewer qualifications.

LIC Behind the Conspiracy?

Peerless always felt the RBI's chase after it was instigated by LIC. This is evident in BK's letter to Ajit Kumar Chatterjee, on 3 August 1983:

> "We have been treating the first year's subscriptions as 'income' and all second and subsequent years' subscriptions are credited to the certificate holder's fund. This fund, together with the compound interest, credited to it every year will be more than sufficient to meet any kind of contractual liability to the certificate holder. Therefore, even after spending the first year's subscription, the company is in a commanding position to meet its all liabilities to the certificate holders. This procedure has been followed by the company for the last 25 years or so and (we) have also paid taxes on that basis.
>
> Recently, and rather suddenly, the Company Law Department asked the company to show cause why the legal action should not be taken against the company and its directors, for wrongful accounting procedure. Smelling another conspiracy behind it (engineered, perhaps by the LIC), we ourselves filed a suit against the Company Law Department for a declaration that the system consistently followed by the company for the last 25 years on the basis of actuarial accounting

principles was correct."

In his office at Peerless Bhavan, 3 Esplanade East, bang opposite Governor's House in Kolkata, SK Roy, who was awarded the Padma Shri, India's fourth highest civilian award, in 2009, in recognition of his distinguished services in social work, told me, "Peerless followed the accounts on actuarial basis – first year's liability was spent following the norms of life insurance accounting practices and the RBI initially found the system scientific."

Peerless, he said, was very disciplined in its approach and always invested the money collected in bank deposits and government securities and bonds. "In fact, the RBI got the idea from us when it told RNBCs to put in a bulk of their deposits with scheduled commercial banks and in government bonds."

He showed me the photocopy of a September 1992 'liability certificate' of United Bank of India that says Peerless had kept ₹760.44 crore worth of fixed deposits receipts and government bonds with the bank and this money could not be withdrawn without the consent of the bank.

Roy consciously stays away from politics and the glare of media. His business ethic is fairly simple. On a Sunday evening in 1968, over tea at Dum Dum residence in north Kolkata (Roy now lives in Southern Avenue), his elder brother BK told him that it was all public money and he was nothing more than a trustee.

However, YV Reddy, who became the RBI governor in 2003, was not impressed with Peerless's record. He decided that

RNBCs had fulfilled their role as a financial intermediary and had no business to be around anymore. In 2007, the RBI told Peerless to stop taking fresh deposits from March 2011 and close its RNBC business by 2015. It prescribed the same medicine for the Sahara group the next year. Wiser with experience, Peerless did not move the court. By April 2013, Peerless had trimmed its balance sheet and had about ₹1,900 crore worth of deposits liability to be repaid.

Sahara too gave up its RNBC business in 2007 but once again started raising bonds in 2008, for which it has been fighting with the market regulator Sebi. It had earlier raised bonds in 2001 with approval from the Registrar of Companies; some 19.8 million investors put in money in its first OFCD in 2001.

Dipankar Basu has no great feeling of discomfort; he knows what is happening at Peerless. After the crisis of 1996, when the Supreme Court ruled against the company, Peerless's promoters became keen to be on the right side of the regulator and have been "generally cooperative". The RBI's shock therapy had worked.

Another RNBC Shuts Shop

Ahead of charting out its plan to close Peerless in July 2005, the RBI shut down another RNBC, Ennoble India Savings and Investment Co. Ltd, by cancelling its registration. In doing so, the regulator used its powers under Section 45-IA of the Reserve Bank of India Act, 1934, which allows it to cancel registration.

This was done seven years after the RBI found the Bellary, Karnataka-headquartered Ennoble India violating norms, both in taking deposits and investing in government bonds, and banned the company from accepting fresh deposits. Its net worth, too, had turned negative.

While prohibiting Ennoble India from taking fresh deposits from 5 October 1998 in any form, the RBI also directed the company not to sell, transfer or mortgage its assets, except for repayment of its deposits on maturity, without the regulator's approval.

The company was floated by Gali Janardhana Reddy when he was just 21 years old. Reddy, the youngest son of a police constable from Andhra Pradesh, had learnt the business as an agent for a local chit fund company. He eventually transformed into a mining baron, dabbled in politics and became Karnataka's tourism minister – a pauper-to-prince story paling many mafia dons into insignificance. He was finally arrested in 2011 by investigating agencies for the alleged violation of mining laws.

To be fair to Reddy, unlike Peerless and Sahara, his company never challenged the regulators. He closed shop without a murmur when he was asked to do so. He had more important issues on his plate than fighting the RBI. But that's a different story.

3

THE TWO MEETINGS THAT CLINCHED THE DEAL

When India's banking regulator was fighting it out with Peerless in the country's apex court in the 1990s, Yaga Venugopal Reddy, an Indian Administrative Service officer of the 1964 batch, was the banking secretary in the ministry of finance. Manmohan Singh was finance minister and C Rangarajan was the governor of the Reserve Bank of India.

There was tremendous political pressure on the RBI to back out. The support of the Left Front that was ruling West Bengal then was critical for the Congress government at the Centre, headed by PV Narasimha Rao. The Congress had ushered in economic reforms in the early 1990s to pull India out of an unprecedented balance of payment crisis. Rao's government couldn't afford to upset Jyoti Basu, then chief minister of West Bengal for whom Peerless was even playing the role of lender of the last resort. Some government officials nudged RBI to begin a dialogue with Peerless.

The RBI's stance was clear – Peerless had dragged it to the Supreme Court and it could not enter into a dialogue with the company while the case was being heard. You could not negotiate with somebody who had gone to the Supreme Court against you. If you did, how could you protect your accountability?

By late 1995, political pressure on the RBI had increased to unilaterally pull out of the Supreme Court case. Both Singh and Reddy were foursquare behind governor Rangarajan. The RBI deputy governor, SS Tarapore, was directed to attend a meeting in the finance ministry where Peerless would be present, but both Tarapore and Reddy declined to be there.

Reddy was appointed the 21st governor of the RBI on 6 September 2003 and served in that position for five years. By that time, Peerless was back on the profit track and had started growing, albeit slowly. On the other hand, SIFCL was growing at a rapid pace. Reddy's one-point agenda was to finish off Sahara and Peerless, which by then accounted for 70% of all deposit-taking companies in the country and were quickly growing to be too big to fail.

Reddy, known for his differences with the finance ministry on many critical issues, always felt that the two groups were holding the regulator to ransom. There were three other RNBCs – much smaller in size – that the RBI wanted shut. These three firms accepted the exit plans charted out for them. They were based in Calcutta, Guntur (Andhra Pradesh) and Bellary (Karnataka). The Calcutta one was the last of the three to shut shop.

Peerless, after losing its legal battle, couldn't grow much. It became more of a holding-on operation for the Roys. But Sahara continued to grow at a breakneck speed. With Reddy at the helm, the RBI's job was to entice, incentivize and enable Sahara to slow its growth momentum. Its winding down had to be drawn out, as a sudden move would have disrupted the entire financial system and created a social chaos with millions of depositors losing their money and lakhs of collection agents losing their jobs.

People in the industry say that before the Reddy regime at the central bank, Roy used to be invited to meetings on the non-banking industry and his advice was sought both by the RBI as well as the government.

Sometime in 1998, when Bimal Jalan was governor of RBI, his deputy, the late SP Talwar, strongly voiced his concerns on the state of affairs in non-banking finance companies, including RNBCs, at a social gathering in the Mumbai home of actor and chairman of Balaji Telefilms Ltd, Jeetendra. Talwar was highly annoyed. Nobody could blame him as thousands of investors had lost money at Chain Roop Bansali's CRB Capital Markets Ltd that went bust a year back. Subrata Roy, present at the do, strongly reacted to Talwar's statement. He even challenged Talwar to send whoever he wanted to check Sahara's books. Talwar took up the challenge and a sent a team of inspectors who stayed put at Sahara's Lucknow headquarters for more than two months.

Roy told me that the RBI team was happy and found nothing wrong with Sahara.

Two meetings – running for hours – at the RBI headquarters on Mint Road, Mumbai, on 12 and 16 June 2008, sealed Sahara's fate. Of course, these two meetings were preceded by a courtroom drama, both in the Allahabad High Court and the Supreme Court. However, unlike the legal battle with Peerless that lasted nearly two decades, the legal cases in this instance were more of an interlude in the prolonged closed-door negotiations between the RBI and Sahara. The legal fight lasted just for a day each – on 5th June in the high court and on 9th June at the Supreme Court.

Let's focus on the last round of the meetings.

Neither the then RBI governor Reddy nor his deputy V Leeladhar attended the meetings of 12 and 16 June 2008. The first meeting, on a Thursday, lasted six hours, from 4pm to 10pm. The second and final meeting, on a Monday, began earlier, at 3pm, and went on till nearly midnight.

The venue of the meeting was a relatively small room on the 15th floor of the RBI office in Mumbai, adjacent to the large conference room where the RBI brass meet bank chiefs every April and October for the annual monetary policy and the half-yearly review.

Subrata Roy – who came along with his trusted lieutenants Anupam Prakash, Pallav Agarwal and Vandana Bharrgava (executive directors of Sahara India Pariwar) – looked tired but never lost his composure. Prakash handled all legal matters for SIFCL while Agarwal's forte was finance. He played a critical role in the Air Sahara-Jet deal. Bharrgava was in charge of Roy's secretariat in Lucknow. Her husband,

Ashok K Bhargava, was the chief executive officer of Sahara India Power Corp. Ltd.

The RBI was represented by G Gopalakrishna, executive director in charge of the department of non-banking supervision (DNBS); P Krishnamurthy, chief general manager; GS Hegde, the legal head; and two other officers – Shekhar Bhatnagar and Reena Bannerji.

The RBI Strategy: No Confrontation

The RNBC model had inherent weaknesses, according to the RBI. The Indian central bank's strategy was simple: no confrontation; Sahara had to be convinced through discussion.

The RBI team had studied Roy well: he had a superb understanding of his business, but Sahara was too big to be left unscathed this time.

Gopalakrishna started the meeting with a warm welcome address and a brief on the agenda for the meeting. After that, Krishnamurthy took over.

A 1981 batch RBI officer, Krishnamurthy had closely worked with Bimal Jalan when the latter had been the RBI govenor, and with Reddy when he had been deputy governor, on exchange rates for successive years: first, during the Asian financial crisis of 1997; then in 1998 when the US imposed economic sanctions on India after the Bharatiya Janata Party-ruled government conducted a series of underground nuclear tests; and, finally, during the Kargil war with Pakistan in 1999. He had been sent to Oman on deputation in 2003–2004 to advise the local central bank on reserve management.

After a small stint in the RBI's Bangalore office, the tall, dark and shy Krishnamurthy was transferred to Mumbai to oversee DNBS in June 2005, replacing OP Agarwal, who was made regional director in Jammu.

"You are free to ask any question you wish and we will respond," Krishnamurthy told the Sahara team. Roy was anxious, but he gave no sign of losing his calm even though it was not easy to give up a ₹20,000-crore empire.

Throughout the meeting, Krishnamurthy harped on the same point: in the absence of a rectification of its operations, the RBI couldn't allow Sahara to grow. He appealed to Roy: "Sir, please cooperate with us. We are not comfortable with the RNBC model. Please convert it into a non-banking finance company. Please stop taking fresh deposits."

Unlike NBFCs, which are required to follow many regulations in terms of raising and investing money, RNBCs enjoyed too much freedom. Apart from the capital adequacy ratio that does not allow NBFCs unbridled asset creation without an adequate capital base, these financial intermediaries also need to follow norms on deposit mobilization as well as on giving loans to firms. For RNBCs, created by an RBI directive in 1987, the regulatory tools were capital adequacy ratio and investment norms. Until March 2005, an RNBC needed to invest 80% of the money raised in government bonds and other securities approved by the

RBI. In April 2005, the limit for such investments was raised to 90% and a year later, to 100%. The capital adequacy ratio was 12%. This means, for creating assets worth ₹100, an RNBC needed a capital of ₹12.

Krishnamurthy recognized Roy's role in building a big RNBC, was extremely polite and made Roy feel he would be doing the regulator a big favour by closing his RNBC. But Krishnamurthy was firm on one count – the RBI had nothing to do with the employees and the agents of Sahara; the regulator's only concern was Sahara's depositors.

The RBI team counselled Roy, cajoled him, and when nothing else worked, started appealing: "Sir, please give up the business."

Roy knew he had little choice, but was ready to fight for every penny. Since Peerless was given four years to stop taking fresh deposits, and Sahara had grown to be much bigger than Peerless, it must be given at least five years, Roy argued.

The RBI was willing to give him a three-year window for deposit-taking, till June 2010, and wanted Sahara to close shop in five years, by 2015.

"Sir, you are a business tycoon and the economy can't flourish without you... It's a very small adjustment for you," Krishnamurthy told Roy. But the deadlock could not be broken at the first meeting. That the RBI didn't care much about Roy's 1.1 million workforce was pretty evident and it was also certain that Sahara would have to close down its RNBC, but they bargained hard on the time frame for doing this.

The RBI also did not want to project itself as a regulator in a hurry to force its decision down Sahara's throat. It wanted to come to a decision through discussion, even though it was firm on the final outcome of the meeting. So, the RBI team told Roy to discuss matters with his people over the weekend and assemble again the following Monday, 16th June, at 3pm.

On that day, when the RBI governor, Reddy, finally left his office at 9pm, there had been no progress in the matter as both sides were adamant. Leeladhar stayed put in his cabin on the 18th floor. Wily Reddy knew that Roy was trapped, and it was a matter of time before he accepted the RBI's road map for winding down Sahara. He dropped a subtle hint while leaving office that the three-year time frame could be stretched to four, but no further concessions could be given to Sahara, even if that meant a no-deal.

Roy's team took intermittent breaks to discuss their strategy in an adjacent room. Tea and coffee were served every half an hour and there were cookies. Roy was keen to continue taking deposits and close shop after seven years, but he had to succumb to the RBI's pressure. At around 11pm, Roy signed on the closure deal. He was given four years – the same time frame that Peerless had been given. A small victory for Roy.

However, it was a technical victory. Although Sahara was allowed deposit-taking activities for four years, till June 2011, it had a really three-year window for all practical purposes. This was because the minimum maturity for deposits raised by an RNBC was one year. Since it was decided that no fresh deposits would mature beyond June 2011, Sahara could effectively take deposits only till June 2010.

It was also decided that the last deposit would mature in 2015, when Sahara had to close shop. So, the maximum-maturity, seven-year deposits could not be taken after 2008.

Once Roy gave his nod to the scheme, the RBI team felt like a tiger that had just tasted blood but it could not roar as the job was only half-finished. The next step was recasting the Sahara board and changing the auditors. Roy was agitated. The RBI knew it did not have the power to do this and that it had to convince Roy to do this on his own, saying it would enhance his credibility.

You Are the Sector

As was his wont, Krishnamurthy told Roy, "Sir, you are the sector. We are trying to get you more credibility... We won't force you. You will do it voluntarily... You give us the names (of directors)."

For once, Roy turned emotional. Once the board was reconstituted, what would he be left with?

Like the Sahara team, the RBI team was also taking breaks to discuss the developments and strategies. Krishnamurthy left the meeting for a few minutes, took the lift and went to the 18th floor where Leeladhar was waiting patiently.

When Krishnamurthy returned, the final outlines were discussed and both teams drafted a note on plain paper on the changes to be made in the Sahara board and its auditors.

Roy was requested to write down everything on a Sahara letterhead and bring it back the next day. Only after that would the RBI issue a press release. Roy agreed to send the note, but bargained hard to extract a promise from the RBI team that the statement would say that Sahara had volunteered the changes.

In retrospect, it was a model discussion for both the RBI and Sahara – their teams fought hard on virtually every point, but in the end they settled it amicably. The RBI established the regulator's supremacy with dignity and Roy gave up his empire with a smile.

At well past midnight, Leeladhar sent a text message to Reddy, who had not yet gone to bed, "Sir, mission completed. Strictly as you wanted." He had dictated the message to Krishnamurthy, who typed it on Leeladhar's mobile while taking the lift down from the 18th floor. "Great job. God bless you," Leeladhar's mobile phone flashed back as the deputy governor left the RBI headquarters at 12.30am.

Reporters of television channels were waiting for their sound bytes, but Leeladhar and Roy kept quiet. A reserved Leeladhar didn't want to talk and Roy preferred to silence as he was eyeing a banking licence and didn't find it worthwhile settling scores with the RBI through the media.

Another person was very happy that night – Leeladhar's wife, Savithri. She found him smiling when she opened the door. He had been tense the past few days and tossing sleeplessly in bed, though Savithri did not ask him about it. Both in the office and at home, Leeladhar was a reserved man.

On the next day (17th June), Alpana Killawala, chief general manager, communications, at the RBI, issued a formal statement on the agreement with Sahara. Earlier that day, finance minister P Chidambaram had been told of the development.The RBI release said:

> SIFCL (Sahara India Financial Corp. Ltd) is hereby directed not to accept any new deposit which matures beyond 30 June 2011, and to stop accepting installments of existing deposit accounts also with effect from that date. The aggregate liability to depositors (ALD) will not exceed ₹15,000 crore as of 30 June 2009; ₹12,600 crore as of 30 June 2010; and ₹9,000 crore as of 30 June 2011.
>
> SIFCL shall repay the deposits as and when they mature and bring the ALD to zero on or before 30 June 2015.
>
> SIFCL shall not treat non-payment of installments under any running daily deposit or other recurring deposit schemes by depositors after 30 June 2011 as a default by depositor and SIFCL shall be liable to pay the agreed rate of interest on the amounts actually held by it for the entire term of the deposit as if there was no default.
>
> SIFCL shall continue to comply with the requirements of directed investments... with respect to its ALD.
>
> SIFCL shall ensure 100% compliance with the KYC (know your customer) norms for all new deposits...

The RBI said it had incorporated in its order the offer made during the hearing by the managing worker and chairman of

SIFCL (Roy) and the company's senior executives.

Keeping in view quality corporate governance, Sahara offered to reconstitute the board of directors of SIFCL within 30 days from 16 June 2008, inducting independent directors acceptable to the RBI. It would get the appointments of these directors ratified at Sahara's ensuing annual general meeting and the arrangement would remain in place till all its depositors had been repaid.

Sahara also agreed to replace the company's existing auditor by an audit firm approved by the RBI at its forthcoming annual general meeting by 31 August 2008.

The RBI forced all these changes on SIFCL because of its continuing alleged violations of investment norms. The banking regulator had accused Sahara of not following rules regarding the payment of the prescribed minimum rate of interest to depositors, asset-liability management guidelines, KYC norms for opening deposits, and failing to intimate depositors when their deposits matured.

Roy says the main allegation was about a ₹1,100 crore shortfall in directed investment that happened because the income tax department in Lucknow was treating Sahara's deposits as revenue. The RBI had earlier allowed Sahara to treat the amount of TDS as directed investment, but suddenly it stopped this practice.

"We sought the RBI's permission to infuse ₹1,100 crore from other group companies as debt, but the RBI insisted that it should come in the form of equity. We managed to bring in ₹600 crore, but still the RBI issued its prohibitory order barring us from taking deposits. The whole action was pre-decided, filmy style. All other allegations had no substance," says Roy.

There followed a series of 11 meetings, spread over three years at periodic intervals, and an inspection of books. By May 2008, the RBI had lost its patience and served a show cause notice to Roy on 9th May. The confidential note, signed by the RBI executive director, Gopalakrishna, said:

> "... You are hereby called upon to show cause before the close of business on 26 May, 2008, why your company should not be prohibited from accepting deposits... If your company fails to show sufficient cause before the aforesaid time, (the) Bank (RBI) will be constrained to proceed to issue such orders as it deems fit and necessary in public interest to protect the interest of the depositors. In case the Bank does not receive any reply from your company before the aforesaid time, it will be deemed that you have no cause to show and the Bank will be constrained to proceed to issue such order as it deems fit and necessary in public interests..."

The notice enclosed 14 letters written by the RBI to Sahara between 16 April 2007 and 28 April 2008. Referring to a 7 May 2008 Sahara letter, it said, "The workable plan or moving out of the business model and pursuing other business model has not been specified (in Sahara's letter) though we had advised your company more than a year ago on 16 April, 2007. The proposed plan does not reflect the requirement conveyed in our letter... The present plan also contemplates acceptance of deposits for another six years..."

The Show Cause Notice

The show cause note listed some 28 alleged violations by Sahara, including not fulfilling investment norms and the absence of records of depositors and branches to violations of KYC norms, taking exposure to group companies, inadequate asset liability and risk management, lack of records for unclaimed deposits, factually incorrect financial figures used in advertisements, and so on.

The note pointed out that as on 31 March 2007, the company had substantial exposure to Sahara India – a partnership firm to which Sahara had outsourced collecting deposits from the public (a security deposit of ₹575 crore and loans of ₹58.88 crore); Sahara India Commercial Corp. Ltd, a group company (₹50.72 crore); and Sahara Airlines Ltd (₹48.52 crore).

Besides, Sahara had raised its equity capital by ₹5 crore to subscribe to the equity shares of Sahara Asset Management Co. Ltd, the group's mutual fund arm. This indicated the absence of arm's length relationship with group companies, in violation of corporate governance norms and the so-called connected lending norms.

"The... violation of (the) Bank's directions and instructions issued from time to time, financial position of the company being not very sound, poor risk management system... and far less than adequate governance principles followed by the company are not in the interest of the depositors," the note pointed out.

Sahara responded to the show cause notice, but before that, Roy wrote a letter to "Respected Shri V Leeladharji" on 15th May in which he "most humbly" submitted that he had always respected the directions of the RBI and the efforts would continue. He also affirmed that Sahara would exit from RNBC activities and would in no way defy any of the RBI's directions, though keeping in mind the size of the company and its large field staff, it had proposed to accept fresh deposits till fiscal 2014.

Roy also said the group's life insurance and mutual fund businesses had started absorbing people and the moment he was ready with another business model, he would approach the RBI for regulatory approvals. Meanwhile, he sought an appointment with Leeladhar "to bridge the gaps between the requirements of the RBI" and Sahara's submissions.

Leeladhar did not grant his wish but the RBI gave Sahara a hearing on 20th May where Roy asked for one more week, till 2nd June, to respond. The meeting was attended by Gopalakrishna, Hegde and Krishnamurthy. After the meeting, the RBI reissued the show cause notice.

The Sahara response, a long and detailed note signed by Roy, tried to address each and every concern of the RBI. It iterated Sahara's commitment to exit the RNBC business and cover the gaps in its investments by generating cash through internal accruals and selling equity holding in a group company (Sahara One Media and Entertainment Ltd – a Hindi general entertainment channel of the group) by December 2008.

Sahara also said it had been exploring an alternative business model in the form of a bank and for this it had engaged consultancy firm E&Y, but on the RBI's advice, it did not pursue the proposal.

Leeladhar had actually pushed SIFCL to engage E&Y, as the RBI wanted to explore the possibility of converting the Sahara firm into a bank to avoid any systemic instability. E&Y made a presentation listing many conditions that SIFCL would have to fulfill to become a bank; it was not happy with the KYC procedures adopted by SIFCL, but could not detect a single case of violation.

Sahara's response was that a majority of its deposit service centres were in rural and semi-urban areas, and depositors in these pockets belonged to no-risk or low-risk categories. They were personally known to Sahara's field agents and some of them were ignoring the pleas of the agents for documents saying the post offices did not ask for such papers. Sahara said it was, however, determined to be KYC compliant.

Roy requested the RBI to drop the proceedings and implored Gopalakrishna to give him a personal hearing to explain the case. He hoped that in view of Sahara's 21 years' existence as an RNBC and in the interest of lakhs of employees and millions of investors, the central bank would not go ahead with its plan to shut Sahara. The RBI wasn't impressed with Roy's explanations.

As a last resort, Roy wrote to Prime Minister Manmohan Singh on 26th May, seeking his intervention "for protection of interest of millions of workers" of SIFCL. In the letter,

Roy said there could be a run on SIFCL as depositors may rush to withdraw money if the RBI imposed a prohibitory order. However, he gave a committment to exit from the RNBC business and sought Singh's intervention to obtain an acceptable time frame for winding down the business. He even agreed to settle for a winding down period of fewer than seven years.

"We are just seeking reasonable time for an orderly and honourable exit from the RNBC business," he wrote and urgently sought a "few moments" with the Prime Minister; but did not get any response.

A restless Roy wrote to Gopalakrishna on 2nd June – a 35-page letter imploring a personal hearing and the dropping of proceedings keeping in mind the interests of the depositors and employees, field staff and agents.

The Prohibitory Order

On 4th June, the inevitable happened. Gopalakrishna issued the prohibitory order that Roy had been dreading. That morning, before Gopalakrishna gave final touches to the 20-page prohibitory order, Reddy spoke to finance minister Chidambaram to keep him informed.

Gopalakrishna asked the company to submit a weekly statement on deposits. The first such statement had to be updated until 6th June and submitted by 9th June. He also indicated that there might be a monthly inspection of SIFCL.

– Sahara was prohibited from accepting any deposit under any scheme either from existing or new depositors with immediate effect.

– Sahara was directed to redeem all deposits as and when they matured.

– Post the order, Sahara could not treat non-payment of installments by depositors as defaults.

– Sahara was, however, allowed to carry on with its other businesses.

An hour before the RBI took the decision to ask Sahara to stop its business with immediate effect, Krishnamurthy asked DPS Rathore, the RBI's regional director in Lucknow, to inform the state administration about this.

Rathore called up the then chief secretary of Uttar Pradesh, Atul Kumar Gupta, and cautioned him on a likely public disturbance in the state. For the next few hours, Rathore was inundated with telephone calls from almost every government official. One of them was cabinet secretary Shashank Shekhar Singh, the first non-IAS officer in UP to have risen to that unique position created by then chief minister Mayawati.

The bureaucrat was upset and said that he should have been informed earlier of such a critical decision that could have enormous impact on public order. Rathore politely told Singh that the central bank was not seeking any help from the state administration and that the information could not have been shared in advance for the sake of confidentiality; the RBI merely wanted to keep Singh in the loop to prevent any public disturbance. Singh allegedly threatened to put the entire RBI administration behind bars. Rathore told him in that case, he would need to take action against the Mumbai office as the top brass sat there.

JB Bhoria, the regional director of Kanpur, was not involved in this matter.

Rathore was summoned to the state secretariat at 11pm that night, but at the last moment he was told his presence was not required.

There was no law and order problem. However, on the same night, at 9pm, SIFCL company secretary Shiv Kumar Pandey circulated a board resolution that authorized director OP Srivastava to take legal action against the regulator's move.

The RBI had sensed that Sahara would file a writ in the Allahabad High Court against the prohibitory order. So, that very evening, immediately after issuing the show cause notice, Krishnamurthy and Hegde flew to Lucknow. Had the RBI not tied up with a lawyer before they landed in Lucknow, it would have been difficult to find one as almost all of them had already been hired by Sahara.

Sahara, on 5th June, moved a vacation bench of the court for interim relief. Prashant Chandra, senior advocate, assisted by Piyush Kumar Agarwal, representing Sahara, filed a petition that ran into 600 pages. Krishnamurthy and Hegde briefed advocate SK Kalia in their car.

The application for interim relief was taken up at 2:30pm and the RBI's counsel requested the bench to defer the matter by at least a day as he had not yet gone through the entire Sahara document; but his prayer was not granted.

In a crowded court room, Chandra said that the RBI had passed the impugned order in a hurried manner and that it was a violation of the fundamental right guaranteed under Article 19 (1) (g) of the Indian Constitution for any person to practise any profession or carry on any occupation, trade or business. He also said no Sahara depositor had filed any complaint with the RBI.

UK Dhaon and Shabihul Hasnain of the bench stayed the RBI's directive and ordered the petition to be listed in the last week of July for hearing. They said:

> "As large number of investors/depositors will be affected by the impugned order as they will be deprived of depositing their money... in various schemes launched by the petitioner, and large number of employees, agents, staff will lose their livelihood, we have no option except to stay the operation and enforcement of the... order dated 4.6.2008 till further orders of this court. The petitioner shall not accept any new deposit whose maturity will be beyond June 2010.
>
> Since the RBI mentioned... that the deposit taking activities of the petitioner are not in conformity with the practices and directions and guidelines issued by the RBI, we direct that the petitioner shall complete all the required formalities and will follow the directions issued by the RBI from time to time."

The moment the court proceedings were over, Krishnamurthy called Leeladhar seeking his advice on the next step. The next moment, Leeladhar was seen walking into Reddy's room for a quick discussion.

The Krishnamurthy-Hegde duo flew to Delhi late that evening. They first met advocates at a law firm that the RBI had engaged for fighting the case in the Supreme Court and reached the RBI guesthouse on Sansad Marg at almost midnight. They then worked till 4am on the special leave petition they planned to file in the apex court. Early on 6th June, a Friday, Krishnamurthy and Hegde met senior advocate TR Andhyarujina, who decided to harp on a critical point in the case – that the investors were not being paid their dues.

The RBI moved a special leave petition at 10:30am in the Supreme Court for an urgent order against the Allahabad High Court's stay. In the absence of a copy of the high court order, the Supreme Court decided to hear the case on 9th June.

Andhyarujina's main argument was that Sahara was collecting money from people such as shopkeepers, fruit vendors, manual workers and villagers through a network of agents and that these small depositors were being penalized for any irregularity in payments of installments by the imposition of so-called liquidated damages. The provision of liquidated damages allows for the payment of a specified sum should one of the parties breach a contract. Such irregular accounts formed 73.79% of all Sahara accounts at that time and deposits in such accounts were to the tune of ₹7,289.85 crore, according to RBI's special leave petition in the Supreme Court.

On top of that, unclaimed deposits of small investors were to the tune of ₹522.39 crore as on 1st March 2007. Finally, Sahara's KYC compliance level was only 12.5%.

Roy rubbishes this, saying they were absolutely baseless points. "In three years between 2008 and 2011, the RBI could not find even one case of KYC violation out of four crore investors."

Supreme Court judges Arijit Pasayat and PP Naolekar, after hearing both sides, asked the RBI if it would give another hearing to Sahara or wait for the hearing at the Allahabad High Court. The RBI counsel was willing to give the company a hearing, but Sahara panicked as it knew that the RBI would only repeat its old order.

Admitting that the principle of natural justice was followed, the judges said it would be appropriate for Sahara to have the opportunity of another hearing. They even fixed the date as 12th June.

> "Till the matter is disposed of afresh by the Reserve Bank of India, the order dated 4 June, 2008, shall not be given effect to. At the same time, the interim protection given by the high court to respondent one (Sahara) shall also not be operative. Since the entire matter is being disposed off in this appeal, there is no need for the high court to deal with the writ petition. We make it clear that we have not expressed any opinion on merits."

The case was disposed of in 15 minutes flat. According to Roy, this is the first instance since independence when the RBI had to withdraw a prohibitory order and two deputy governors – Shyamala Gopinath and Usha Thorat – took it as their personal defeat.

"The vengeance was so much that once Ms Gopinath asked the State Bank of India not to accept a ₹500 crore investment from Sahara. She was on the bank's board. And Ms Thorat was on the Sebi board at the time we moved the market regulator with our proposal to list Sahara Prime City," says Roy, distinctly unhappy with the way the banking regulator treated Sahara. "The worst form of Talibanism."

As directed by the court, the RBI called Sahara for a hearing. "We are here to hear you," RBI officials said, but they knew what would happen. So did Sahara.

On 20th June, three days after the RBI released the road map for closing Sahara and recasting its board, the Mayawati government in Uttar Pradesh went on a demolition drive and the target was the Sahara group, known for its proximity to Mulayam Singh Yadav's Samajwadi Party. The state government demolished the left wall built on an area of 30 metres around the high profile Sahara Shaher at Gomtinagar, Lucknow, as it wanted to build a zonal road there.

Just hours later, the Sahara group got a reprieve from the Allahabad High Court and the demolition drive was suspended. Coming down heavily on the Lucknow Development Authority, the court asked the UP government to return the land and explain why it demolished the walls without giving any notice to Sahara. This was symbolic – one could scratch the surface and even break the walls, but it would not be easy to dismantle Roy's citadel.

Between March and June 2008, the RBI went into a silent zone and nobody spoke about Sahara in the executive lunchroom or in the corridors of the central bank. The discussions were in hushed tones – mostly in Leeladhar's office and rarely in the rooms of Gopalakrishna, Krishnamurthy or Hegde.

The regulator, however, kept all agencies informed at every stage. This included the Board for Financial Supervision, a sub-committee of the central board of the RBI, which oversees the work of the department of banking supervision and non-banking supervision; Sebi; the Forward Markets Commission; the Insurance Regulatory and Development Authority; the High Level Coordination Committee of the regulators (which was replaced in 2012 by the Financial Stability and Development Council); and, of course, the finance ministry.

For many within the RBI, it was still a mystery: why did it have to act so fast? What was the provocation? One officer raised a critical issue before anybody was aware of what was happening. Reddy was to retire in September 2008 and his deputy, Leeladhar, in December. Would the RBI continue to chase Sahara after the change of guard with the same zeal? Nobody knew of course. So, could the chapter be closed before that?

"Can we do it?" Reddy asked Leeladhar. His deputy, after checking with the legal department, confirmed that the RBI was ready for the final onslaught. Reddy and

Leeladhar wanted to shut down Sahara. For them, it was mission accomplished.

4

RBI TIGHTENS THE NOOSE

On 11 July 2008, Sahara India Financial Corp. Ltd (SIFCL) made public its unaudited financial results for the first time in its history. This happened after the country's banking regulator set a three-year sunset window on SIFCL, allowing it to accept fresh deposits maturing until June 2011. SIFCL now has to repay its deposits when they mature and bring down the liability to zero on or before 30 June 2015.

A "fact sheet" gave the company's unaudited financial results as of 30 June 2008. SIFCL had capital and reserves worth ₹1,711.12 crore. Its non-performing assets (NPAs), were a minuscule 0.04% of its aggregate deposit liabilities and its total assets were to the tune of ₹19,886.28 crore.

Since inception in 1978, it has redeemed deposits and interests worth ₹41,563 crore and its deposit (and interest) liability in June 2008 was ₹17,513 crore spread over 39.4 million accounts, the "fact sheet" claimed.

The firm had invested ₹17,584 crore in government securities, government-guaranteed bonds, bank deposits and rated bonds and debentures of listed corporations, in accordance with the RBI norms, which require an RNBC to invest 100% of its deposits in such securities. SIFCL had invested its entire deposit portfolio and more in such securities, it claimed.

These numbers do not say much. This is because an RNBC's investments are calculated with a six-month lag. So, for the quarter ending 30 June 2008, its directed investments were based on the amount of deposits collected till 31 December 2007. Within this period, it could have raised more deposits and invested the money where it wanted.

In other words, SIFCL did not need to invest its entire deposits in approved securities every quarter. People familiar with the way RNBCs function claim SIFCL had used the six-month lag to its advantage by aggressively mobilizing fresh deposits and investing new money in instruments of its choice.

Sahara says this was done to provide cash flow for taking care of premature redemptions of deposits and service loans, which used to come without notice. "This way we maintained smooth cash flow and ran the business competently," one Sahara executive explains.

A perception was created among many depositors that investing in RNBCs was safe as 80% of the deposits in the early years and 100% later on were to be invested in government securities, deposits with banks, etc. – safe and liquid. This perception was strengthened by the fact that the RBI regulated such companies.

The audited financial statements of SIFCL would typically carry the following certificate, signed by the statutory auditors of the company: "Though deposit liability is grouped under unsecured deposits, but because of strict compliance of Residuary Non Deposit Companies (RBI) Directions 1987, issued by RBI, in fact, they are fully secured as the aggregate deposit liability has been invested as per RNBC directions. The FDR (fixed deposit receipts)/scrips, etc., are kept with designated bank/depository. Therefore, deposits are fully covered by value of such investment."

Let's examine to what extent this perception is true. An August-2004 RBI "master notification" on RNBCs highlighted the "security of depositors", referring to a 1997 directive:

"Every residuary non-banking company shall invest and continue to invest an amount, including the amount invested in assets under section 45-1B of RBI Act 1934 (2 of 1934), which at the close of business on any day of the quarter ending June 30, 1997 and thereafter on any day of each quarter shall not be less than the aggregate amounts of the liabilities to the depositors, outstanding at the close of business on the last working day of the second preceding quarter (whether or not such amount have become payable) in securities or other types of instruments which are unencumbered and valued at price not exceeding the current market price..."[1]

---

[1]Residuary Non-Banking Companies (Reserve Bank) Directions, 1987. Master notification amended up to 1 July 2004. RBI/2004-05/90, August, 2004.

But 100% directed investment was not 100%. What does this mean? Let's suppose the aggregate liability to depositors on 30 September 2004 was ₹10,000 crore. The reporting date would be the last working day of the second preceding quarter 31 March 2004. If the liability on that day was ₹8,000 crore, then even if 100% is "directed investment", the mandatory investment was to be made in ₹8,000 crore and the balance ₹2,000 crore added during the last two quarters was available to the RNBC for any investment it wanted to make.

So, even though technically directed investment is 100%, in practice, it is much less. And the more aggressive a company is in deposit mobilization, more money is available for investing in wherever it wants. In contrast, a company that is cautious and happy with a slower growth rate will have less money to play with.

In 2005–06, SIFCL received ₹7,923 crore from the public. Assuming a uniform growth of ₹2,000 crore per quarter, about ₹4,000 crore was available to the company to freely invest – because of the two-quarter lag in-built in the fulfillment of investment norms – and SIFCL could still be religiously following the mandate of the regulator.

When Peerless was big and thriving in West Bengal, SIFCL was small. Unlike Sahara, Peerless was even a lender of the last resort for many state governments. The RBI was always wary of the opaqueness of RNBC operations. It wanted to close them but could not because the law of the land did not allow the regulator to do so. So, it found ways to make them non-viable.

Immediately after he took over as deputy governor of the RBI in September 2004, Leeladhar, former chairman of Union Bank of India, signed a directive allowing RNBCs to classify disputed income tax refund (due from the government) as directed lending. Until then, it had been part of discretionary lending. Once it became part of directed lending, the actual quantum of directed lending came down, as the money was not with the company. As a result of this, the quantum of indirect lending rose. Once he realized the mistake, Leeladhar went on an overdrive to correct it.

The Regulator Slips Up

How did that happen? In December 2004, the department of non-banking supervision (DNBS) of the central bank had moved up an apparently innocuous and reasoned-out note on the income tax refunds of SIFCL.

The note brought to Leeladhar's notice the following facts:

- The income tax department had been creating tax demand by adding/disallowing deposits, interest on deposits, expense reimbursement to the agents, etc.

- The company preferred to appeal before the authority, and in one case (involving a small amount of a few crores) the issue was decided in favour of the company. Tax refund has been determined and adjusted against the tax demands of the pending assessment.

- The company has assessed the refunds at ₹992.88 crore –

the amount due to it from the government.

- These refunds were now to be treated as discretionary investments.

- These refunds were similar to investments in government bonds, which are treated as direct investment.

The department recommended treating such tax refunds as directed investments, provided the statutory auditors of the company certified the correctness of the refunds.

Leeladhar, just about two months old in the RBI, was carried away by the fairness of the recommendation and signed off a circular allowing RNBCs to include IT refunds in tax directed investment category.

What was the impact of this decision? SFICL could move close to ₹1,000 crore of disputed IT claims to the directed investment category. That freed up an equal amount from directed investments already made in the form of fixed deposits of banks and highly rated corporate debentures. They were liquidated and the cash was transferred to the discretionary investment category for investments in projects of the promoter's choice.

The next day a newspaper reported this, and Leeladhar carried the paper to Reddy's room worrying, will he fire me? Will he strip me of the DNBS portfolio? Leeladhar was trying to gauge Reddy's reaction as, by that time, he knew the implications of the move, and Reddy had not been consulted. The governor laughed and told Leeladhar to be careful in future and not be fooled by others. "You have learnt your lesson," were his exact words.

Immediately, all efforts were made to pull out the modification, and the direction was withdrawn 15 months after it was modified.

This was not the RBI's only slip up. When the insurance regulator IRDA asked for its so-called no-objection certificate (NoC) for Sahara's application to float a life insurance company, the RBI gave it without batting an eyelid. A regulator asking for an NoC from another regulator in such cases is a routine affair and the lower rung of the RBI treated it as such, giving it the stamp of approval. However, it was not a routine affair, considering Sahara's background and the history of its fight with the RBI. The governor should have been consulted before the NoC was issued.

That's the RBI version, but Roy has a different story to tell. According to him, executives at all level at the RBI harassed Sahara and refused to issue the NoC. Roy had to approach Bimal Jalan, "the most upright governor of RBI" and only then was the NoC issued.

Both Reddy and Leeladhar reshuffled staff and transferred some who they suspected were leaking information. A new crack team was formed. Krishnamurthy was brought in from Bangalore to head the Mission Sahara team; Reena Bannerji and Shekhar Bhatnagar were the other members.

As deputy governor, Leeladhar was also looking after HR and personnel. It was not difficult for him to call for records of intelligent officers and select for the job people with impeccable integrity. Parallely, the RBI began holding quarterly RNBC meetings.

A Report Never Made Public

Around the same time, a high-profile panel, appointed for a performance audit of public services and headed by former RBI deputy governor SS Tarapore, was asked to take a closer look into the RNBC issues, even though that was not part of its official mandate. The panel's report formed the bedrock of the RBI action against SIFCL and Peerless.

Not too many people have seen the report and it was never placed in the public domain as it was not part of the panel's official mandate. Former managing director of ICICI Bank Ltd HN Sinor, former Sebi chairman CB Bhave, former Bank of India chairman MG Bhide, and Mukund Manohar Chitale, partner of chartered accountancy firm Mukund M Chitale and Co., were the other members of the panel.

The key finding of the report, I am told by a few who have eyeballed it, was that the RNBC business model was essentially a play on liability (deposits) and not assets (loans and investments). Typically, the forfeiture clauses were the main source of income as the defaulters did not receive interest and, in some cases, even the principal amount. The interest was forfeited even if payment was delayed by a day, and even for those who could not deposit their installments not because they did not have the money but because the agent didn't turn up to collect it.

It also found that KYC norms were not followed and suggested that many politicians may have been parking their money with Sahara – an allegation that has never been proved.

Politicians' Money?

The suspicion that Sahara is a parking space for politicians' ill-gotten gains is as old as the organization, but no investigative agency has conclusively proved that. In December 1996, the IT department asked Sahara to furnish a list of MPs and MLAs who were supposedly keeping money with the group with hundreds of names mentioned in the annexure.

Prasenjit Singh, the then assistant commissioner of income tax, central circle III, Lucknow, signed two notices that were sent to Sahara on 4th December and 23rd December. Both the notices had the same text:

> You are requested to furnish the following information along with documentary evidence:
>
> a) The total investment made by the MLAs, MLCs and MPs as per annexure attached, from 1.4.1994 to 31.10. 1996.
>
> b) You are also required to furnish the above mentioned details regarding the deposits made by the mayors of Lucknow and the corporators of Lucknow during this period.
>
> The information should be given in the following format:
>
> 1) Name and address of person
>
> 2) Amount invested
>
> 3) Name of the scheme

> 4) Mode of payment
>
> 5) Date of deposit the money
>
> 6) Whether the money has been received back/or not.
>
> This information about the deposits of the honourable MLAs, MLCs and MPs, mayors and corporators, is in reference to deposits made by them during the above period in the different deposit schemes run by the assessee or the above of the sister concerns. Your reply should be furnished within a week of the receipt of this notice, failing which penalty proceedings will be initiated against you. (The) date of compliance is within ten days of the receipt of this letter.

The list in the annexure included three former Prime Ministers of India – PV Narasimha Rao, AB Vajpayee and Chandra Shekhar.

It also had ministers Mulayam Singh Yadav, Beni Prasad Verma and Gyaneshwar Mishra; speaker of the Lok Sabha PA Sangma; president of the All India Congress Committee Sitaram Kesri; Bahujan Samaj Party president Kanshi Ram; former chief ministers of Uttar Pradesh Kalyan Singh and Mayawati; and many others.

On 2 February 1997, about two months after the first notice was issued, Sahara wrote back to the IT department, saying, "In spite of our best efforts we have not been able to link any depositors in our accounts for and on whose behalf the names and addresses supplied by your honour along with aforesaid notice in respect of deposits."

The IT department wrote back on 8th February, saying, "The answer has to be specific and not loose-ended replies." It also said Sahara had not denied that leading politicians deposited black money with it.

Don't Throw Stones at a Bee Hive

The Sahara Pariwar retaliated by releasing two full-page advertisements in national newspapers in February and March. Signed by Roy, the 14th February ad carried an illustration of stones being thrown at a honeycomb and bees flying out, with a headline that read: "Till such time that the bees do not react to these stones throwers." It also said, "We do no injustice nor tolerate injustice," and "We chase quality, quantity chases us."

Written by Roy himself, the text of the advertisement said:

> "I, as the chief executive of the organization, claim with total steadfastness that our intention has always been to abide by the rules and regulations of the land...
>
> It is unfortunate that instead of encouraging us for our multidimensional success – maintaining such ideal norms – a few officials of certain departments have been regularly behaving in such a contemptible manner that it would not be possible to describe the degree of such meanness. We will never bow our head to their unjustified demands...
>
> We would love to abide by the directive of income tax

officials within seven days but we would like to inform that the complete control of our establishments (more than 1100 offices...) is done through our command office at Lucknow. For effective controlling... the computer department runs two shifts, 30 days a month. Our computerized system is based on a unique account number. In order to get a report based on names, it would definitely take more time. Besides, there is yet another point that the list provided by the income tax department is in Hindi whereas all our entries are in English.

Under these circumstances, when we translate from Hindi to English and then match the... name... it is quite possible to commit an error... In such a system, if there is a single wrong entry... the computer is unable to give the correct information. We have still made all efforts and in the preliminary we have not been able to find even a single name in our depositors' list in accordance with the list provided to us.... Many of the names in the list are of very important personalities with whom it is difficult to communicate in such a short time. Hence, we are publishing the names of the honourable citizens whom we believe will fully cooperate in abiding with the rules and regulations of the country to avoid any embarrassment to us and inform us at the earliest if they have deposited any amount in any scheme run by Sahara India."

The ad carried the list of people mentioned in the IT notices.

On 15th March, the group issued a second ad: "Hear No Evil, See No Evil, Speak No Evil" – reminding one of the three monkeys, Mizaru who sees no evil, Kikazaru who hears no evil and Iwazaru and who speaks no evil. It added, "Do No Evil, Tolerate No Evil."

The ad claimed Sahara India had given a 10,000-page reply to the IT department.

It challenged the tax office: "If any shortcoming, wrong doing, weakness, dishonesty is found in our intention, which is against the nation's interests... we should be hanged at once, but we should not be harassed everyday... by misusing one's powers."

I am not aware of what the IT notices finally led to. The Sahara ads demonstrate the group's obsession with volume: a 10,000-page answer to an IT notice; 16 years later, it would send 127 truckloads of 31,000 cartons carrying documents to Sebi, running into millions of pages – for a list of investors in the OFCDs of its two group companies.

It also highlights the group's strategy when any clarification is sought – the delaying tactic. Computerizing its entire data base in 1996 with unique identity numbers is laudatory, but it is difficult to accept the argument that such numbers did not have a name tag, or that converting English versions of names into Hindi would create chaos in the system.

The group used a similar tactic when Sebi asked for its list of OFCD investors. First, it said such investments were not under Sebi's jurisdiction; then, that its employees were on vacations ; and finally, under Supreme Court's deadline, that even with its 1,500 people and 50 photocopying machines, it would take 275 days to compile the data!

Incidentally, even today, Roy continues to say, "Prove we are doing wrong and hang us." The onus is on the regulator to prove Sahara wrong, not on Sahara to prove itself innocent.

Roy is firm on one ground: Sahara refused to give any information to Sebi as its regulator for OFCDs was the ministry of corporate affairs and it had taken advice from legal luminaries to vindicate this stance.

The Quarterly Meetings

There were frequent complaints from the RNBCs that, unlike banks and even NBFCs, they did not have a forum for discussing their problems with the regulator. Reddy saw in their demand an opportunity to get a peek into the workings of RNBCs and build a rapport with the promoters through periodic meetings – so that they wouldn't rush to the courts to get stay orders even on trivial issues.

It was a platform for discussion, quick decisions and building confidence. A place for moral suasion. The objective was to convince them to convert to NBFCs without taking deposits, focussing on fee-based activities such as distribution of insurance and other financial products. These meetings were headed by Leeladhar.

Why did the RNBCs agree to participate in such meetings? They wanted their voice to be heard and it was indeed the right forum as an RBI deputy governor was there to lend his ear, every quarter. But, more importantly, both Sahara and Peerless had the ambition to become a bank; they did not want to be on the wrong side of the regulator.

The first such meeting with SIFCL was held in April 2005. Leeladhar and then executive director for the non-banking division of the RBI, AV Sardesai, represented the RBI while Sahara was represented by Amitabha Ghosh, a member of the board.

Later on, Krishnamurthy joined the RBI team and three senior group executives – Anupam Praskah, Pallav Agarwal and Vandana Bharrgava – joined Roy who attended all meetings barring the first one. Roy was always cool, carrying himself with grace and dignity, never losing composure even once till the last meeting that sealed the fate of SIFCL.

These meetings took place in a small room on the 15th floor, starting typically at 3pm and lasting little less than an hour.

At the first meeting, Amitabha Ghosh – who was the RBI governor for three weeks in 1985 – spoke about how he controlled NBFCs during his tenure. Sardesai, who had worked with him, kept quiet. Leeladhar heard him out for a few minutes and said, "We invited Roy to attend the meeting... Let's stick to the agenda items and discuss business."

Leeladhar asked about a partnership that SIFCL had with another firm – Sahara India – for collection of deposits. Ghosh was not aware of that. He also said he did not have the mandate for agreeing to RBI proposals. That was the first and last time that Ghosh attended the quarterly meeting.

The first commercial banker to be a deputy governor, Ghosh was the longest serving deputy governor (between 21 January 1982 and 20 January 1992). He also served the shortest-ever term served by any RBI governor.

Son of Jugal Kishore Ghosh, a barrister at the Calcutta High Court, Ghosh had a chequered career. A commerce graduate from City College in Kolkata, he did his chartered accountancy at KN Gutgutia & Co., but instead of becoming a CA, he joined Allahabad Bank in July 1951 as a probationary officer at a monthly stipend of ₹150. By 1969, he was one of the four general managers in the bank; by 1974, the sole general manager; and in 1977, the chairman of the bank.

In 1982, the then Prime Minister, Indira Gandhi, insisted on taking a commercial banker as a deputy governor of the RBI. Ghosh was made deputy governor along with Rangarajan, but was senior to Rangarajan as he had joined two weeks before the latter. When Manmohan Singh stepped down as the RBI governor in January 1985 to join the Planning Commission as its deputy chairman, Ghosh moved to the corner room for three weeks, before RN Malhotra took over the mantle.

BV Chaturvedi, a CA in Kolkata, requested Ghosh to join Roy, then a rising entrepreneur. He joined the SIFCL board in 1994 along with KS Bhatnagar, former secretary, ministry of law and company affairs, and former chairman of the Company Law Board, and Brijendra Sahay, former chief secretary of Uttar Pradesh, a close friend of Roy.

After a couple of years, Ghosh resigned as public perception was not good about Sahara, but joined SIFCL again in 1998, only to resign in 2008. However, he continued to remain on the boards of other group companies. Why did he come back in 1998? Ghosh says he was convinced by people he knew well in the group. Besides, he was given the freedom to choose which group companies he would be associated with as a board member.

Long-Time Directors Resign

In April 2013, Ghosh finally severed ties with the group by stepping down from the boards of five Sahara firms along with S Mohan, retired Supreme Court judge and Arun Chand Mukherjee, former chairman of New India Assurance. All three cited either health or personal reasons for putting in their papers. Mohan was, however, persuaded to stay back.

Ghosh was a director in Sahara Prime City Ltd, which is in the business of developing commercial and residential properties; Sahara India Life Insurance Co. Ltd; Sahara Mutual Fund; Sahara Hospitality Ltd, which runs Hotel Sahara Star, a venue of many board meetings; and Sahara Infrastructure & Housing Ltd.

Mukherjee was an independent member on the board of the life insurance firm while Mohan is an independent trustee of the asset management company.

Ghosh, it seemed, was unhappy on many counts, including with the appointment of a legal firm – Athena Legal – by Sahara Prime City for advice and services at an annual fee much higher than the company's net profit. In a dissent note to the company secretary of Prime City, CB Thapa, Ghosh wrote that his understanding was the resolution to appoint the firm was withdrawn for deliberation at a subsequent meeting but in the draft minutes of the 30th March meeting, "it was shown as an approved item, which is not correct."

The domain name athenalegal.org is owned by Sahara India Pariwar, according to DomainTools, an online database of registered domain names and hosting data. It was registered by Rajat Prakash Srivastava, son of Om Prakash Sirvastava, on behalf of Sahara India on 12 October 2011. Its registered address is the same as Sahara India's Lucknow address.

Srivastava, an MA in old Indian history from Gorakhpur University, is the last word on legal issues in Sahara; he is also the trouble-shooter. A deputy managing director at Sahara India Pariwar, Srivastava has been supervising and monitoring para-banking and other businesses since the inception of the group. He is the third-most important employee of Sahara India Pariwar, after Roy and his wife Swapna, and ahead of Roy's brother and sons in the hierarchy. Swapna Roy is the vice chairman of Sahara India Pariwar.

"If for any reason this item finds a place in the minutes as an approved item, please note that as I have not agreed to the said item, my dissent should be recorded and it should be noted that I am not a party to this decision," Ghosh wrote.

He was also upset with the way the chief of Sahara India Life Insurance was appointed and one particular transaction among group companies. Sanjay Agarwal was made the insurance chief, replacing NP Bali. Sahara India Life was granted licence by the insurance regulator in February 2004: the first Indian company without any foreign collaboration to enter the Indian life insurance market. Roy is its chairman.

Apparently, Agarwal was made the CEO without the approval of the board. In an email to company secretary Parakh Tandon in March 2013 Ghosh wrote:

> "... Both Mr (Arun) Mukherjee and myself have been urging from time to time for appointment of a permanent CEO but this could not be finalized by the management. A few days back I received a message from you which indicated that a decision has been taken to appoint Mr Sanjay Agarwal as CEO consequent on resignation of Mr Bali w.e.f 7 March, 2013, and a resolution has to be passed in this regard by circulation instead in a board meeting and the resolution would be ratified at the next board meeting in the month of April, 2013, to which both Mr Mukherjee and myself objected as we felt that such an important matter should not be passed by circulation and subsequently ratified at the next board meeting.
>
> Both of us insisted that a board meeting must be convened to pass an appropriate resolution before we write to IRDA. Thereafter, you advised me that the proposal to appoint Mr Sanjay Agarwal as CEO has been dropped and our query regarding replacement of Mr Bali remained unanswered.
>
> This morning you contacted me and mentioned that IRDA has raised certain points regarding the appointment. In the letter of IRDA, it has been written that (the) appointment of CEO must be supported by (a) board resolution. It appears from the letter of IRDA that you recommended appointment of Mr Sanjay Agarwal as CEO without a board resolution. It is inappropriate and

irregular to approach (the) regulator for appointment of (the) CEO without a proper board resolution which must be within your knowledge... The way the matter has been handled is unsatisfactory...

In view of the seriousness of the matter, a board meeting shall be convened forthwith to discuss this subject in all its aspects before sending a reply to IRDA. Await your advice. Keep your top management informed what have been stated in this communication."

Under Section 289 of Companies Act 1956, a resolution can be passed by circulation but this does not dispense with the need for holding a meeting at least once in three months, as required by Section 285. Such a resolution should also find a place in the minutes of the next board meeting.

In another letter to Prime City's Thapa, Ghosh wrote:

"This is in connection with the matter discussed in the board meeting held on 30 March 2013 at your Mumbai office. One of the agenda item(s) – No 6 of the audit committee agenda – was for approval of unaudited financial statement of the company... I observed... that a sum of ₹1,500 crore had been received by the company from Sahara Credit Cooperative Society as advance for business development. However, contrary to the understanding, an amount of ₹500 crore out of the aforesaid sum of ₹1,500 crore has been invested in the unquoted equity share capital of Sahara India Commercial Corp. Ltd. The matter was not discussed in any previous meetings either of the committee or board.

I sought a detailed explanation for this deviation but did not get a satisfactory response. Accordingly, I would like to place on record my dissent in this matter.The company secretary may please be directed to note my dissent."

Sahara India Commercial Corp., which has its registered office in Kolkata, is into real estate (especially integrated townships), media and entertainment, and trading through its countless subsidiaries, a few of which are overseas.

According to Abhijit Sarkar, the corporate communications head of the Sahara group, Ghosh and other directors resigned when the "Sebi matter became hot". He also says Ghosh has been trying to reach Mr Roy through various sources for his re-induction on the board but "Mr Roy is not even taking his calls".

What is the Problem?

After writing these letters and email on 30th March, Ghosh called Roy to say he wasn't comfortable with the way the Sahara group companies were being run – decisions were being taken without discussion. "What is the problem?" Roy asked him. Ghosh answered that he did not like the style of functioning in the group companies he was associated with.

Other independent directors on the Sahara Prime City board were Madhukar, former chairman of United Bank of India; Justice KN Singh, the 22nd Chief Justice of India; Debi Prasad Bagchi, former chief secretary of Orissa; and Devi Dayal, former banking secretary.

Ghosh, insiders say, was concerned about the lack of KYC norms fulfillment by the SIFCL depositors and raised his voice when the company was buying government bond at high prices. He insisted on setting aside money to provide for mark-to-market or MTM losses in case the interest rates were reversed. MTM is an accounting practice of valuing a financial asset in accordance with its market value and not the value at which it was purchased. In a rising interest rate scenario, bond value goes down as prices move in the opposite direction of its yield.

Ghosh and fellow board member KS Bhatnagar protested against and scuttled SIFCL's plan to invest in Aamby Valley Ltd. A township developed by Sahara, Aamby Valley City is spread over 10,600 acres of hilly terrain in Maharashtra's Pune district, about 120 km from Mumbai.

Overall, Ghosh tried to bring in a semblance of discipline within the RNBC. The chief financial officer of the company, RP Singh, used to say, "*Ghosh-saab bahut tung karte hain.*"(Ghosh gives us too much trouble.) Srivastava was brought into the audit committee to neutralize Ghosh.

The RBI held 11 quarterly meetings that tightened the noose around the neck of Sahara's RNBC arm and led to a forensic audit by KPMG. At every meeting, the RBI would convince Roy on certain things; he would then go back to his office and agree to the new terms and conditions imposed by the regulator, write that on his letterhead and circulate the minutes of the meeting.

Who Owns the Partnership Firm?

Sahara used to outsource deposit collection to a partnership firm run by Roy and his relatives – Sahara India. The company is registered as a partnership firm under the Indian Partnership Act, 1932, and housed in Sahara India Bhawan, 1, Kapoorthala Complex, Aliganj, Lucknow.

The partnership firm used to operate out of SIFCL branches, but the RBI could not inspect the books as they technically belonged to a separate company on which the banking regulator's writ did not work. There used to be at least 60-day delays between the collection of money by the firm and its transfer to SIFCL. The RBI forced Sahara to terminate the outsourcing agreement. This gave the RBI team a direct entry into SIFCL branches to introduce KYC norms.

SIFCL is an RNBC registered with the RBI to conduct the business of collecting deposits from the general public. Roy, his wife Swapna Roy and brother Joy Broto Roy (representing the promoters) and Ghosh, Sahay and Bhatnagar had been independent directors on SIFCL's board for most of its existence. Sahara India is a partnership firm with Roy, his wife and brother as partners and this is not regulated by the RBI.

Under the outsourcing agreement between SIFCL and Sahara India, the collection agents were employed by Sahara India while the branch premises were owned or leased by SIFCL and made available to Sahara India for deposit collection and other related activities on rent. The deposit mobilization expenses were paid to Sahara India while

SIFCL received rent from it for using its branches.

In other words, Sahara India, the unregulated partnership firm, was collecting deposits, redeeming matured deposits, completing KYC requirement and keeping accounts, but the RBI was kept away from looking at its books. The RBI also could not access details on individual depositors and other aspects like KYC compliance, details of brokerage paid to agents and payment of interest, and forfeiture of interest for non-payment or delayed payments of installments.

All that the RBI could get were macro details but there was no scope for cross-checking or verification from branches as the regulator did not have an entry there.

Roy vehemently denies this, saying every year, five senior RBI inspectors used to inspect Sahara headquarters and up to 200 branches in about two months.

Outlining the history of Sahara India partnership firm, he says the arm was created when it was lawfully taking public deposits. By the time the RBI banned unincorporated bodies from taking public deposits by amending Chapter IIIC of Banking Regulation Act 1949, Sahara India had opened thousands of branches, employing lakhs of people. It became a popular brand and took up the agency work for deposit collection of the RNBC. The branches could not be transferred to the RNBC as Sahara India had the tenancy agreement for such branches.

The RBI got wind of this arrangement in September 2004 when it insisted and got a copy of the 2002–03 annual report of SIFCL. Just ahead of that, the RNBC had signed a two-year arrangement with Sahara India on 1 April 2004, till 31 March 2006.

In four years between 2002 and 2006, SIFCL paid close to ₹1,061 crore to Sahara India, the unregulated partnership firm, data extracted from the audited financial statement of the company, appearing under related party disclosure, show.

The money collected as deposits by Sahara India was expected to be passed on to SIFCL immediately, but the RBI had no means to check whether this had been done. If the money collected is not paid to SIFCL entirely and immediately, the fund would become available for the partnership firm to use as it wished.

As long as such money did not come into the accounts of SIFCL, it did not count for the directed investment mandated by the RBI.

The audited annual account of the company disclosed a significant amount of money pending with Sahara India: collected but not passed on to SIFCL. For the fiscal year ended March 2002, it was ₹474 crore, 14% of the amount collected; and for fiscal 2003, it was ₹353 crore, or 7% of the amount collected. The money was lying at 1,400 collection centres with agents at the close of the year.

Financial companies usually resort to the so-called year-end window dressing to manage their annual accounts. So much money might not have been lying with Sahara India round the year but the regulator took exception to it as the deposits collected by Sahara India should have been passed on to SIFCL immediately. RBI, however, could in no way check this.

Later, after the agreement ended in 2006, and the RBI did inspect the branches, it found that the time lag between collection of deposits and remittance to SIFCL was 60–90 days. No interest was paid for this period to SIFCL.

Till March 2006, when the arrangement was in place, each time the regulator asked for details of brokerages paid to collecting agents, the interest paid to the depositors, and KYC procedures, the standard answer was "all of them are available in the branches", but the regulator could not inspect any of them.

"If this is true, it means that our balance sheet and quarterly liabilities were always wrong, which was not the case," says an agitated Roy. "Did the RBI suddenly discover this? What was it doing for 18 years – between 1987 and 2005?" he asks.

There was no list of agents or details of brokerage paid to these agents at the corporate office, where the RBI had access to, as the agents were not on the payroll of SIFCL, the regulated entity. Even the branches did not have the complete list of "workers" as they were on the payroll of the partnership firm.

Most of the deposits of SIFCL were either daily deposits or monthly deposits with a tenure of seven years – the maximum allowed by the RBI. The definition of default was unfair as even a single day default under a daily deposit scheme would have made a depositor forego the interest for seven years. This could have happened for no fault of the depositor – an agent's lethargy to collect money could make a depositor a defaulter. They were always vulnerable.

Typically, as agents receive a high initial commission, it is normal that they would always be eager to get new depositors. Roy, however, claims that Sahara's commission structure was "very low" compared with Peerless. A Sahara official says there were different deposit raising schemes, such as daily and monthly, and different tenures, between one year and 15 years, and for all such schemes, the agents' commission varied between 1.5% and 4%.

Going by the RBI's norms, a minimum 8% interest was to be compounded annually on amounts deposited in lump sum or monthly or over longer periods. For the daily deposit scheme, it was 6%. The RBI mandated these rates in November 1997 and they were revised periodically, in sync with the prevailing interest rates in the banking system.

SIFCL, however, has its bullet-proof explanation. In a letter to the RBI on 26 August 2004, Anupam Prakash, the senior Sahara group executive, clarified:

> ...The company is paying interest/bonus on the accounts which are for the full term of the scheme as per the provisions of the RBI directions. The defaults and lapses on the part of the depositors are governed by terms of schemes duly agreed between the depositor and the company. In the event of default... the company is entitled to the liquidated damages as per (the) law of the land.
>
> The rate of interest/bonus on lapsed account is being calculated after considering the investment opportunity loss, etc. to the company due to non-deposit of installments by the depositors in accordance with the terms of the scheme.

The matter has earlier been discussed with RBI and it was found that the above rules of the company are in conformity with the law of the land and do not in any matter impinge upon the RBI directions...

You would kindly appreciate that the RBI directives deal with only completed contracts. We are advised that in the case of banks also, RBI directions on interest rates on deposits do not cover discontinued recurring deposits contracts and such matters have always been left to the banks... It may also be incidentally mentioned that the banks do not accept daily deposits. When they accepted such deposits, they used to pay simple interest rate of 1.5% to 3.5% per annum on regular contracts, leave aside the discontinued deposits. The defaults in the deposit contracts have to be discouraged (as) otherwise there will (be) no encouragement to the depositor to adhere to the terms and conditions of contract.

The regulator heard of the arrangement between SIFCL and Sahara India in September 2004, but instead of immediately pressing the cancellation button, it decided to wait for over 18 months, allowing the agreement to run its course till 31 March 2006. Why? Nobody in the RBI is willing to discuss this. Repeated requests for certain facts did not elicit any response. Certain information sought through the Right to Information Act (RTI) was also not entertained.

Possibly, the regulator did not want to rush, fearing that Sahara may go to court, get a stay, and grow too fast in the intervening time. Besides, till the last moment, the RBI did not want to confront SIFCL. Indeed, the RBI wanted to introduce stringent norms and bring in better control over these companies, but the plan was to do it amicably and through discussions with the RNBCs. The quarterly dialogue offered a platform for this.

The Tax Demand

Another contentious issue was income tax assessment and the tax demand made by the tax authorities.

The contingent liabilities of SIFCL declared in the audited financial statements in the company's balance sheets contain details of assessment completed and demands raised by IT authorities. These demands were increasing at an alarming pace and had no relation to the net profit declared by the company. For instance, for fiscal 2003, the company's net profit was ₹6.11 crore but the cumulative tax demand raised from assessment year 1991 to 2000, mentioned in the 2003 balance sheet, was ₹517 crore. In 2007, the cumulative tax demand till assessment year 2004 rose to ₹5,288 crore while the profit for the year was a paltry ₹17.75 crore. The year in which income is earned is the fiscal year and the year in which it is taxed is called the assessment year. The fiscal year precedes the assessment year.

Since the IT authorities were not able to identify many of the depositors physically at the addresses given by the company, they added to the company's taxable income the entire new deposit accounts generated by it in an assessment year. They also disallowed interest paid to new depositors.

Simply put, the IT authorities had strong reservations against the so-called deposits added by the company every year.

Schedule 17 forming part of the accounts for the year ending 31 March 2005 shows this statement: "The income tax department has been creating tax demands by adding/disallowing deposits interest on deposits, expenses reimbursed to the agents, etc." The IT department was treating part of the deposits mobilized by the company as undisclosed income and was adding them to the income of SIFCL to calculate its tax liability. The department also disallowed interest payment on such deposits. Incidentally, the company never made any provisions for these demands.

The RBI was curious about Sahara's claim of high capital adequacy ratio. In 2003, it was 26.97%; in 2004, 25.40%; and in 2005, 31.30%. The computation of the capital adequacy ratio is not certified by auditors. The annual reports cite data of shareholders' funds and fixed assets like land, buildings, plant and machinery, vehicles, communication equipment, recording equipment, etc. Many of these were not connected to the core business of SIFCL and were leased out to group companies for their activities. For instance, recording equipment owned by SIFCL had a book value of ₹112.52 crore, or 23% of its total fixed assets of ₹435.75 crore. A great way of helping group companies.

Roy scoffs at the suggestion that the capital adequacy ratio was not certified by auditors. "The RBI inspection team and offsite auditors always calculated threadbare the capital adequacy ratio of the company," he says, insisting that maintaining ideal capital adequacy ratio was very important for an RNBC and Sahara's capital adequacy ratio was always very high

Both NBFCs and RNBCs had 12% capital adequacy ratio, but unlike RNBCs, NBFCs have a cap on their leverage ratio: to what extent they can raise public deposits is linked to their net worth or capital and reserves. Besides, RNBCs investments were largely confined to zero-risk government bonds.

In March 2008, SIFCL had a capital adequacy ratio of 28.78% which progressively rose to 180% in March 2011 when it was winding down its business. In March 2013, it was 106.09%.

Forensic Audit

At the tenth quarterly meeting, the RBI made Roy agree to the idea of a forensic audit of SIFCL, to be conducted by the regulator as it would supposedly help Sahara prevent fraud, which was a probability in the absence of its adherence to KYC norms.

KPMG conducted a forensic audit of SIFCL – the first such exercise in the Indian financial system. A parallel audit was conducted in Peerless by an India arm of Deloitte.

In one Delhi branch, it was found that the namesake of former Bihar chief minister Lalu Prasad Yadav had kept at least 200 accounts of ₹19,500 each with SIFCL. There were many such accounts. An unfazed Roy says that there are many people in India who have similar names. For instance, thousands of Atal Bihari Vajpayees, all namesakes of the former Indian Prime Minister, had kept deposits with Sahara in the past.

Under norms, up to ₹20,000 can be kept in cash with a financial intermediary. This means one can keep one's unaccounted money this way and won't get caught as there is no cheque transaction.

One can use bank branches too in the same way. In fact, a 2013 investigation by the RBI of digital magazine *Cobrapost's* allegations about three large Indian private banks – ICICI Bank Ltd, HDFC Bank Ltd and Axis Bank Ltd – being involved in money laundering, revealed that front-desk employees were selling large amounts of gold and high-value insurance policies without following the KYC norms, and allowing high-value cash transactions. In March 2013, *Cobrapost* had released videos of its undercover sting operation that captured on camera bankers suggesting they could help clients avoid tax and convert black money into white. Later, the digital magazine released reports, implicating more private and public sector banks.

An RBI investigation did not reveal any evidence of money laundering, but the regulator penalized these banks as they were found to have violated RBI regulations in terms of their correspondent banking relationship with cooperative banks, certain aspects of KYC norms and anti-money laundering guidelines, among others.

Reacting to media reports on KPMG conducting a forensic audit of Sahara, India's apex audit body, the Institute of Chartered Accountants of India (ICAI) wrote to the RBI saying KPMG was licensed to do consultancy as a corporate entity, approved by the body, but it was not registered with ICAI to do audit. The RBI could not ignore what a self-regulatory body of auditors was saying. It decided to conduct its own inspection and validate the KPMG findings. A group of three RBI officials, under RN Kar, a general manager in Hyderabad, audited 15 Sahara Financial branches in three weeks.

Their findings were presented to the Board for Financial Supervision (BFS), a part of the high profile RBI board. A senior central banker carried the KPMG findings in four CDs and the printouts in four fat files one evening in March 2008 to the finance minister's office in Delhi. It was raining heavily. By the time the RBI official left North Block on Raisina Hill, which houses the finance ministry, it was well past 8pm.

For most of the time, Leeladhar was handling DNBS directly along with the department of payment and settlement system. During the Reddy regime, the RBI instituted a system whereby each deputy governor would handle a few departments directly – cutting down the layer of executive director – to move things fast. Towards the end of the battle with Sahara, Gopalakrishna was given the charge of the department as an executive director.

It was a tactical move. Had Leeladhar continued to oversee the department directly, Reddy would have been the appellate authority in case Sahara wanted to appeal against any of the deputy governor's decisions. By making Gopalakrishna responsible for the department, Reddy was spared from any appeal against the DNBS decision. Gopalakrishna's boss

Leeladhar became the appellate authority.

Gradually, the time taken by the meetings became longer, often beyond an hour, as they always did a review of the previous meeting – what Roy had agreed to do and whether SIFCL actually met the commitments. Many a time, SIFCL did not do what it had committed to.

KYC was the weakest point in SIFCL's armour. For the RBI, violation of KYC norms was the strongest weapon to bring Sahara down. The other big issue was non-payment of interest to depositors or forfeiture.

Roy says Sahara had never failed in any of its commitments except for once when for many months RBI controlled Sahara's bank account and it could not withdraw money without the clearance of the RBI-nominated statutory auditors. "Only for those months we could not make timely repayment." He also says there was absolutely no forefeiture of deposits at all.

SIFCL claimed that most of its depositors were from among the poorest of the poor, residing in remote areas where banks had no reach. Its collection agents are reported to reach their depositors on a day-to-day basis and attend to their needs. Almost all SIFCL director's reports include a statement saying there was no unclaimed and/or overdue deposits with the company during the period under review.

Unclaimed Deposits

At the RBI's insistence, the company began giving data on unpaid depositors in its annual reports from 2004–05. In the fiscal year 2005, there were 25,99,097 such depositors, and the money involved was ₹145.48 crore. The next year, the number of depositors who did not claim their money from SIFCL swelled to 31,72,788 and the kitty rose to ₹224.19 crore. In subsequent years, the corpus expanded even more. As on 31 March 2011, there were 93,43,776 depositors who hadn't submitted their claims for ₹952.86 crore.

No interest is paid on the overdue deposits from the date on which the deposits mature. Typically, all director's reports say, "...the company has instructed its officials situated at each centre to contact such hon'ble depositors for payment against these request at the earliest possible. (The) company has also started sending advance intimation to all its hon'ble depositors informing them the due date of maturity of these deposit with the company so as to minimize such cases in future."

Incidentally, under norms, a deposit that remains unclaimed for seven years needs to be transferred to the government's Consolidated Fund, but this rule is applicable only to banks. The RNBCs could keep such money with them – a unique source of free funds.

The RBI would list out all points, however trivial, at every quarterly meeting and Sahara would contest all. But the RBI would not accept the Sahara argument and insist on compliance. Wiser from the Peerless experience, the RBI wanted to engage Sahara in discussion, close the loop slowly but surely, and not allow it to approach the court. Every meeting had minutes and the BFS was kept informed.

Typically, Roy would talk the least at such meetings; others would do the talking. He was, however, very keen to invite Leeladhar and others to Aamby Valley City and Sahara Star hotel to impress on them his contribution to the Indian economy. He even offered to host the regional directors' conference, an annual ritual at the RBI, at Aamby Valley. There were no takers for such proposals. Roy was also very critical of the KYC norms. "How would vegetable vendors furnish KYC documents?" he would often ask.

He is still critical of the RBI and cannot forget those days in the Indian central bank under the Reddy regime. "It first allowed us to treat the income tax demand as part of the directed investment. It had asked us to give them at least two examples of refund but later withdrew this," Roy told me in January 2013 at his secretariat at Sahara Shaher in Gomti Nagar, Lucknow.

"The RBI first issued a show cause notice, and on the third day clamped down the prohibitory order. We had to go to the high court and they ran to the Supreme Court. They had to change the order... It never happened in RBI's history."

There were lighter moments too. For instance, when Sahara One, the Hindi general entertainment channel of the group, was relaunched, and Leeladhar congratulated Roy, the Sahara supremo feigned surprise and said there's hardly anything about Sahara that the deputy governor didn't know.

When the group spent ₹300 crore to sponsor the Indian cricket team, Roy announced the money hadn't come from the RNBC, even before Leeladhar could say anything. And, after selling his loss-making airline to Jet Airways Ltd, Roy asked the RBI team whether it was a good move or not.

Leeladhar lost his cool only twice – once at the very first meeting when Roy did not turn up and Ghosh wanted to impress his team, but he managed to not show his annoyance; he merely told Ghosh to stick to facts and asked him why Roy could not come.

The second time he got livid when Vandana Bharrgava, one of the three senior Sahara group executives, claimed that 100 SIFCL branches in UP were connected through technology and could reconcile data as she had promised in the previous meeting. Leeladhar stood up and said that was a false claim and that SIFCL had done nothing to improve on the technology front. He also said that the meeting was meant for Roy, and others who had been attending the meeting should stop doing that if they did not have any information to share.

In December 2008, at the RBI's annual executive directors' conference in Mumbai, after a day-long meeting, there were lighter moments in the evening over drinks and dinner. Gopalakrishna did a skit on how to make the normally calm, never-agitated deputy governor angry, acting out the Bharrgava incident. Everybody, including the new RBI governor D Subbarao, burst into laughter. This was a few months after Subbarao had joined and weeks before Leeladhar called it a day.

A Sahara official says Leeladhar had no business of getting upset with Bharrgava as the company updated technology continuously and aggressively. It had Asia's biggest V-Sat network and not a single payment could happen without the advise of the headquarters.

Fit and Proper

According to the company director's reports, SIFCL's philosophy on corporate governance envisages the attainment of high level of transparency and accountability in its functions and conduct of its business. These include close interactions with the depositors, creditors and employers with due emphasis on all legal and regulatory compliance.

The nomination committee which was formed for the first time on 29 March 2005, according to a director's report, "... had noted that Shri Amitabha Ghosh former deputy governor of RBI and Shri KS Bhatnagar, former secretary, ministry of law and justice and corporate affairs ... both aged above 70 years. But on the basis of their robust health, professional knowledge and expertise and in the interest of the sound and prudent management of the company, should continue as members of the board of SIFCL. These facts have already been communicated to RBI that all directors of the company are fit and proper for appointment/continuing to hold appointment on the board."

This is the Sahara way of conforming to the "fit and proper" norm – old professionals should remain on board by virtue of their "robust health", apart from other qualifications.

The group also boasts of a unique committee that no other company in the world would have – the Kartavya Council. Members of the council include actors Amitabh Bachchan, Aishwarya Rai and Raj Babbar; cricketers Kapil Dev and Saurav Ganguly; tennis player Leander Paes; former election commissioner TN Seshan and former Tata Steel Ltd (formerly Tisco) head Russi Mody.

How often the council meets, the attendance of its members, and the sitting fees they earn are not known. The council advises on matters relating to quick redressal of grievances. An inhouse publication of Sahara says the Kartavya Council works "as a query, grievances and suggestions cell". It also gives a chart on the number of grievances received by the council and solved every year. Between 2003 and 2005, there were about 7,500 complaints received every year and almost all of them were solved. Since then, the number has come down.

In an interview with this author, Roy explained why he chose actors and cricketers for the council. "We have to take care of human psychology in every aspect – whenever the platform is strong, the faith is more. Renowned people give them security. Glamour plays a positive role. People jump on to film actors, they go mad. We believe in glamour."

He also said the council takes care of justice for one million people. "Sitting here, I cannot ensure that. Anybody who has any problem can approach them. Here a director is punished if he misbehaves with his driver. My brother did that once and he was punished severely. When I heard that he had misbehaved with the driver, I asked him why he did this. There is an assembly every Saturday. I told him either he would have to tender an apology to the driver with folded hands or I take administrative action. He preferred to apologize," he said.

Sahara holds an open house to deal with such issues every week. The open house is held on Saturdays at Lucknow, where activities of the group, general and medical awareness, personal finance, etc. are discussed. It's an interactive platform.

5

NEW BOARD, NEW AUDITORS, NEW SAHARA

The RBI wanted SIFCL to reconstitute its board with 50% independent directors, acceptable to the regulator. In early July 2008, after consulting the RBI, SIFCL invited HN Sinor, former managing director of ICICI Bank Ltd; TN Manoharan, a chartered accountant and the founding partner of Manohar Chowdhry & Associates, and former president of Institute of Chartered Accountants of India; and Arvind KD Jadhav, a 1970 batch IAS officer, and former secretary mining and chairman of Maharashtra Water Resources Regulatory Authority, to join its board.

Leeladhar wrote to all three, thanking them for consenting to join the SIFCL board, and assured them that they were acceptable to the regulator.

Even though all three had the endorsement of the RBI, they were not nominees of the central bank and that made them a little wary when famed investment banker Nimesh Kampani, an independent director on the board Nagarjuna Finance Ltd (NFL), was hounded by the Andhra Pradesh police in 2009 and, for long, Indian courts refused to grant Kampani an anticipatory bail. Kampani and other directors on the NFL board were under investigation for the firm's alleged failure to return ₹98.3 crore collected from 85,160 depositors in 1997–98.

Kampani, chairman of financial services firm JM Financial Ltd, was one of the NFL directors till April 1999. JM Financial applied for a banking licence to the RBI in June 2013 when the Indian banking regulator opened its window for the third round of private banks. Indian born American banker and former Citigroup chief executive officer Vikram Pandit would drive the initiative.

Can an independent director face criminal charges for the actions of a company well after he has quit? Section 5 of the Andhra Pradesh Protection of Depositors of Financial Establishments Act 1999 says, "Where any financial establishment defaults in the return of a deposit either in cash or kind, or defaults in the payment of interest, every person responsible for the management of the affairs of the financial establishment, including the promoter, manager or member of the financial establishment, shall be punished with up to 10 years' imprisonment and up to ₹1,00,000 fine."

The Andhra Pradesh police issued an "international lookout notice" against Kampani in January 2009 when he was in Dubai on official work. He had to stay overseas for long to avoid arrest.

Jadhav quit eight months after he joined the Maharashtra Water Resources Regulatory Authority; the other two remained on the board for a little over three years – between August 2008 and October 2011 – and resigned on 31 October 2011. They wanted protection from the RBI in case of any default. After all, they were overseeing SIFCL's repayment of money to millions of depositors. The banking regulator did not make them RBI nominees, but issued a comfort letter, throwing a protective ring around them.

After Jadhav stepped down, Roy's brother Joy Broto too had to quit the board to maintain the balance between insiders and outsiders. Roy and his Man Friday, Srivastava, remained on the board representing the promoter.

The RBI also forced SIFCL to change its auditors of 25 years, Chaturvedi & Co and DS Shukla & Co – both based in Lucknow. The new auditors were GD Apte & Co and Kalyaniwalla & Mistry, based in Pune and Mumbai, respectively.

Before the trio took over as independent directors of SIFCL, on 28th July, the RBI executive director Gopalakrishna called them to the 15th floor conference room at its headquarters in Mumbai and explained the road map to them.

Smooth Repayment of ₹18,000 crore

The primary job of the directors was to ensure that the depositors' interest was protected by smooth repayment of the ₹18,000 crore by selling government bonds and securities and to ensure that there was no default. The biggest challenge was monitoring the asset-liability mismatches, when the new money flow dried up.

Indeed, the directed lending norm under which SIFCL was to invest 100% of its deposits in government bonds and other approved securities ensured liquidity as bonds can be sold at a short notice, but it had a negative side too.

As investment in government bonds are subject to market or MTM losses, if a company wants to redeem bonds ahead of maturity to pay off depositors, there could be asset-liability mismatches because of value erosion.

Investment in government bonds depreciates with the rise in interest rates and any premature redemption erodes value. This means, money in the kitty could be less than what was needed to pay off the depositors. The absence of fresh cash flow could make matters worse.

Sahara was forced to sell some assets to generate liquidity but even that was not enough to pay off the depositors. By 2010, Sahara got a ₹1,800 crore refund from the income tax authorities, which it had paid under protest.

The money offered it a huge cushion against redemption. By the time Sinor and Manoharan left the board, very little money was left to be paid.

In January 2013, Roy said the exercise was almost complete as of December 2012 and only ₹700–800 crore was left to be paid. "We are tracing some depositors.... It will take a while."

The First Board Meeting

The first meeting of the new board took place on 13 August 2008, roughly a month after SIFCL revealed its numbers for the first time through publication of a "fact sheet", purportedly to instill confidence in the depositors and field workers. Both Manoharan and Sinor were already on the board (Manoharan was also made the chairman of audit committee), but Jadhav was yet to join formally. He was present at the meeting as a special invitee.

The venue of the board meeting was the Sahara Star Hotel at the Mumbai airport. The directors got a red carpet welcome and were ushered in to the second floor ACES Presidential Boardroom of the hotel. Roy made a dramatic entry through a lift that descends directly from Sky Lounge, the penthouse of Sahara Star where he lives when he is in Mumbai. The atmosphere was charged.

The meeting was action packed – the board was reconstituted, the auditors changed and the audit committee recast. The board also approved a new business plan drafted with assistance from Ernst & Young Pvt Ltd. Of course, most of the decisions were subject to shareholders' approval at the annual general meeting later that month in Lucknow, but that was a formality as Roy owned SIFCL.

The new board met at least 18 times in the next four years and most meetings were held at Sahara Star. At the end of one such meeting, lunch was served at Roy's penthouse from where one can see planes taking off and touching down at the airport.

Sahara Star has an interesting history. In October 2002, the Sahara Group bought over the 300-room Centaur Airport Hotel on a 30,000 square metre plot, from the Delhi-based Batra Hospitality Pvt Ltd for ₹115 crore. The deal included the Centaur Airport Hotel, six flats in Andheri east and dealership of a petrol pump across the hotel. Batra Hospitality had bought over this hotel, along with the flats and petrol pump – whose ownership is disputed with Indian Oil Co. Ltd – for ₹83 crore in February that year.

The sale of the airport hotel, belonged to the Hotel Corp. of India Ltd, the wholly-owned subsidiary of Air India, was part of then Bharatiya Janata Party-led National Democratic Alliance government's disinvestment programme, overseen by disinvestment minister Arun Shourie. This marked Sahara's entry into the hospitality space.

The directors received a compensation of ₹20,000 as sitting fee for each meeting. A generous Roy suggested to offer monthly compensation and other perquisites but both Sinor and Manoharan declined the offer. There was also an invitation from the company secretary of Aamby Valley to Manoharan offering him a board seat but the chartered accountant did not respond to the letter; declined it orally.

Roy missed very few meetings, including the last one, on 31 October 2011, when Manoharan and Sinor were around. In his absence, OP Srivastava chaired the meeting. One can imagine what he must have felt when the RBI forced his nominees out and recast the board but he was never bitter towards the independent directors and showed the courtesy of seeing them off at the end of every board meeting that he attended.

Manoharan found Roy polite, courteous and genuinely affectionate. "I have seen people touch Roy's feet – it's not a boss-subordinate relationship; he is a fatherly figure. I have never seen in him an attitude of non-cooperation. He never confronted; he accepted reality," he told me in his Chennai office on Subramaniam Street, Abirampuram, over an "executive lunch" sent from a nearby restaurant, complete with pickle, *sambar, rasam*, curd rice, *papadum* and *payasam*.

According to him, Roy had a very practical approach, but he had his anguish as a businessman. "His continuous concern was on restrictions imposed on him and his thought process was if only government doesn't clip his wings, he could expand and do more things. He can work wonders. There was no reason to disbelieve him... He is ambitious... He has a burning desire to grow... He wants to touch as many lives as possible."

"He often wondered, why does the government curb business and create bottlenecks? He also said if the government continues to do that, he will find ways to grow outside India. Mr Roy always said the government should not be a regulator, it should be facilitator," Manoharan told me.

Roy invited the independent directors to every family function and offered accommodation and flight tickets for such do's, but Sinor and Manoharan politely declined such offers. He was generous in hospitality.

The new board initiated the process of sale of bonds and securities – about ₹500–700 crore every month and started paying the depositors. It also closely monitored the cash flow and the RBI was kept informed at every stage. By the time Manoharan and Sinor resigned in October 2011, SIFCL's deposit liability came down to about ₹2,000 crore and net owned funds rose ₹3,000 crore.

Under the arrangement, the RBI had to approve all bond sale and it was contingent on the previous month's utilization of sale proceeds. The board found that clause an irritant as it took a few weeks to disburse the funds and another few weeks for the auditors to verify the disbursement. They moved the RBI, made a presentation to executive director Gopalakrishna and got it relaxed. The regulator agreed to accept the utilization certificate after a month.

The board also noticed that while deposits were being repaid, on a few occasions, some money was coming back to Sahara group companies as the depositors were reportedly not interested in getting their money back. Apparently, they wanted the funds to be invested in group companies. The board put its foot down and said let the depositors directly issue cheques to those group companies after realizing their monies in their bank accounts.

The independent directors also noticed that many deposits remained unclaimed for six years; in the seventh year, the company could locate some of the depositors and pay them their money.

This took place even though, unlike banks, RNBCs are not required to deposit unclaimed deposits with the goverment's Consolidated Fund after seven years. The board therefore asked the auditors to look into this.

The RBI used to take stock of the situation periodically. One such meeting took place on 2 August 2010. Roy, Manoharan and Sinor were present at the meeting. Uma Subramanian and D Mishra, and a few other officers, were on Gopalakrishna's team. The RBI executive director expressed concern that SIFCL was not able to meet the directed investment norms. He also wanted Roy to pay back depositors through cheques, but Roy pointed out that it was impossible as most depositors did not have bank accounts.

Pune Warriors

At that meeting, Subramanian asked Roy whether he was in a position to sponsor Pune Warriors India at the Indian Premier League (IPL) while SIFCL was on a winding down mode and had to meet deposit liabilities. Roy assured the RBI that no financial load would fall on SIFCL and the group companies would make funds available. At that point, Sinor said that the independent directors too had raised the issue and found that the commitment of SIFCL was in the form of a performance guarantee and not a direct exposure.

In fact, there had been occasions when the directors wanted to know why Roy was spending so much on cricket sponsorship. Roy's answer was that he had strong emotional bond with sports, and while such activities do not add to the profits, they help valuations rise.

In March 2010, Sahara Adventure Sports, a group company, successfully bid ₹1,700 crore for the Pune franchise for ten years, the highest bid by any company in the history of IPL.

In May 2013, Sahara announced its withdrawal from the IPL after the Board of Control for Cricket in India (BCCI) moved to encash a bank guarantee as Sahara did not pay the full franchise fee for the year. Sahara had made the ₹1,700 crore bid, according to its statement, on the basis of revenue that could be generated from the 94 matches per season that had originally been envisaged. This was reduced to 64 matches, following which, Pune Warriors requested the BCCI to reduce the bid price proportionately to make it a more viable proposition for them.

The discussions ended in a stalemate and Sahara announced its withdrawal from the league in February 2012. The two parties agreed to arrive at a solution and started an arbitration process, but the question of the franchise fee remained unresolved. In January 2013, Sahara paid around 20% of the year's franchise fee, ₹170.20 crore. It told BCCI that it would pay the remaining amount by 19th May but did not do so as it was waiting for the arbitration proceedings. That led to the IPL governing council encashing the bank guarantee on 20 May. A Sahara press release issued at the time said, "We would not keep the IPL franchise even if the entire fee is waived off."

Later, in June, Sahara Adventure, the owner of Pune Warriors India, moved the Bombay High Court, seeking arbitration.

Sahara had considered withdrawing its sponsorship of the national Indian cricket team as well, but didn't do so immediately on grounds that it would not be in the interests of the players or the sport. "We have given time to the BCCI to get the new sponsorship in place from January, 2014, as we will continue the national team's sponsorship only up to December 2013," Sahara said. "That's the expiry date of the present agreement." The group has been the sponsor of Indian cricket team since 2001.

At the August 2010 meeting, the RBI was critical of SIFCL's functions on many counts. For instance, Mishra pointed out that SIFCL transferred ₹150 crore to one group company from its account with Punjab National Bank in Lucknow. He wanted to know the reason behind the money transfer. Roy explained that SIFCL had borrowed the money from the group company to repay the depositors.

The RBI executive director Gopalakrishna was concerned that 53% of the deposits were discontinued, the auditors did not have access to SIFCL's applications systems from where they could generate data, and finally, the KYC norms were still not being strictly followed. Sinor, however, pointed out a perceptible change in SIFCL's KYC process since 2009.

The first thing the new board members did was tightening the KYC norms – photographs were taken of all depositors, branches were audited and random checks, technically called "in-person verification", were conducted, but not a single case of violation was detected, Sinor told me.

They also forced the company to stop the practice of forfeiture of interest. SIFCL was asked to pay at least what a savings bank depositor earns. The RBI freed the savings bank deposit rates in October 2011, but most banks pay around 4%, the last mandated rate. This burdened Sahara with an additional cost of ₹400 crore. The board also made it mandatory that all deposits unclaimed for seven years should go to the government. The company had to sell some fixed assets to take care of its asset-liability mismatches and pay off the depositors.

The board declined to give its nod to Roy's proposal seeking a banking licence. Roy was keen to reach out to rural India and offer doorstep service to customers. He wanted Sinor and Manoharan on the board of the proposed bank.

A Bloomberg report in May 2013 quoted Roy as saying he wants a banking licence. The Sahara group's financial-services companies, which have 100 million depositors and investors in villages and small towns, are part of India's largely unregulated $670 billion shadow-banking industry. "We are fighters and we will remain so," Roy said of his quest for the licence in an interview with Bloomberg at his home office in Lucknow. "In three years, we will be – asset-wise, cash asset-wise and profitability-wise – among the top few companies in the world." He said his employees were preparing the application. Eventually though, he refrained from seeking a licence for a new bank.

At the 31 October 2011 board meeting, SIFCL presented a paper on the group's views on the RBI's draft banking licensing norms, which, among other things, suggested a five-year window for the listing of new banks, as "India has a cycle of five years in capital market, directly or indirectly impacted by Lok Sabha elections."

Unique Lab of Financial Inclusion

The board members, I am told, received full cooperation from the group and they did not discover any politicians' money kept with Sahara – an apprehension shared by many. Sinor says Sahara was a unique lab of financial inclusion: it inculcated the habit of savings in poor people. The company apparently snatched money from the pocket of alcoholics in rural UP and offered money when their daughters got married.

Since it has about 600,000 agents, at least 2.4 million people were depending on the group for their livelihood if each agent has three persons in his or her family. Apparently, Roy makes it a point to attend family functions of many of the depositors and there, in everybody's presence, he touches the feet of elderly family members. The board also did not come across a single complaint of a customer losing money.

In rural UP, Roy is a messiah of the poor who helped them develop the habit of saving. He is an entrepreneur who doesn't like to be regulated. Some people see in him a shadow of Dhirubhai Ambani, the patriarch of India's biggest private sector company by revenue, who indulged in regulatory arbitraging to develop business. In Roy's own words, had he not been banned by the regulators so many times and forced to float different outfits, he would have built a financial intermediary larger than the State Bank of India, the nation's largest lender.

Roy has challenged the regulators, kept the money flowing

any way he could and used that to buy fancy hotels, float a cricket team, hobnob with Bollywood actors, politicians and cricketers, and help widows of Indian soldiers who died in the Kargil war and of the Mumbai policemen who died in the November 2008 terrorist attack.

In some sense, he is a lone warrior whose empire is built on money collected from millions. He met his nemesis in Reddy, a champion of depositors. As a central banker, Reddy's prime focus was to keep the banking system strong and ensure that nobody lost money.

Post script: Roy told this author that he always wanted his financial business to be regulated and claimed that he had written several letters to the banking regulator to allow Sahara to float money raising schemes under the RBI regulations, but that he never got any reply. He wrote one such letter to former RBI governor D Subbarao on 25 June, 2013, urging him to give Sahara "an opportunity to work under RBI in any suitable scheme" and requesting him for reintroduction of RNBCs in Indian financial system.

PART II

6

THE IPO THAT NEVER WAS

The RBI sealed the fate of SIFCL in June 2008, but the entrepreneur in Subrata Roy knows how to open another door when one closes. Money, the raw material of his business, does not grow on trees. Nor does he have a note-printing machine at Sahara Shaher, the fortified, 360-acre, self-supporting township in Lucknow that Roy lords over. But he knows how to collect money the way seasoned gardeners gather leaves in the fall.

Sahara Shaher boasts of everything that one needs for a comfortable living – a helipad, a cricket stadium, a mini sports complex, a lake 11-km in circumference, an 18-hole mini-golf course, a revolving open-air stage, a state-of-the art auditorium that can accommodate 3,500 people, a 124-seater cinema theatre and a five-bed health centre with an ambulance, besides a fire brigade station and a petrol pump.

When SIFCL was hibernating, two of the group companies, Sahara India Real Estate Corp. Ltd (SIRECL), known earlier as Sahara India Commercial Corp. Ltd (SICCL), and Sahara Housing Investment Corp. Ltd (SHICL), started raising money through OFCDs, a hybrid financial instrument.

There is no interest payment during the life of the instrument, usually three or five years. The investor in such an instrument has the option to decide at a predetermined time – after one or two years from date of issuance – to convert the debenture at a formula, linked to the market rate. Usually, it is at a discount to the assumed market price on the date of conversion. Since the investor does not earn interest, the earning is a function of differential pricing.

How does the company benefit? The company does not have to service the debt until it is converted into equity; this arrangement protects the annual cash flows. However, if an OFCD is not converted by the investor, the company needs to redeem it at a premium to the issue price, factoring in the interest payment. This usually happens when the market price of equity is less than the conversion price as the investor loses incentive to convert OFCD into equity.

In contrast, FCDs or fully convertible debentures, are converted on a predetermined date at a fixed price and the investors get interest at regular intervals till the date of conversion into equity.

Sick and tired of the RBI's insatiable appetite for information and endless scrutiny, a nimble-footed Roy chose to move into the fold of Registrar of Companies (RoC) in UP and Uttarakhand, under the ministry of corporate affairs, an entity that polices all of India's registered companies.

The listed companies, by virtue of being traded on stock exchanges, are looked after by Sebi as well. Incidentally, Roy has under his belt 4,799 establishments, almost equal to the universe of listed companies in India, the largest market for listed entities in the world.

It might have gone unnoticed but for Roy's plan to list one of his group companies, Sahara Prime City Ltd. On page 640 in the disclosure section in the 934-page Draft Red Herring Prospectus (DRHP) of Prime City filed with Sebi, one critical piece of information was tucked away that India's capital market regulator latched on to – certain tax-related issues in regard to OFCDs which SICCL was fighting out with the income tax authority. This was related to a ₹35.57 crore disputed income tax that was imposed on the company for accepting OFCDs worth ₹20,000 or more from many investors through cash and not account payee cheques or demand drafts, as is required under the Income Tax Act 1961.

When Sahara Prime City filed the DRHP, SICCL was holding a 13.7% stake (7,46,46,889 equity shares) in it. SICCL had also on 30 January, 2008 entered into a service agreement with Sahara Prime City to provide all government or other regulatory permits, licences and approvals required in connection with the development of the proposed integrated townships of Sahara Prime City.

Sahara submitted the DRHP on 30 September 2009. It gives us a peek into the business model of the group where hundreds of unlisted companies cohabit and some undergo name changes periodically. For instance, Sahara Prime City was incorporated on 9 March 1993 as Sahara India Financial

Corp. Ltd (SIFCL) and, since then, has changed its name thrice – first to Sahara India Corp. Ltd on 20 October 1994, then Sahara India Investment Corp. Ltd on 5 August 2005. The latest name was taken up on 15 February 2008.

Incidentally, SIFCL, which is being forced by the RBI to wind down its business by 2015, was incorporated in 1987 as Sahara India Savings and Investment Corp. Ltd. It changed its name to SIFCL on 23 November 1994. This means that only for six weeks in 1994 – between 10th October and 23rd November – did the group not have a company named SIFCL in its fold.

The DRHP claimed that Prime City was one of the largest real estate development companies in India with 8,484.65 acres of land reserve – bigger than seven countries in the world: Tuvalu, Nauru, Tokelau, Gibraltar, Pitcaim Islands, Monaco and Vatican City. This includes a vast tract of land the company either owns or holds contractual development rights over. Sahara Prime City wants to develop 88 integrated townships under the Sahara City Homes brand and 15 residential complexes under the Sahara Grace brand, across 99 cities.

It owns its greatest stretch of land – 274.53 acres – in Vasai on the outskirts of Mumbai, followed by Muzaffarnagar (213.75 acres) and Kanpur (212.76 acres) in Uttar Pradesh, and Kurukshetra (201.05 acres) in Haryana. It has land banks of at least 100 acres or more each in 18 Indian cities, including the metropolitan Kolkata.

Its plan was to raise ₹30,000 crore from the capital market through an initial public offer (IPO) to meet the expenses of construction and development of ongoing and new projects. Had the plan been successful, this would have been the group's fifth company to be listed on the bourses.

The four listed companies are Sahara Infrastructure and Housing Ltd, Sahara One Media and Entertainment Ltd, Sahara Housingfina Corp. Ltd and Master Chemicals Ltd.

Sahara Infrastructure and Housing is listed on Calcutta Stock Exchange Ltd and UP Stock Exchange Ltd in Kanpur; Sahara Housingfina Corp is listed on BSE Ltd; and Sahara One Media is listed on BSE, Delhi Stock Exchange Ltd and Calcutta Stock Exchange.

BSE has frozen the trading of Master Chemicals. The scrip was moved to the so-called Z category after the company failed to submit information related to its shareholding for 1998, 1999 and 2000 to the exchange, mandatory under listing norms. In July 2007, Master Chemicals moved an application to BSE to shift it to trading as the relevant documents that Sebi had asked for were "lost" in a fire at the company's office. Subsequently, it was shifted to the so-called T category where scrips are settled on a trade-to-trade basis. It has not been traded after 29 December 2009.

Global coordinators and book-running lead managers of the proposed IPO were Enam Securities Pvt Ltd (which subsequently merged with Axis Bank Ltd, a new generation private bank) and JM Financial Consultants Pvt Ltd. The high profile issue had four book-running lead managers: Edelweiss Capital Ltd, IDBI Capital Market Services Ltd, Daiwa Securities SMBC India Pvt Ltd and Kotak Mahindra Capital Co. Ltd. The legal advisors to the issue included Amarchand

& Mangaldas & Suresh A. Shroff & Co., Luthra and Luthra Law Offices and Milbank, Tweed, Hadley and McCloy LLP.

Sahara Prime City's auditor is Lucknow-based DS Shukla & Co., the entity that had worked with SIFCL for 25 years till the RBI forced SIFCL to change its auditor.

Roy is the chairman of Sahara Prime City, holding a 40.23% stake. Other directors include his wife Swapna Roy (6.17% stake); brother Joy Broto Roy (4.22% stake); and two sons – Sushanto Roy and Seemanto Roy – 3.24% stake each. Sushanto is the executive director worker and head of international business and Seemanto is executive director and worker head of corporate control and management.

The DRHP carries the voter identification number of all directors. It also mentions the driving licence number of all, barring Swapna Roy.

The DRHP lists 120 promoter group companies, including Maa Chhabi Chhav Foundation, named after Roy's mother.

Sahara Prime City has 298 subsidiaries under its fold, the oldest being Sahara Hospitality Ltd, incorporated in 1989, which owns Sahara Star hotel in Mumbai. Barring a few, they are all tiny as an auditor's report, part of the DRHP, says 285 subsidiaries had a total assets of ₹574.17 crore as on 31 March 2009 and a revenue of ₹116.18 crore.

Most of these subsidiaries were floated between 1996 and 2008 and many were incorporated in October and July 2005; 4th, 5th and 6th October, and 4th and 6th July in 2005 seem to be the favourite dates for Roy to incorporate his companies in hordes. This possibly stems from Roy's belief in numerology.

Too Many Holes

When a company seeks Sebi's nod for an IPO, the market regulator looks up all information about the company's parent group. It puts up this draft prospectus on its website, making it available to the public; separately, the merchant bankers handling the issue also put it up on their websites. This norm was introduced in 1995–96.

The logic behind this is: Sebi cannot scrutinize all information on its own, but at the same time, it would not be fair to stop an issue at the last moment, based on a discovery. By putting up the prospectus on its website, the regulator creates a window for the public to air their grievances, genuine or malicious. At the next stage, Sebi looks into the issues raised and, accordingly, seeks information from the company and its merchant bankers.

Internally, the Sahara's OFCD issue was discussed at Sebi and a routine enquiry went to merchant bankers, but Sahara was reluctant to part with information and that made Sebi suspicious. Two other things happened around the same time. Firstly, on 4 January 2010, Roshan Lal, a resident of Indore, Madhya Pradesh, sent a note to the National Housing Bank, requesting that it look into housing bonds issued by two companies of the Sahara group.

A chartered accountant, Lal wrote in Hindi that he found that the bonds, bought by a large number of investors, were not issued according to the rules. The National Housing Bank forwarded the note to Sebi.

Secondly, the regulator received another, similar note from the Professional Group for Investor Protection, based in Ahmedabad, questioning Sahara's money-raising through OFCDs.

Sahara was not forthcoming; its stance was that unlisted companies had issued the OFCDs and they were not regulated by Sebi. Sahara claimed to have obtained the ministry of corporate affairs' permission for issuing the OFCD and legal opinion to back it. Salman Khurshid was the corporate affairs minister then. The relationship between Sebi and the ministry has been of "friendly tension", a euphemism for turf war.

Later, Sahara lawyers pointed out that Enam Securities, the merchant banker to the Sahara Prime City IPO, had sent a response to Lal's Janata Colony address in Indore, but the letter could not be delivered as the address could not be found. N Sundaresha Subramanian, a journalist with financial daily *Business Standard*, in a report on 8 September 2012 wrote that he "tried hard to locate him but in vain". However, for Sebi, at that stage, the information and not the identity of Lal was important. Sebi was also not getting into legal issues; it wanted information in order to decide on the fate of the IPO.

There was pressure from various quarters. And, there were frequent phone calls – Why are the clearance for the IPO pending? Why can't the issues be sorted out? Be gentle with Sahara – and many innocuous queries and gentle persuasions, without any paper trail.

But Sebi stood by its decision; Sahara's unwillingness to give information was not acceptable. Roy sought to discuss matters with the Sebi chairman CB Bhave, but their brief meeting did not yield any result. After the meeting, where Bhave made his intention clear, phone calls to the chairman's office stopped, but there was no let up in the pressure.

The case was being handled by KM Abraham, a fulltime director in charge of surveillance and investigation at Sebi. Under him, a small team, led by executive director Usha Narayanan, started the probe. There were weekly meetings in Abraham's office at Sebi headquarters – targets for the investigating team being set and closely monitored.

"We knew something was amiss but never knew the scale of concealment. There was always suspicion that Sahara is into money laundering but nobody dared to question them. Nobody was allowed to investigate – income tax, enforcement department and even ministry of corporate affairs," Abraham, an additional chief secretary in Kerala government since February 2013, told me at his office on third floor of the Kerala sacretariat annex in Thiruvananthapuram.

Sahara Banned

Abraham issued his first order on 24 November 2010, banning the group from raising money from the public in any form. The 34-page order explains how Sebi tried to get information from Sahara on the OFCDs, but the group declined to furnish anything primarily on two grounds: a)

Section 55A of the Companies Act, 1956, empowers Sebi to seek information only from listed companies; and, b) under Section 60 B of Companies Act, one can file a prospectus with the Registrar of Companies and raise money if one does not want to list the securities through which the money is raised and Sebi has no jurisdiction over this.

Sebi's investigation, outlined in the November order, revealed that the OFCDs were not the so-called private placement as had been claimed by Sahara, as they involved more than 50 investors, and by not listing them, Sahara was violating Section 73 of the Companies Act. It also found that SIRCEL had raised₹4,843.37 crore and SHICL, ₹32,355.55 crore between fiscal years 2005 and 2009.

Since the OFCDs raised a massive amount of money, Sebi wanted to ascertain the source of such funds and ensure protection of investors in such issues but the company, it alleged, did not provide any information. The Sebi order restrained SIRCEL and SHICL from mobilizing funds from the public; prohibited the promoters and directors of the two companies – Subrata Roy, Vandana Bharrgava, Ravi Shankar Dubey and Ashok Roy Choudhary – from soliciting money from anybody; and asked the two companies to show cause why action should not be taken against them.

"Astonished" at the "irresponsible and wrongful ex parte order," Sahara first issued an advertisement in national newspapers on 26th November and moved the Lucknow Bench of the Allahabad High Court on 29th November, saying Sebi lacked jurisdiction to pass such an order, that too without any hearing. Justice Virendra Kumar Dixit and

Justice Devi Prasad Singh granted a stay on the Sebi order on 13 December, 2010.

Sebi quickly moved the Supreme Court with a special leave petition on 4th January. It was almost a re-run of the 2008 Sahara-RBI spat with one difference: by this time, the image of the Allahabad High Court had taken a beating.

This happened after a Supreme Court bench of Justices Markandey Katju and Gyan Sudha Misra issued a strong indictment in November 2010 of a judge of the Allahabad High Court for passing orders on extraneous considerations. The Supreme Court asked the Chief Justice of Allahabad High Court to take action against the judge concerned and some other judges facing complaints. A New Delhi datelined Press Trust of India report, on 26 Novemer 2010, quoted a bench of justices Katju and Misra saying, "Something is rotten in the state of Denmark, said Shakespeare in Hamlet, and it can similarly be said that something is rotten in the Allahabad High Court," and the high court "really needs some house cleaning."

The bench also asked the chief justice of the Allahabad High Court to take some strong measures, including recommending "transfers of the incorrigibles". It flew into a rage while scrapping a single-judge bench order of the Allahabad High Court that had asked a Bahraich-based Waqf Board to temporarily allot a portion of its land in May–June 2010 to the proprietors of a circus for its show during an annual fair.

"The faith of the common man in the country is shaken to the core by such shocking and outrageous orders," said justices Katju and Misra. "We are sorry to say but a lot of complaints are coming against certain judges of the Allahabad High Court relating to their integrity," they said, without disclosing the contents of complaints.

Referring to the rampant 'uncle judge' syndrome[1] allegedly plaguing the high court, the 12-page order made the insinuation that, "Some judges have their kith and kin practising in the same court... And within a few years of starting practice, the sons or relations of the judge become multi-millionaires, have huge bank balances, luxurious cars, huge houses and are enjoying a luxurious life. This is a far cry from the days when the sons and other relatives of judges could derive no benefit from their relationship and had to struggle at the bar like any other lawyer."

Typically, India's apex court does not hear an appeal on a stay; it hears appeals on a judgment, a substantive decision. In 2008, too, the RBI had moved against a stay order given by the Lucknow bench of the Allahabad High Court.

The Supreme Court made it clear that the Sebi was entitled to seek any information, including the names of OFCD investors, and the Sahara lawyers agreed to provide such information. Disposing off the petition, the apex court requested the high court to hear and decide on the case expeditiously. Thus, the Supreme Court solved Sebi's problems without any interference from the stay given by the high court.

---

[1] The uncle judge syndrome refers to judges passing favourable orders for parties represented by lawyers known to them.

Sahara gave a committment to share the requisite information, but did not actually do this. Owing to this, the high court dismissed the petition in April 2011.

The Sub-plot

Bhave stepped down as Sebi chairman in February 2011 and UK Sinha stepped in. With the change of guard, something else happened in Sebi that is no less interesting than the Sahara case.

After the November 2010 order, it was fairly certain that Abraham would not get a second term as a board member at Sebi. And ditto with Bhave. Both names apparently went to the Appointments Committee of the Cabinet, but the files were called back.

One day in November, just before the order was released, Abraham received a call from TKA Nair, then principal secretary to Prime Minister Manmohan Singh – an apparently innocuous call. After exchanging pleasantries, Nair asked what was happening on Sahara and ended the call saying, "Shall I tell the PM that everything will be done fairly?" He did not ask for a favour, nor did he tell Abraham to go soft on the group.

That was before he signed off on the report. A month after the report was published, in late December 2010, Abraham received an unusual visitor at his home in Mumbai's Bandra Kurla Complex – a senior office bearer of the housing society at Maker Tower, Cuffe Parade, in south Mumbai, where he was staying in a Sebi accommodation before moving to his own flat. Abraham thought the gentleman had come to wish him on Christmas. Over a cup of tea, the person introduced himself as a CA working for Sahara and pleaded with Abraham to clear the Sahara DRHP as the group has been doing a marvelous job and contributing to India's economy.

With a new chairman at the helm, pressure mounted from various quarters to go soft on Sahara, claims Abraham. Bhave, too, was under pressure, but he never allowed his colleagues to know what he was going through. As Abraham started feeling that Sebi was turning into an agency of some people in the finance ministry, he first reached out to cabinet secretary KM Chandrasekhar (on 16th May) and then Nair (23rd May). Chandrasekhar advised him to write to the government; Nair's advice was to meet Omita Paul, special advisor to finance minister Pranab Mukherjee.

Abraham wrote a letter to the Prime Minister on 1st June and another on 24th June.

After he wrote to the PM, pressure mounted on him from every quarter. The Prime Minister's principal secretary Nair called him on some official matter and casually asked him how things were in Mumbai. Abraham pleaded with him to take his letter seriously.

A fortnight after receiving Abraham's letter, the Prime Minister's office sent a copy of the letter to the economic affairs secretary in the finance ministry, R Gopalan, for his comments. That's how the 1st June letter to the Prime Minister found its way to the finance ministry, and subsequently Sebi, and was leaked to the press. A whistle blower was compromised. This led him to write to the Prime Minister again on 24th June.

Maharashtra additional chief secretary (home) Umesh Chandra Sarangi offered him police protection, but Abraham declined. The state administration wanted a statement from Abraham saying that he did not want police protection, but Abraham declined to do that also. He wrote to all board members of Sebi twice on the finance ministry pressure and wanted to discuss at the board, but no board meeting was held till he left Sebi on 20th July.

A day before the last letter was written, Abraham released his 99-page order on 23rd June, asking the Sahara group to pay back investors with 15% interest. The order was sent to all regulatory agencies including the RBI, MCA, income tax authorities and the enforcement directorate. The Sebi chairman was not aware of the contents of the order till it was put up on the website.

The department of personnel and training wanted to take disciplinary action against Abraham for violating service code and writing to the PM unsubstantiated scandalous things about the finance minister's office. Both the chief vigilance commissioner (CVC) and the income tax department also started enquiries.

In the eye of the storm was Abraham's purchase of a 1 crore flat at BKC from the Kohinoor group. The National Stock Exchange Ltd (NSE) had purchased a few flats at the same complex – the insinuation made was that Abraham had compromised himself. The NSE is a regulated entity and Abraham's previous boss Bhave was perceived to be close to the NSE. His colleague MS Sahoo, another fulltime member of Sebi, who also bought a flat at the same complex, came under the IT scanner as well.

There were questions about Abraham's source of money. How could a bureaucrat of his rank, entitled to a payscale of ₹67,400–79,000 a month, buy a ₹1 crore flat? The IT authorities served him a notice to explain his source of funds.

I asked him the same question. As a fulltime director in Sebi, he received a market related salary (around ₹24 lakh a year). Had he got the National Institute of Securities Management (NISM) job, his salary would have been even higher (around ₹30 lakh a year). Since that did not happen, he is back to his bureaucrat salary. How would he repay the loan? Abraham said he had taken a home loan of ₹88 lakh from the State Bank of India, which was being repaid with earnings from his salary, his parents' pension and by renting out the flat.

The investigations did not lead anywhere and both the CVC and the IT department had to close them. In fact, Abraham was refunded ₹1.25 lakh for paying excess income tax.

His plan was to shift to NISM, an institute set up by Sebi, after his three-year stint as fulltime director. A three-member search committee had selected him for the assignment six days before Bhave demitted his office. Bhave, the chairman of the committee, didn't sign off the appointment; he left the matter to his successor to decide. The other two members of the search committee were Uday Kotak, vice chairman of Kotak Mahindra Bank Ltd, and Dr Pritam Singh, director general of International Management Institute in Delhi. The 11 February 2011 meeting of the search committee was attended by Bhave and Kotak, and Singh gave his consent even though he was not present at the meeting.

Even though the search committee selected Abraham for the top job at NISM in February 2011, by December 2010, after the finance ministry blocked Bhave's extension proposal, Abraham started sending feelers to Delhi for an opening. On a trip to South Africa for the International Organization of Securities Commission meeting in Cape Town, Abraham told Sinha that he had a feeling that he would not get the NISM job and he would keep looking for opportunities outside bureaucracy.

Even after his tenure ended in July, he stayed in Mumbai till August, pinning his hopes on an opening at the National Intelligence Grid (Natgrid) in Delhi. This is an integrated intelligence grid that links the databases of several departments and ministries of the government to collect comprehensive patterns of intelligence that can be readily accessed by intelligence agencies. When that didn't work out, he went back to Kerala in September 2011.

What is his take on Sahara? "It would not have been caught had it been careful about systems and processes; even a skilful creation of fictitious account holders would have done but Sahara did not do that. But, above all, it exposes the vulnerability of the financial system in India. It also underscores the need for all agencies – IT department, enforcement directorate, RBI and Sebi – to collaborate closely to prevent ravages of the delicate fabric of the financial system."

Roy finds in Abraham the most sadistic and biased person he has ever come across who can only concoct allegations.

Whistle Blower's Letter

In the 1st June letter to the Prime Minister, Abraham, who was in charge of the primary market, parts of secondary market, investigation and surveillance at Sebi, said he had issued at least 380 quasi-judicial orders and 300 consent orders during his tenure and the entities involved in his orders and investigations included the Sahara group, companies of Mukesh Ambani and Anil Ambani, Bank of Rajasthan Ltd and stock exchange MCX-SX Ltd.

> "I am humbly aware that it is unusual for a person serving on a regulatory body set up by Parliament to approach the honourable Prime Minister directly. But such is the gravity of the situation, that I make myself bold to do so, and entreat your kind indulgence.
>
> Supervising the investigation and surveillance function in the securities markets as the whole time member of Sebi for the last three years, has made me deeply conscious of the fact that the securities market in India is still fragile... Several attempts continue to be made by powerful groups to misappropriate wealth...

> Personally, I have been exposed to, what I believe sincerely, are attempts to harass and intimidate me in the discharge of my duties..."

Alleging that the Sebi was "under duress and under severe attack from powerful corporate interests," Abraham wrote that the regulator's victory over Sahara at the Lucknow bench of Allahabad High Court and Supreme Court was not celebrated and he was not allowed to issue newspaper advertisements for the benefit of the investors and instead had to settle for a news release.

Sebi insiders say the idea of a news release came from Abraham himself. They also say Sinha, as the Sebi boss, did not show much emotion either in "victory" or "defeat". That's his style of functioning.

Abraham's letter also went on to cite examples related to other corporate houses to justify his argument that Sebi had been under pressure from the finance ministry. Towards the end of his nine-page letter, he wrote, "I am willing to testify to the above facts, under oath in an appropriate judicial or administrative forum, should I be called upon to do so."

Sinha responded to charges levelled by Abraham in a letter on 8 July 2011, 12 days before Abraham stepped down, where he dismissed the allegation that he "discouraged" Abraham from issuing a public notice about the fact that the stay on Sebi's order was vacated by the Lucknow bench of the Allahabad High Court as a "figment of imagination".

Writing to economic affairs secretary Gopalan, Sinha described the allegations as baseless and "an attempt to tarnish the image of the government". According to Sinha, Abraham was upset over the income tax investigation and was suffering from a feeling that everybody was out to harm him. He was also anxious that without the NISM assignment, it would be difficult for him to maintain his family and repay the home loan.

Many consider Abraham's 99-page order against the Sahara group as one of the boldest in Sebi's history. What did it say?

– It directed two companies, SIRECL and SHICL, and their directors to refund money to the investors in OFCDs with 15% interest.

– Such repayment would be done through demand draft or pay order.

– The two firms needed to publish advertisements on how they planned to make the refund.

– They would not access the securities market till the money was paid back to the OFCD holders.

– Subrata Roy, Vandana Bharrgava, Ravi Shankar Dubey and Ashok Roy Choudhary would not access the securities market till Sebi was satisfied with the mode of refund.

– If the two companies failed to comply with these directions, Sebi would take appropriate action, including the launch of a prosecution proceedings against the companies and their directors.

Abraham's order clearly stated that OFCDs were securities on which Sebi's writ held and as they were issued to more than 50 people, this route of money-raising could not be called private placements. And, since they were not private placements, the securities needed to be listed.

It also said that though the Sahara group companies claimed the OFCDs were issued to persons related or associated with the companies themselves, money was actually mobilized from millions of investors through thousands of service centres and that these subscribers had no connection with the Sahara group.

The order came down heavily on the group's "lackadaisical and cavalier attitude to investor identification" and the scant respect for KYC norms, an issue on which different regulators have been fighting Sahara.

Roy defended his Pariwar, saying Sahara was reaching out to those pockets of investors where banks feared to tread. These unbanked people, belonging to the poorest of the poor strata in the world's tenth largest economy, often had no official identity barring their names. He also said they were all associated with the group as depositors in some scheme or other.

The 23 June 2011 Sebi order stunned Sahara and kicked off a fight in the Supreme Court and the Securities Appellate Tribunal (SAT), the appellate body of Sebi – no-holds barred and far more complex than what the banking regulator had experienced in 2008. Soon after issuing the order, Abraham stepped down, but Sebi did not show any slackness in taking the fight to its logical end.

A young and dashing Subrata Roy, from his NCC days

Roy and his wife Swapna with NCC cadets

Roy with an animated Prince Charles

In discussion with US President Barack Obama and First Lady Michelle Obama

Roy & his wife smile for the camera with the charismatic, sherwani-clad Bill Clinton, former US president

A calm and collected Roy at a meeting with British Prime Minister David Cameron

Roy was devoted to the Blessed Mother Teresa

Roy fondly looks on at His Holiness, the 14th Dalai Lama

Roy in a light moment with close personal friend Amitabh Bachchan

The Birlas and the Roys share the limelight

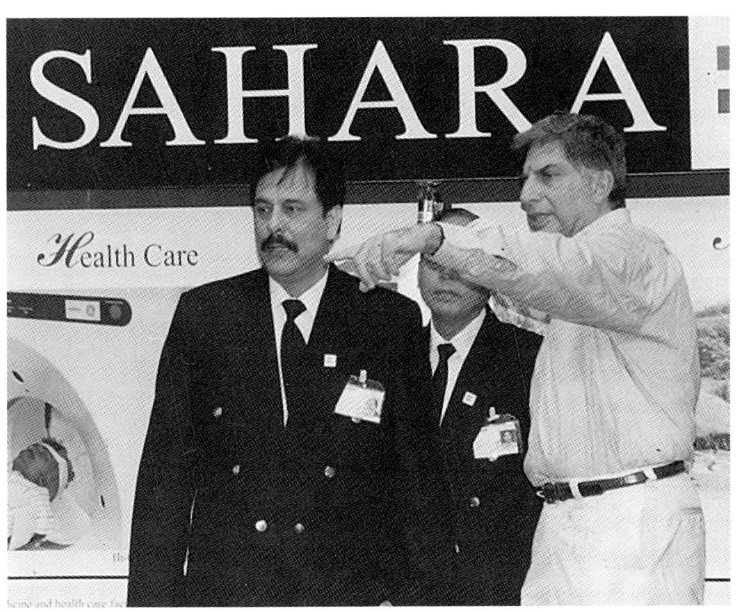

Ratan Tata and Roy in discussion at a Sahara Health Care event

With famed industrialist and tycoon Dhirubhai Ambani

Roy with former Indian PM Atal Behari Vajpayee

Bala Saheb gestures dramatically while Roy looks on

Roy with former RBI Governor, whose one-point agenda was to shut down Sahara's non-banking arm

Roy and Bimal Jalan, the "best among RBI governers"

At each Samuhik Vivah Samaroh, the Sahara India Pariwar organizes the marriages of 101 girls from weaker sections of society

हार्दिक अभिनन्दन भारतीय रिजर्व बैंक को

और

हार्दिक अभिवादन उच्चतम न्यायालय को

30 जनवरी '92 के फैसले के लिए जिसमें देश के जमाकर्ताओं की जमा धनराशि को पूर्ण सुरक्षा प्रदान करने हेतु भारतीय रिजर्व बैंक द्वारा 15 मई '87 को जारी रेजिड्यूरी नान बैंकिंग कम्पनी (आर.एन.बी.सी.) डायरेक्शन '87 को वैध करार दिया गया है।

आर.एन.बी.सी.डायरेक्टिव, 1987

जमाधन को पूर्ण सुरक्षा प्रदान करने हेतु

निर्देश :

प्रतिभूतियों की सुरक्षा :

जमाधन का शेष 20% :

प्रमाणीकरण :

स्मरण

भ्रांति

सच्चाई

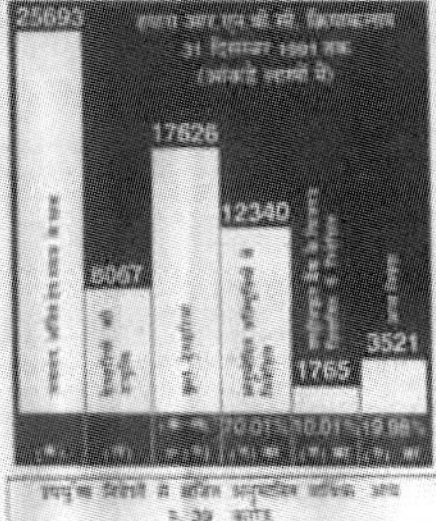

सहारा इण्डिया परिवार

भावनात्मकता से संघठित भारतीय परिवार

हमारा आरंभ :

हमारा वर्तमान :

वृद्धि दर :

हमारा भविष्य :

हमारा बल

हमारा विश्वास :

हमारी उत्पादकता :

हमारा स्वामित्व :

हमारा मुनाफा वितरण :

हमारा संतोष :

हमारी उपलब्धि :

ऐसे बने हम देश में अग्रणी

Sahara publicly congratulates RBI & the Supreme Court on legitimizing "Residuary Non-Banking Companies (RNBC) Directions, 1987" on 30th January, 1992

289

ANNEXURE – P/81

11.04.2007

MUMBAI

Dr. Y. V. Reddy
Governor
Reserve Bank of India
Central Office
Mumbai

Dear Hon'ble Governor,

We have taken a serious note of the concerns of Reserve Bank of India in regard to the growth in deposits of our company. We have ourselves taken a number of steps to moderate the growth like stoppage of both the fixed deposit schemes, direct interface of the company with the depositors (as against earlier through our agent), discontinuing opening of new accounts under RD schemes, etc.

We have all along been complying with all the provisions of RBI Directions and guidelines issued from time to time. We have made a number of changes in our systems, processes and procedures in deference to the instructions of RBI either in the form of written communications or oral advices and renew our commitments to RBI for the same in future also. We have always been rendering best of services to the Depositors.

I would feel obliged if you permit me to have the benefit of your vision and guidance in speeding up the mitigation of the concerns of our Guardian Institution. I may kindly be granted an audience with you on any day between April 12 and 17, 2007.

With Warm Personal Regards,

Yours sincerely,

(Subrata Roy Sahara)

Above & Opposite: *Rare exchange of letters between former RBI governor YV Reddy and Subrata Roy*

ANNEXURE-P/82

भारतीय रिज़र्व बैंक
RESERVE BANK OF INDIA
www.rbi.org.in

April 11, 2007

गवर्नर
Governor

Dear Shri Roy,

I have received your kind letter dated April 11, 2007. I am very happy to note that you are having interactive dialogue with our officers. As you are aware, we are totally convergent in terms of our objective to have a strong financial sector in general, and NBFCs sector in particular.

As a large player in the sector, your fullest co operation will make the task easier for all of us.

I have been briefed by our team led by Shri V.Leeladhar, Deputy Governor about their periodical discussions with you and I must say that the dialogue has been active even though more intensive efforts may be needed to fully and expeditiously realize our objectives.

I have no personal vision or guidance that could be considered other than what has been articulated in public and also in the series of discussions between us.

With regards.

Yours sincerely,

(Y.V. Reddy)

Shri Subrata Roy Sahara
Sahara India Pariwar
Sahara Shaher
Lucknow 226 010

Fax No. 0522 2398174

केन्द्रीय कार्यालय भवन, शहीद भगतसिंह मार्ग, मुम्बई 400 001 भारत
Central Office Building, Shahid Bhagat Singh Marg, Mumbai 400 001 INDIA
Tel: (022) 2266 0868 / 2266 1872 / 2266 2644 Fax: (022) 2266 1784 e-mail: rbigovr@bom3.vsnl.net.in

7

THE NEVER ENDING BATTLE

Sahara's defence for its massive fund-raising was that the OFCDs were made to "friends, associates, group companies, workers/employees and other individuals associated/ affiliated or connected in any manner with the Sahara India group of companies", and hence the investments were private placements and beyond the jurisdiction of Sebi.

At the core of the dispute is the question, who has the jurisdiction over fund-raising activities by two unlisted Sahara group entities, SIRECL and SHICL, through the "private placement" route – Sebi or the ministry of corporate affairs? The other question is, should raising money from more than 50 people, even if through the private placement route, be construed as a public offering? This is because for all public offers, it is mandatory to get the Sebi nod.

The first time Sahara started collecting money through this route was in 2001 and the window was closed in 2007. A year later, in 2008, the two companies once again took permission from the Registrar of Companies to raise funds through OFCDs. They raised money from about 30 million investors, all of whom, they claimed, were people associated with the Sahara group.

Let's take a closer look at the Sahara side of the OFCD story. It had filed returns for 19.8 million OFCD investors in 2006 for the money raised since 2001after getting clearance from the Registrar of Companies in Kolkata. In 2008–09, once again, it obtained permission for raising money through SIRECL from the Registrar of Companies in Kanpur and SHICL from the Registrar of Companies in Maharashtra.

In fact, on 21 April 2010, R Anand, a manager in the division of issues and listing at Sebi's corporation finance department wrote to the regional directors in northern and western region in the ministry of corporate affairs saying the market regulator had received complaints alleging that SIRECL and SHICL Ltd have issued OFCDs "violating statutory requirements".

> "We have understood that the Sahara India Real Estate Corporation Ltd has filed its red herring prospectus with Uttar Pradesh and Uttrakhand on 13 March, 2008, and Sahara Housing Investment Corporation Ltd has filed its red herring prospectus with registrar of Maharashtra, on 6 October, 2009. Since both ... these companies are unlisted ... and have not filed their DRHP with us, we hereby enclose the copy of complaints and other documents to your office for examination and necessary action."

The minister of state, finance, Namo Narayan Meena, too, in a different context told the Lok Sabha, the lower house of India's Parliament, that privately placed debentures by unlisted companies, issued under the Companies Act, were under the regulatory purview of the ministry of corporate affairs, not Sebi. So, the ministry of corporate affairs is the gatekeeper for such activities.[1]

Sahara, reached out to a battery of legal eagles seeking their opinion on this case. The list includes, among others, the late C Achuthan, former presiding officer of Securities Appellate Tribunal; SP Kurdukar, former judge of the Supreme Court of India; and AH Ahmadi, former Supreme Court Chief Justice.

Almost unanimously, they said that Sebi had no business overseeing the fund-raising of unlisted entities even if they were raising money from more than 50 investors as that didn't qualify such fund-raising arrangement as private placement.

Sahara also wrote to the ministry of corporate affairs seeking clarification on whether the two firms were governed by the ministry or Sebi. The corporate affairs ministry, in turn, referred the matter to the ministry of law and justice and Mohan Parasaran, then additional solicitor general of India, observed that Sebi has no *locus standi* over unlisted companies. Media reports suggest that then law minister M Veerappa Moily endorsed this view.

Parasaran was appointed solicitor general of India in February 2013, the third incumbent in less than two years

---

[1] Lok Sabha unstarred question No. 5872, answered on 4 April 2010.

after two of his predecessors – Gopal Subramaniam and Rohinton F Nariman – resigned over reported differences with successive law ministers.

All this boosted Sahara's chances of keeping the shadow of Sebi miles away from its massive money-raising activities from its "associates and friends" through the so-called private placement route after the RBI blocked the RNBC window. Or, so the group thought.

A little more than a year after Sebi asked Sahara to refund the money to investors with 15% interest – and the case moved back and forth in a triangle of Sebi, its appellate arm and the Supreme Court – India's apex court delivered its verdict on 31 August 2012, taking the wind out of Roy's sails. The Supreme Court, to a large extent, reiterated what Abraham had said in his June 2011 order. Fali S Nariman represented SIRECL at this case; Gopal Subramanium, SHICL; and Arvind P Datar, Sebi.

SIRECL collected close to ₹19,401 crore between 25 April 2008 and 13 March 2011. As on 31 August 2012, the company had ₹17,657 crore on its books as money collected through OFCDs net of premature redemption from over 22.10 million investors. This was done through three debentures called Abode Bond, Real Estate Bond and Nirman Bond.

SHICL, too, floated three bonds after filing draft prospectus with the Registrar of Companies in October 2009: Housing Bond, Income Bond and Multiple Bond.

The total amount due to the investors as on 31 August 2011 was ₹24,029.73 crore. Out of this amount, SIRECL owed ₹17,656.53 crore and SHICL owed ₹6,373.20 crore.

The apex court asked the two firms to refund ₹24,029.73 crore along with an interest of 15%. Sebi lawyer Pratap Venugopal pegs the interest quantum at around ₹14,000 crore. So, the total liability of the two Sahara firms was a little more than ₹38,000 crore in August 2011. Both had a paid-up capital of ₹10 lakh each and had no other assets or reserves. And both of them were loss-making companies.

Roy claimed to have cleared payments to 90% of the bond holders. And, all in cash. This means, only ₹2,620 crore needs to be paid. This is why he had given Sebi ₹5,120 crore: an extra ₹2,500 crore as a cushion.

Indeed, Sahara's ability to reach out to 30 million investors – who, it claimed, were the group's friends and associates – is extremely creditable. India's oldest mortgage lender, Housing Development Finance Corp. Ltd (HDFC), incorporated in 1977 and one year older than Sahara, boasts of 4.4 million home loan takers. India's most valued bank by market capitalization, HDFC Bank Ltd, with over 50% retail assets in its books, has 25 million customers.

The State Bank of India, the nation's largest lender, however, has at least five times Sahara's customer base in savings account holders.

Sebi dashed off its first letter to Enam Securities, the merchant banker handling the proposed IPO of Sahara Prime City, seeking information. Enam's response was that the money was raised keeping the appropriate authorities – in this case, Registrar of Companies – informed and with their permission; and that they did not fall under Sebi's jurisdiction: a stance that Sahara stuck to all along.

CDs without Passwords

In the meanwhile, however, Sahara sent to Sebi password-protected CDs containing the names and addresses and investment details of the 30 million investors – not once, but twice. The first time, the regulator could not open the file as the password was not given. On the second occasion, Sahara could give only partial information because of the "enormity of the work and the time taken in collating and compiling the data."

The Supreme Court order was delivered by two judges – KS Radhakrishnan and Jagdish Singh Khehar. The 263-page judgment has three parts – observations by the two judges, and the order.

Let's look at their observations first. Shorn of technicalities and complex legal jargon, what did Radhakrishnan say? Here's a verbatim reproduction:

> Sahara, in the bonds, sought for a declaration from the applicant that they had been associated with (the) Sahara group. No details had been furnished to show what types of association the investor had with the Sahara group. (The) bonds also required to name an introducer, whose job evidently was to introduce the company to the prospective investor. If the offer was made to those persons related or associated with (the) Sahara group, there was no necessity of an introducer and an introduction.
>
> If the offer was made only to persons associated,

> related or known to Sahara group, then they could have furnished those details before the fact finding authorities.
>
> ...(The) Saharas having failed to make application for listing on any of the recognized stock exchange (s)... become legally liable to refund the amount collected from the subscribers...
>
> (The) Saharas have no right to collect ₹27,000 crore from thirty million investors without complying with any regulatory provisions contained in the Companies Act, Sebi Act, (and) rules and regulations already discussed.

Now, the observations of Khehar. They seem to be more interesting. These too are reproduced verbatim:

> When the first communication was addressed by Sebi to Enam Securities, the merchant banker for Sahara Prime City, the reply... referred to the fact that the same was based on legal opinion. It is therefore apparent, that right from the beginning, legal opinion came to be sought before replies were furnished... It is in the aforesaid background, that one needs to evaluate the responses of the two companies...
>
> An astounding reply was submitted by the companies in May 2010. "In the months of May and June, most of the staff remains on long holidays with their children due to summer holidays of schools/colleges. In our case also the concerned officials are on vacation and gone out of station."

One wonders whether the appellant companies were running a kindergarten, where their staff was expected to be unavailable during the summer. ... In spite of the fact that Sebi was responsible for the development and regulations of the securities market, the appellant-companies could brush aside Sebi's demand for information in such a brash and audacious manner, is quite frankly difficult to comprehend. ... It is difficult to swallow that the two companies had not even maintained records, pertaining to investments in the range of ₹40,000 crore.

What was placed before the Sebi in the compact disc... has now been made available to this court as a hard copy... It was not possible to persuade oneself to travel beyond the first page of the voluminous compilation... For facility of reference extracted hereunder details of "Kalawati", one of the investors disclosed in the hard copy.

Serial No: 6603675

Investor's Name: Kalawati.

Investor's particulars: Uchahara S K Nagar, UP

Introducer's agent name: Haridwar

Introducer's agent code: 107511425

Investor's/agent's address: Bani Road, Semeriyawa, Sant Kabir Nagar.

First and foremost, the data furnished by the appellant-companies does not indicate the basis of the alleged "private placement". It is impossible to determine whether Kalawati... was invited to subscribe for (sic) the OFCDs as a friend or associate of group companies or worker/employee.... Neither her parentage nor her husband's name has been disclosed, so that the identity of Kalawati could be exclusively determined...

The address of Kalawati indicated is of a general description, as it does not incorporate a particular door number, or street, or locality. The name of the introducer/agent leads to a different impression altogether. Haridwar, as a name of a person of Indian origin, is quite incomprehensible. In India, names of cities do not ever constitute the basis of individual names. One will never find Allahabad, Agra, Bangalore, Chennai or Tirupati as individual names... One would not like to make any unrealistic remark, but there is no other option but to record that the impression emerging from the analysis of the single entry ... is that the same seems totally unrealistic, and may well be, fictitious, concocted and made up.

...It is essential to express that there may be no real subscribers for (sic) the OFCDs.... Or, alternatively, (sic) there may be an intermix or real and fictitious subscribers. The issue that would emerge in the aforesaid situation (which one can only hope is untrue) would be, how the subscription amount collected.... Even though I hope that all the subscribers are genuine, and so also, the subscription amount, it

> would be necessary to modify the operative part of the order issued by the Sebi which came to be endorsed by the SAT (Securities Appellate Tribunal), so that the purpose of law is not only satisfied but also enforced.

Both Kalawati and Haridwar, however, have filed affidavits at Ahata court at Sant Kabirnagar, confirming their identity.

Haridwar's affidavit (No. 58AB 115736, dated 24 August 2012), written in Hindi, said that Haridwar was from the village of Uchahra Kalan, *tehsil* Khalidabad, district Sant Kabir Nagar, Uttar Pradesh. He was a resident of this address and an agent with Sahara Company. The company had given Haridwar a unique identification code (107511425). He deposited the money saved by the people associated with the company, with Sahara India along with receipts.

His father, Ram Lakhan, gave him the name Haridwar as he was born following his father's prayers at that holy city. It was derived in the same way as Kashinath and Kashiram are derived from Kashi (a neighbourhood in Varanasi; also called Old Varanasi). Along with the affidavit, he attached a copy of his voter identification, issued by the election commission of India, and his photo.

Going by her affidavit (No. 58AB 120513, dated 31 August 2012), Kalawati is the daughter of Ram Shankar. Her affidavit, also written in Hindi, said that no one in her village had the same name as hers; that the village had no house numbers so people just called each other by names and the postman delivered letters to them. She deposited money in Sahara through 'Haridwar Babu' and claimed that

Sahara was very popular in her area as banks did not open accounts easily without proper identification. The proof of her residence had been provided by the head of the village *panchayat* who claimed to have known Kalawati for the past three years and ten months.

The affidavits did not mention the age of Haridwar or Kalawati, but Haridwar's voter identification card put his year of birth as 1968 without any reference to date or month.

For the record, the Sant Kabir Nagar district – named after the 15th century mystic poet and philosopher whose writings greatly influenced the Bhakti movement – was created on 5 September 1997, by carving out 131 villages from *tehsil* Basti and 161 from tehsil Bansi of the Siddharth Nagar district. It lies between Gorakhpur in the east, Basti in the west, Siddharth Nagar in the north and Ambedkar Nagar in the south.

The name Kalawati hit the national headlines when Congress vice president Rahul Gandhi met a Dalit widow of the same name on his trip to Vidarbha in eastern Maharashtra, known for its arid land and farmers' suicides. Gandhi mentioned her plight in Indian Parliament in 2008 to explain how things had not changed for poor people in rural India. Since then, Kalavati Bandurkar – she spells her name differently – has become a mascot for the Indian poor.

However, investments made by Sahara's Kalawati (or, should we say, Kalawatis?) who figures 5,984 times in different locations across north and west India on the list of investors that runs into 112,000 pages, are worth ₹5.5 crore. According to an *Indian Express* report, this name is mentioned at least 55 times against one address.[2]

– Kalawati first appears at Serial No. 90 in the list of those who subscribed to the SIRECL OFCD. An investment of ₹15,000 is credited against a "Kalawati Singh, Rajapur Dillipur Bhojpur BR". The same entry then appears 17 more times on the list.

– The Kalawati entry then appears at Serial No. 6603675, with the address "Uchahara, S K Nagar, UP". Another entry at Serial No. 1968216 in the name of 'Mairunnisha' bears the same address.

– Kalawati figures several times against the address "Civil Lines Buxar BR". There are 150 other entries from this address with different names.

– A Kalawati Devi, wife of Dharam Bhagwi Ch. Dadri Bhiwani HR, appears 55 times with an investment of ₹15,000 per entry except for once when the figure is ₹10,000.

– Kalawati Devi, 140 VPO Bhagwai Ch. Dadri HR is listed 16 times. Ch. Dadri presumably stands for Charkhi Dadri, the largest *tehsil* in Bhiwani district of Haryana.

– One Kalawati Bhusari surfaces in "Jaipur Nagpur Maharashtra" once; another Kalawati lives at "187 Aurangabad Lucknow UP" (Serial Nos. 118507 and 6612830).

– The address for Kalawati Ahir (Serial No. 1887125) is "W No 12 Nepalganj Banke UP".

---

[2] "The curious case of 5,984 Kalawatis in Sahara list", Appu Esthose Suresh: New Delhi; Wednesday 1 May 2013

– The Kalawati Chamar of Serial No. 306151 appears to live in "W No 13 Nepalganj Saigaw Nepal". Nepalganj is a municipality in Banke district, Nepal, on the Terai plains near the southern border with Bahraich district in Uttar Pradesh.

The operative part of the Radhakrishnan and Khehar judgment ran into five pages. It told Sahara to refund ₹17,500 crore with a 15% interest within three months. The group was also asked to furnish details of investors who have got their money back and Sebi was to check the correctness of such claims. If Sebi does not find the documents produced by Sahara to be genuine, it would be presumed that the two companies have not refunded any amount, the judgment said.

The court also gave Sebi freedom to appoint external agencies and experts to sift through the documents and validate them – all at Sahara's expense.

In case genuine investors were not found, the money not owned by anybody would go the Consolidated Fund of India for investor protection.

Finally, in case Sahara was not able to refund the money to investors, Sebi was empowered to take legal actions, including attachment and sale of properties and freezing of bank accounts to realize the money.

The court also appointed retired judge Justice BN Agarwal to oversee the entire recovery process and directed Sebi to file a status report and seek further directions, if necessary.

The appointment of Agarwal to oversee the recovery process can be interpreted either as the court's lack of faith in

Sebi's ability to implement its order or its efforts to create the impression of fair play. The third person would vet all actions of the regulator in possibly the toughest recovery process in Indian financial system where millions of investors are involved but identities of many of them are shrouded in mystery.

The Supreme Court judgment clearly said that "in the event of finding that the genuineness of the subscribers is doubtful, an opportunity shall be afforded to Saharas to satisfactorily establish the same as being legitimate and valid. It shall be open to the Saharas, in such an eventuality, to associate the concerned subscribers to establish their claims. The decision of Sebi in this behalf will be final and binding on Saharas as well as the subscribers."

Once the onus was put on Sebi to ensure that all genuine investors should get back their money (within a time frame too) and that wherever the identity of an investor was suspect, the money should flow into the Consolidated Fund of India, the job became very complex.

Relatively, the RBI's task of winding down the RNBC arm of Sahara was easier as the banking regulator reconstituted the board of the company and left the job of paying back depositors to the company itself as long as the board was satisfied with the KYC norms followed.

Just the Beginning

The August 2012 Supreme Court judgment was not the end but the start of a new chapter fraught with Sahara's defiance, missing deadlines and sending truckloads of documents that took weeks to collate and even longer to read and make sense of. And rounds and rounds of fights both at the court and the appellate body of the Sebi on non-compliance of the Supreme Court order by Sahara, contempt petition filed by the regulator against the group, the apex court giving extension to Sahara for a phased repayment in three stages, and Sebi freezing bank accounts of Sahara companies and their directors.

A frustrated Sebi even moved the Supreme Court seeking detention in 'civil prison' of Roy and two other directors, Ashok Roy Choudhary and Ravi Shankar Dubey. The regulator wanted the court to direct the trio to deposit their passports with the court. "In view of the open, continued and consistent defiance of the orders of this court and the orders of Sebi, it is necessary that drastic measures are taken to protect the interest of three crore investors."

Shortly after that, Sebi summoned Roy and three directors, including Bharrgava, to its office. To keep the psychological pressure on, Sinha was not on the scene; they met Prashant Saran, a fulltime member of Sebi, for an hour. Roy made a rather theatrical appearance, in a convoy of four cars – a Mercedes and three Toyota Innovas, all white – and with a small army of bodyguards wielding machine guns.

Out of the meeting, Roy told reporters outside the Sebi headquarters that he had asked Sebi to speed up the verification of investors' documents and made the famous remark "*Aaj ek ghanta Sebi ne bithaya humhe. Ummeed thi ki ek pyali chai ke liye poochenge; lekin woh bhi nahi poocha.*"

(Today, Sebi made us wait for an hour. We had hoped that they would offer at least a cup of tea; we were not offered even that.) For Sebi, this was not an informal chat over a cup of tea; a fulltime director, a quasi-judicial authority, had summoned Roy. It was more like a court proceeding.

After the meeting was over on that day in April 2013, Roy was seen simultaneously on all major business television channels exuding energy, confidence and transparency. Roy, a trophy for business channels, listed out his personal assets: he had gold and jewellery worth ₹3 crore, cash and bank balances worth ₹34 lakh and fixed deposits of ₹1.59 crore. Besides, he had advanced ₹11 crore towards the purchase of a sugar mill in Badhauli in Ambala district of Haryana.

Roy said there was not a single complaint from any of the 110 million investors in the group. He also said that all his businesses would grow at a faster pace from then on and reminded the media that it had a "big responsibility" to uphold the truth. He ducked all critical questions though and dished out these homilies and told the media, "prove me wrong and hang me".

"You are Manipulating the Courts"

A few days later, Justices Radhakrishnan and Khehar of the Supreme Court, once again, pulled up the Sahara group for not furnishing details of the depositors to the Sebi and reiterated that if there were untraced depositors, the money should be remitted to the central government.

When senior counsel Aryama Sundaram appearing for Roy pointed out that Sebi was attaching his personal property though Roy was not a party in the case, Khehar observed: "We are not interested in parties. If you have approached the high court, then it is contempt of this court. You are not cooperating with Sebi, and you are not obeying our order. You are manipulating the courts. I am surprised at what you are doing."

Radhakrishnan, expressing his anguish, said Sahara's attempt to overreach the orders of this court is contempt and "Sebi has its obligations to fulfil".

Later in May 2012, in an interview with Reuters, Roy said that Sahara was looking to bring equity and debt investment into its businesses as the fight with Sebi had set back its growth. "Out of turn, when you have to make payments, it affects the cash flow," Subrata Roy said.

The company was looking to bring in corporate or financial equity partners to take minority stakes in some Sahara group businesses, including its Q Shop retail chain, a large dairy project in India and real estate ventures. He, however, did not identify any potential investors, but said he may offer stakes of 10–20%.

Sahara had earlier not been interested in bringing in equity partners, but would now look for investors to bring debt, too. Roy said the tussle with Sebi had set back its growth by a year or two. "We have now said, yes, we will give equity, provided equity also brings a bigger amount of debt with it," he said.

This marks a shift in Roy's stance. In an interview with this author in January 2013, Roy had stated that cash flow was not a problem with the group.

He may have to look for equity infusion – and along with it, debt – because the group may not have enough underlying assets to pay back the bond holders. In its affidavit filed with the Supreme Court, Sahara has listed properties that it owns across India and their valuation, but a Sebi investigation has found too many holes in its claims.

This gives a new dimension to Sahara's claim of a vast land bank. The popular perception was that Sahara is solid, but not liquid – it has land, but it may not be able to sell the land and generate cash – but Sebi's investigation has debunked the theory. The regulator has found that the title deeds of many plots that Sahara claimed to own are not clear.

How would Roy react to this? "It is totally baseless. One or two percent of our land holding might have unclear titles but the rest all are absolutely fine. Why should I go for a stress sale?"

"We gave ₹5,500crore to Sebi. We purchased hotels in the US at thousands of crores. There is no dearth of money," he had said in January. In November 2012, Sahara completed the acquisition of two iconic New York hotels – the New York Plaza and Dream Downtown for around $800 million. It had acquired Grosvenor House in London in 2010.

"Disgusted" with Sebi's move, Roy plans to remove the Indian flag that flies at these three hotels. "There was global news that Sebi had attached our properties, bank accounts. Hearing that, foreign banks recalled loans that they gave us for purchasing these hotels. We are somehow managing to hold the hotels through help from friends. There is huge extra expense. We have to remove Indian flags from all three hotels. Sad," he says.

In the interview, he also gave a couple of examples of appreciation of value of land. Apparently, Sahara got into an agreement with a party (Roy did not name the person or entity) to develop about 106 acres of land at Versova, Andheri, a western suburb of Mumbai. The legal issues involved are all settled and Sahara could make as much as ₹30,000 crore or more by developing this piece of land.

It bought some 220 acres land near Gurgaon in the NCR region at less than ₹100 crore, but people were offering ₹2,100 crore for it in 2013. "We are an unlisted company. There is no need to take care of earning per share. Why should we sell? The appreciation of land price is so huge; maybe Sahara is the richest company in the country," Roy told me.

These two pieces of land – in Versova and Gurgaon – are two of the nine jewels that Sahara listed in a 4 January 2012 affidavit filed with the Supreme Court. They were all acquired with OFCD investors' money. The affidavit gave an undertaking that these nine assets were sufficient to guarantee the repayment of the OFCD holders, with the whole lot being valued at over ₹36,000 crore.

Nine Jewels

Let's take a look at the nine jewels. The first one – Aamby

Valley – is certainly the Kohinoor of Roy's treasure trove.

(1) Aamby Valley Ltd holds the development rights for about 707 acres of land in Pune, Maharashtra. The amount spent on purchasing the land: ₹3,459 crore.

(2) Sahara India Real Estate Corp. Ltd (SIRECL) holds the development rights in 186-acre plot at prime location in Delhi and Gurgaon on behalf of Sahara group companies – Sahara Constructions Pvt Ltd, Sahara India Residential Holding Pvt Ltd., Sahara India Prop. (P) Ltd, Sahara India Dev. (P) Ltd, Sahara India Real Estate (P) Ltd, Sahara India Commercial Corp. Ltd, Sahara Structurals Pvt Ltd, Sahara Township Pvt Ltd, Sahara Residentials Pvt Ltd, Sahara Complex Pvt Ltd, Sahara Land Arts Pvt Ltd and Sahara Enclave Pvt Ltd.

The amount spent on purchasing the land: ₹1,436 crore.

(3) Sahara India Commercial Corp. Ltd (SICCL) holds a 33% stake in Versova Project, comprising 106 acres near Lokhandwala, Mumbai. The amount spent for purchase of land: ₹1,848 crore.

(4) Many companies – partners companies of the Sahara group – hold 90–95 % stake in 64 special purpose vehicles with an equal number of projects in as many cities, measuring 4,378 acres of land. The amount spent for purchase of land: ₹1,105 crore. The (estimated) valuation of SIRECL's share in these projects is ₹21,631 crore (before tax).

(5.1) Sahara group companies hold a 40% stake in four city-home projects in four cities/towns over 318 acres. The enterprise valuation of SIRECL in these projects is about ₹888 crore (before tax).

(5.2) Sahara group companies hold a 50% stake in 15 city home projects in 15 cities/towns, measuring 1,751 acres. The enterprise valuation of SIRECL's stake in these properties is about ₹5,192 crore. The amount spent on purchasing the entire 2,639 acres is ₹180 crore.

(6) SICCL holds a 30% stake in Lucknow district project comprising 170 acres of land. The amount spent for purchase of land: ₹1,000 crore.

(7) The group holds a 100% stake in equity shares of 60 entities having parcels of 515 acres of land across 16 locations in India. The amount spent for purchase of land: ₹532 crore. The enterprise value of SIRECL's share in this project is about ₹3,138 crore (before tax).

(8) The group holds a 100% stake in two entities holding development rights in land measuring about 196 acres and 56 acres at Vasai and Malegaon, Maharashtra. The amount spent for the purchase of this land: ₹62 crore. The enterprise value of SIRECL's share is ₹2,421 crore (before tax).

(9) Sahara Aamby Valley City was conceived in 1996 as an integrated city spread over approximately 10,000 acres. The amount spent on purchase of land: ₹5,207 crore. The valuation of the land is ₹40,460 crore.

A *Firstpost* investigation suggests that the group may have grossly overvalued some of its real assets. It looked into one of the assets declared by Sahara in its affidavit to the Supreme

Court and found reasons to doubt their authenticity.[3]

Firstly, the group has shown the value of the property purchased at a very low price and a making a 23-fold profit without doing anything on it, according to *Firstpost*.

Secondly, some pieces of the land were bought on the same day – one from a man and the other from his widow. Did she sell the plot on the same day her husband died?

Thirdly, some of the sellers who allegedly sold the land to Sahara were untraceable at the addresses mentioned.

Twelve real estate companies of the group had acquired 186 acres of land, most of it in Gurgaon, in phases, by 2007. Land mutation documents available with Firstpost confirm that Sahara paid nearly ₹62 crore for this land over time. These 12 companies are Sahara Constructions Pvt Ltd, Sahara India Residential Holding Pvt Ltd, Sahara India Prop. (P) Ltd, Sahara India Dev. (P) Ltd, Sahara India Real Estate (P) Ltd, Sahara India Commercial Corp. Ltd, Sahara Structurals Pvt Ltd, Sahara Township Pvt Ltd, Sahara Residentials Pvt Ltd, Sahara Complex Pvt Ltd, Sahara Land Arts Pvt Ltd and Sahara Enclave Pvt Ltd.

How did ₹62 crore become ₹1,436 crore? By selling the development rights to a group company for the bloated sum. Sahara, it seems, "manufactured" a deal to sell this 186-acre plot to SIRECL – one of the two companies that raised over ₹17,000 crore in OFCDs – for ₹1,436 crore.

---

[3] "₹62 cr to 1,436 cr: How Sahara inflated land value 23 times", Raman Kirpal, Firstpost, 11 April 2013

Firstpost's investigations into the 186-acre plot in Gurgaon bordering Delhi (in Sectors 111 and 113) reveal not only gross overvaluation of the asset, but also that the 12 Sahara companies that originally bought this land may have made a huge margin by selling development rights to group company SIRECL for ₹1,436 crore. The implication is that SIRECL investors were sold an inflated asset.

Sahara claims that this piece of land can be sold any time for more than ₹2,000 crore. "When an agriculture land is converted into a non-agriculture land for residential purpose, the price escalates 10 to 15 times," a Sahara official points out.

This plot, located behind Village Chouma in Gurgaon's Palam Vihar, is not yet developed and there is no construction whatsoever. Sahara contractors had put barbed wire around it, but the villagers have cut the wire and use the land as a *kuccha* path in the absence of any other approach road.

The Sahara affidavit painted this picture of the plot: "The project is spread on land parcels of approximately 186 acres and is to be developed as commercial space and residential apartments, including group housing, branded villas, luxury apartments, club and hotel projects."

Haryana's town planning office confirmed to *Firstpost* that the Sahara group has "no licence" to execute this project. And the land use shown in the records is still "agriculture". According to land mutation documents, Sahara's first foray into Gurgaon's 186-acre plot began some time in 1997–98 with one Rajiv Saxena transferring a few acres of land to Sahara. This transfer did not involve any monetary transaction. Another person, Nishith Joshi, also contributed about seven acres of land to Sahara. The Delhi addresses of both men are incomplete in the land records.

Sahara built up its real estate empire around the transferred land in Gurgaon. Twelve real estate companies of Sahara were unleashed to cajole farmers into selling their land.

According to the land records, Sahara bought two acres of land from Sahib Singh on 24 December 2003. However, the same land records show that Sahib Singh was dead, and that Sahara appears to have bought the land from Ramrati, widow of Sahib Singh, also on the same day!

In 2003, the Sahara group of companies purchased nearly 25 acres of land for just ₹4.20 crore from local farmers.

The plot further swelled with the acquisition of 10 acres of land for merely ₹1.37 crore in 2005.

Sahara hit the bull's eye in 2006, when it managed to acquire over 100 acres of land for ₹31.22 crore. And in 2007, when property prices were scaling new heights, the final deal was sealed with the purchase of 10 acres for ₹25 crore. This was the front end of the 186-acre plot and thus had cost more to purchase than the rest.

The final purchase value paid for the land is about ₹62 crore. The market value of the land has, meanwhile, increased to about ₹3 crore per acre in this area. Even if one values the Sahara land at current market rate, this amounts to around ₹558 crore and it is unlikely to be ₹1,436 crore by any stretch of imagination, the *Firstpost* investigation concluded.

Sahara did not respond to the *Firstpost* queries for this story, but the Sahara official quoted earlier told the author that this piece of land is today priced at more than what the company had mentioned. This is because it has become a residential zone and a 12-lane highway is now touching the piece of land.

Referring to one particular plot outside Aamby Vally, the group says a valuator, MC Bhide of Pune-based Bhide Associates, pegged the price at ₹8 crore per acre, but when Sebi appointed the same person for valuing the land, the price dropped to ₹54 lakh per acre. The government rate for the land, based on which stamp duty is decided for a transaction, is ₹5 crore. "You can always confuse people using a tag like 'no development zone' and suppress the price," the Sahara official says. "Throughout the country, residential townships and commercial complexes are being built with different FSI (floor space index) in no development zones."

He also refers to the IPO document of Sahara Prime City which was vetted by national and international lawyers and half a dozen top dog investment bankers. "It valued the company at over ₹30,000 crore in 2007 because of its land bank."

Roy is extremely bitter about Sebi. The markets regulator, according to him, will not be able to verify identity of investors in OFCDs in years to come. "The Sebi counsel Mr (Arvind) Dattar has told the court that Sebi does not have so much staff to take care of assets offered by Sahara, so Sebi cannot accept assets. If it does not have suitable people for taking care of assets, how can it handle verifications of three crore investors in a business conglomerate that has more than 4,000 establishments? No private sector agency in India can verify such a large volume," Roy told me.

8

ROLES PEOPLE PLAYED

YV Reddy was the first RBI governor to tackle the bull by the horn. He was ably assisted by his deputy V Leeladhar. Similarly, former Sebi chairman CB Bhave was the first to confront the Sahara group and ask it to furnish information that was not revealed in the draft prospectus of Sahara Prime City. Bhave was supported in this by his fulltime director Dr KM Abraham.

Reddy and Leeladhar finished their Sahara assignment before their term ended. In the case of Sebi, Bhave and Abraham initiated the process, leaving it to the next Sebi chairman UK Sinha to step on the gas.

Many people in the regulatory bodies, judiciary and industry played an important role in making Peerless and Sahara appreciate the importance of regulations in a space that deals with the money of the masses. This chapter profiles a few of them.

Dhruba Narayan Ghosh

DN Ghosh was born in Kolkata, but spent his early childhood in Coochbehar, in northern Bengal. The son of an academician, he studied economics at the famed Presidency College and wanted to follow in his father's footsteps, but drifted into civil service instead.

In the civil services examination, Ghosh opted for Indian Audit and Accounts Service as his first preference, rather than the more widely preferred Indian Administrative Service – a decision he would rue later. In an interview, he was asked why he did not choose the administrative service. Ghosh, who had just finished reading Dudley Dillard's *The Life of John Meynard Keynes*, had a smart reply: "When Keynes appeared for the British Civil Services examination, he indicated the British treasury as his first preference and not the Indian Civil Service."

"Are you comparing yourself with Keynes?" one of the interviewers asked him.

His answer was, "No sir, I am following his example."

After five years in the Indian Audit and Accounts Service, Ghosh joined the banking division of the finance ministry's economic affairs department in January 1958 as an under-secretary. Except for a four-year break, he was attached to the division until March 1975 in various capacities. By the time he left, a department of banking had been created.

A sabbatical and a four-year stint with the Left Front government in West Bengal (1977–81) later, Ghosh returned

Dhruba Narayan Ghosh

to Delhi, but this time to a different ministry – first, steel and mines, and later, defence production.

In 1985, AS Puri, managing director of the State Bank of India, was set to take over as the chairman of the country's largest lender, but at the last moment certain allegations cropped up against him and the then finance minister VP Singh decided to have Ghosh instead as the bank's chairman. Rajiv Gandhi was India's Prime Minister then.

Ghosh, an outsider to head the nation's largest bank, retired in 1989. He also headed Philips India and Larsen & Toubro Ltd, and was the founder chairman of rating agency Icra Ltd.

Ghosh, who turned 85 in 2013, vividly remembers his Peerless days. He was not the RBI's nominee at the company. Peerless promoter Roy had picked him to be the company's chairman. Ghosh, who had the full backing of the RBI, in turn, picked his team. In 1996, when he took over as chairman of Peerless, he was a 68-year-old bureaucrat who ate, drank and slept finance.

Was Peerless his most difficult task? "Not really; the government of India service gives you a tremendous amount of self-confidence. I can pick up any challenge," Ghosh said with a smile. Curiosity about what is happening around him has kept Ghosh going. He can work on many fronts, including writing regularly on finance and working on his autobiography, which is expected to be released sometime in 2014.

His association with non-banking finance companies dates back to the mid-1960s when finance minister Tiruvellore

Thattai Krishnamachari, popularly known as TTK, took the initiative to classify the entities. While amending the RBI Act by inserting a separate chapter (Chapter III B) on non-banking finance companies in 1967, there was an attempt to classify different kinds of non-banking companies – housing finance companies, lease finance, nidhi, chit funds, mutual funds – the defining criteria being the nature of their assets.

Ghosh and RK Seshadri, a bureaucrat in the ministry of finance who later joined the RBI as an executive director and eventually became a deputy governor, found it hard to classify some companies according to their asset criteria. These companies were raising deposits from the public and investing in different kinds of assets. Unable to come up with a better tag, they named the entities as residuary non-banking companies. So Ghosh has been associated with the RNBC genre since its birth.

He is also the severest critic of the model. Ghosh blames the RBI for failing to rein in RNBCs. "Why couldn't the RBI control them? Why did it allow them to grow to monstrous sizes? Clearly, it was a failure on their part," he says.

After Reddy took over as the RBI governor, Shyamala Gopinath, then an executive director, called Ghosh at Reddy's instance to ask his suggestions for the sector. "Why not control the assets?" Ghosh replied. That probably prompted the RBI to change the directed lending norms – from 80% to 100%.

In 2004, Ghosh, while heading Peerless, wrote an explosive article in *The Economic and Political Weekly* that many in the company believe encouraged the regulator to go for the kill against RNBCs.

Ghosh stepped down from Peerless in 2006, ensuring that it was back on the growth path. But for him, the Kolkata company would probably not have survived. Ghosh steered the rescue by changing the business model and downsizing personnel – unheard of in Communist-ruled West Bengal in the 1990s. He had the unstinted support of chief minister Jyoti Basu, who, it turned out, was quite pragmatic. Between Peerless being liquidated with thousands of employees on its payroll and the company bouncing back to health with a trimmer work force, Ghosh chose the latter option; Basu saw logic in the decision.

The phenomenal growth of Peerless and Sahara, Ghosh said, illustrated the inefficiencies of the system, the regulator's indifference and the greed and political influence. His contribution in caging the RNBC animal was no less important than putting Peerless back on the rails.

Chandrasekhar Bhaskar Bhave

In June 2010, in a speech at the Confederation of Indian Industry's annual mutual fund summit in Mumbai, the then capital market regulator CB Bhave rued the inability of the 3,000-odd mutual fund schemes to match investors' needs. "Investors are intelligent," Bhave said. "If we have not been able to convince them, even with thousands of mutual fund schemes, there's some problem with the products. We are not

Chandrasekhar Bhaskar Bhave

getting to the heart of the matter." Bhave's candid talk was directed at inducing the industry to do some soul-searching; instead, it had a different effect on the players in India's then ₹6.75 trillion mutual fund industry. The moment Bhave left the venue, the knives were out. In a chorus, the fund managers blamed the regulator for "killing the industry".

The speech was Bhave's first public appearance after an ordinance on the regulation of unit-linked insurance plans (Ulips) put an end to the spat between Sebi and the insurance regulatory and development authority (IRDA). The 18 June 2010 ordinance had settled the matter in favour of IRDA and said Ulips, hybrid products that combine insurance and equity, fell under the purview of IRDA, and Sebi had nothing to do with them.

Roughly a month later, MCX Stock Exchange Ltd moved the Bombay High Court seeking its intervention on Sebi's inaction on an application seeking permission to serve as a platform for trading in equities.

Bhave's three-year tenure at Sebi was tumultuous. The mutual fund industry bayed for his blood for abolishing the entry load that took away commissions for distributors, the lifeline of the industry. IRDA and Sebi fought a hard battle that the former won with the government's support. And finally, a regulated entity – MCX-SX – dragged Sebi to court for the regulator's silence on its application for equity trading. Bhave had been branded the market's Enemy No. 1.

The Ulip ordinance was promulgated when Bhave was in Canada attending the International Organization of

Securities Commissions conference; he was not consulted on it.

Bhave, a 1975-batch IAS officer of the Maharashtra cadre, had worked at Sebi earlier as well, as executive director in charge of the secondary and, later, primary markets between 1992 and 1996.

Before joining Sebi in 1992, Bhave had been additional industries commissioner of Maharashtra for three years and earlier, had served as an undersecretary in the ministry of finance and as a deputy secretary in the ministry of petroleum. After his first stint with Sebi, Bhave resigned from the IAS (in 1996) to create India's first share depository, which revolutionized the capital market by getting market players to accept a new system of dematerialized shares. The depository, set up at less than ₹100 crore, achieved paperless trading within three years.

A Chittapavan Brahmin – a group traditionally known for integrity and intellectual honesty – Bhave was not keen to be the chairman of Sebi because, as the head of National Securities Depository Ltd, he was fighting with the regulator and there was an evident conflict of interest.

Bhave's stint at Sebi was controversial. He was rigid and inflexible. His obsession with self-righteousness was hubris, Bhave's detractors say. Allegations stacked up against him, that he had a hidden motive for this pro-investor image; that he wanted to teach the intermediaries a lesson; that he was fighting the battle for the National Stock Exchange and didn't want it to lose its monopoly; and finally, that he had done well in terms of investor protection and market development, but had failed in fostering competition.

"In public service jobs, you receive praise as well as criticism," Bhave said in an interview with this author in 2010. "Both can be motivated or genuine. It's not easy to segregate the two but one needs to do that. The human mind pushes you to believe that praise is genuine and criticism motivated. One has to make constant efforts to avoid this and use criticism as an opportunity to improve. At Sebi, we try and take all stakeholders' feedback and then take a decision."

Under him, Sebi doggedly pursued all high-profile cases. Its investigation into a dozen firms linked to Reliance Industries Ltd for possible violations of insider trading norms and questioning of Anil Ambani and four senior officials of his Reliance group for explanation over what it referred to as "certain dealings" stole the limelight. However, Bhave's quiet work on the Sahara group company's IPO did not attract much attention during his tenure, which ended in February 2011.

He initiated the probe into Sahara and stood by his team until the end. While there is no end to the debate within Sebi on whether Bhave was a level-headed regulator with an iron hand or had overstepped his brief, everybody agrees that as a boss, he soaked up all pressure, did not expose any of his colleagues to the strings and pulls of the big bad outside world, and had the gumption to stand up for what he believed was right.

Dr Kandathil Mathew Abraham

KM Abraham graduated in civil engineering from Kerala University, acquired a Masters degree from IIT, Kanpur, became an Indian Administrative Service officer in 1982, and followed that up with a PhD on inter-organizational systems – the hardcore management of technology – from the University of Michigan, Ann Arbor. He would go on to become additional chief secretary in Kerala's higher education and social justice department and vice chancellor of Kerala University, his alma mater.

For all this, Abraham is a chartered financial analyst. Finance has been his passion. As Kerala's secretary of finance between 1996 and 2003, Abraham was associated with nine state budgets, including two interim budgets, a record no other bureaucrat in the southern state has come close to. He also piloted a ₹1,300-crore government programme of the Asian Development Bank modernizing administrative reform, service delivery improvement, asset management and fiscal reforms initiatives in Kerala.

For all his storied achievements, Abraham looks up to former chief auditor of India, Vinod Rai, and his former boss at Sebi, Bhave, as his role models.

In 2007, when India's capital market regulator advertised the position for a board member, Abraham, then principal secretary in the Kerala government, applied for the job. He joined in July 2008. In Sebi's administrative architecture, the chairman sits at the top – he is the primus inter pares, the

Dr Kandathil Mathew Abraham

first among equals. He's accompanied on the board by three fulltime members – the two others with Abraham were MS Sahoo and Prashant Saran. They were quasi-judicial authorities, to whom the executive directors reported.

Abraham evokes strong reactions from within Sebi and outside. While many find him an honest, upright officer, never willing to compromise on ethics, others say he had an agenda. He suffered from a persecution complex and paranoia and "appeared to be under severe emotional stress and a delusion that everybody was out to harm him and his family," UK Sinha, Bhave's successor, wrote to the finance ministry. Abraham had written to Prime Minister Manmohan Singh charging the finance ministry with influencing Sebi.

The whistle blower act overshadowed Abraham's tenure in Sebi (which by all standards was controversial) but nobody can deny the fact that he had the mettle to take calls on influential and highly connected corporate houses. His two orders on the Sahara group in November 2010 and June 2011 form the bedrock of all investigations and actions against the two group companies that had raised money through OFCDs. Members of Sebi's investigation team remember him as a hard task master with an eye for detail and an uncompromising attitude.

Yaga Venugopal Reddy

Yaga Venugopal Reddy

What was YV Reddy's most important moment at the Indian central bank, which he served for over a decade, first as a deputy governor and then as governor? Possibly, it was his 1997 Goa speech. On 15 August 1997, at a gathering of foreign exchange dealers in Goa, he said, "As per the real effective exchange rate, it would certainly appear that the rupee is overvalued." The next day, the currency tumbled. This was the first time the Indian central bank had talked the market. The RBI had wanted to convey a message and gauge how the market reacted, and Reddy was its messenger.

His six-year stint at the RBI as a deputy governor was the longest posting at one place for the 1964 batch IAS officer. He was that rare RBI governor to be offered a five-year stint from the beginning. The last governor before him to get such a stint was IG Patel in 1977.

On 12 January 2005, a foreign expert on Indian stock markets was seen on a news channel tearing into Reddy. The provocation for his reaction was Reddy's academic discussion that evening while releasing the India Development Report 2004–05 of the Indira Gandhi Institute of Development Research (IGIDR). Reddy had said a view had to be taken on capping foreign institutional investors' (FII) inflows into the Indian markets. He also suggested monitoring the "quality and quantity" of FII flows. Finally, he asked the authorities to examine the efficacy of "price-based measures such as taxes (on FII flows)," though their effectiveness was arguable.

He was frank enough to admit that quotas or ceilings on FII flows, as practised by certain countries, might not be desirable at that stage, but there was merit in keeping such an option open and exercising it selectively as needed.

By the time Reddy came back to his office on Mint Road in Mumbai, his mobile phone was ringing and the RBI executives on the lobby of the 18th floor (where the governor's office is located) heard him talking to then finance minister P Chidambaram. The minister later appeared on television to clarify that the government had no proposal to cap portfolio inflows or tax them.

At a hurriedly convened press conference at the RBI headquarters late that evening, Reddy said personally he was "not in favour" of a ceiling on foreign funds inflows. Those who checked the RBI website later found that minor changes had been made to his original IGIDR speech.

Almost everybody in the financial world agrees Reddy's concern about the quality of inflows chasing Indian securities is valid. They wonder whether the speech was a faux pas or a deliberate comment by the governor to measure market reactions on hot money. Reddy always evokes extreme reactions and keeps people guessing.

Bimal Jalan, Reddy's predecessor at the RBI, has high regard for him for two reasons – his complete integrity and his devotion to work.

As a governor, Reddy possibly enjoyed the "creative tension" between the ministry and the RBI the most because of his strong sense of independence. Not many people, even at the

RBI, had a ringside view of such fights, as Reddy is a very private person, one who does not believe in washing office linen in public.

His five-year term, which ended in September 2008, was characterized by the highest average growth rate achieved by the Indian economy and the lowest average inflation since independence. However, he also saw the first signs of the economy overheating and made sure Indian banks were not caught in the bubble. He did not allow Indian banks to take risks that he himself did not understand and didn't care if investment bankers and bond dealers found him a conservative central banker who avoided innovation. He did not allow banks to hawk credit derivatives and securitize loans aggressively to take them out of their balance sheets. As a result of all this, hardly $1 billion of India's $800 billion banking assets turned toxic, while trillions of dollars were being written off globally during the economic crisis that began in 2008.

Reddy also sensed the real estate bubble ahead of other regulators and curbed banks' exposure to the sector by increasing the risk weight on commercial real estate. The higher risk weight called for more capital for banks and this made money more expensive for the borrowers. Similarly, he raised the risk weight on mortgages, consumer credit and capital market exposure. At the same time, he progressively raised provisions for standard assets and did not allow banks to borrow too much from other banks. On top of all that, there was strong and continued moral suasion to dampen banks' appetite for risk. All these measures fenced in the

Indian financial system from the ripple effect of the global financial crisis following the collapse of US investment bank Lehman Brothers Holdings Inc.

As a central banker, Reddy was most careful about three things – the conditions of the market, contagion and the interests of depositors. The day he became the RBI governor, his top agenda was to close down Peerless and Sahara.

Historically, Peerless revelled in court cases, but when it came to business, it was very different from Sahara. So, Reddy had different medicines for the two different RNBCs. He prescribed those medicines from the background, leaving it to his deputy V Leeladhar to administer them. He succeeded in both cases. Reddy became hated by both companies, but the head of the 14th Finance Commission did not let that bother him. His objective was to protect depositors' interests at any cost and he did that without caring about the power and influence wielded by the RNBCs.

Vittaldas Leeladhar

V Leeladhar could have been a high-profile corporate chief. A chemical engineer from Kerala University, Leeladhar had applied for a management trainee's job in Indian Aluminium Ltd in 1969. But the legendary banker TA Pai lured him to a job as a trainee officer at Syndicate Bank, which he was then heading, on a monthly salary of ₹241 – roughly a third of what Leeladhar would have earned at Indian Aluminium. In his application to Indian Aluminium, Leeladhar had used

Pai, with whom his uncle was working, as a referee and that's how Pai got to know Leeladhar.

The engineer did not flounder in the world of finance – his early job was to appraise industrial projects for loan disbursals.

After 11 years with the Syndicate Bank in Manipal, Leeladhar moved to Mangalore when he joined Corporation Bank in 1980, and stayed there till he was appointed executive director of the Bank of Maharashtra in 1996. At 49, Leeladhar was probably one of the youngest executive directors in a state-run bank. Fifteen months later, he became chairman and managing director of the Bangalore-based Vijaya Bank. In 2000, he shifted to Mumbai to head the Union Bank of India.

Leeladhar was possibly the only bank chairman never to have worked in a branch, regional or zonal office. Also, by a strange quirk of fate, Syndicate Bank was nationalized three months after he joined it in 1969; Corporation Bank was nationalized a month after he joined.

Leeladhar's greatest strength was perhaps his penchant for keeping a low profile. He never craved limelight, never raised his voice, but was firm in what he believed and got what he wanted done. Once, while at the executive lunch room at the Union Bank, Leeladhar asked an official of a consulting agency to prepare a report in three days. The task was not easy and the executive told the soft-spoken chairman he would need at least a week. Leeladhar kept quiet, but post lunch, he told his secretary, within earshot of the executive, to pencil

Vittaldas Leeladhar

their meeting in three days for the report. That cut short any scope of arguement with the chairman, the executive told me, and he knew he would have to complete the task if he wanted to keep his assignment.

A proponent of consolidation in the banking industry, Leeladhar, who headed banking operations and supervision in the RBI, forced the merger of quite a few banks. He also worked hard to streamline cooperative banks, many of which were seeing their net worth eroding and turning into a cesspool of politics. But Leeladhar considers the closing down of Sahara India Financial Corp., once the country's largest residuary non-bank finance company, his biggest achievement at the RBI.

He also tightened norms for NBFCs. Like Reddy, he too wanted to protect the interests of depositors and hence his focus was on deposit-taking firms. Unlike bank deposits, NBFC deposits do not have insurance covers. Many big NBFCs do not take public deposits, but they have access to public money in the form of short-term commercial papers and debentures. They were also resorting to heavy borrowings from banks.

Leeladhar was instrumental in introducing capital adequacy and concentration ratios for big, systematically important NBFCs. He also put a ceiling on the amount of bank finance that could flow into NBFCs, introduced disclosure norms, and asked NBFCs to report to the RBI every month on their source and deployment of funds. Some of these companies were in trouble because of their exposure to the real estate and capital markets.

Why did he take on Sahara India Financial? His stance was that the RNBC business model was inappropriate. The RBI could not stipulate any leverage ratio for RNBCs because of a series of court cases that the central bank had to fight with Peerless in Kolkata. So, even with a small capital, such companies could take huge public deposits. To tighten the screw, the RBI stipulated that 100% of such deposits had to be invested in instruments such as government bonds, triple-A rated corporate bonds, bank deposits and so on. Peerless cooperated with the RBI in terms of investments and constitution of the board. The regulator offered it a plan on exiting public deposits over a period of four years.

The RBI discussed a similar plan for Sahara, but it didn't head anywhere. After a brief legal battle at a high court and the Supreme Court, Sahara had no choice but to cooperate with the regulator in terms of agreeing to a time frame to wind down deposits, change the statutory auditor and reconstruct the board with new directors acceptable to the RBI.

If Reddy was the field marshal in the RBI's war with RNBCs, Leeladhar was the crafty general who meticulously planned every move in consultation with his lieutenant general and major general. He preferred to remain in Reddy's shadow, but he was the real executioner – the others merely followed his instructions.

Upendra Kumar Sinha

In February 2013, India's finance minister P Chidambaram in his Budget speech said, "I believe that India's capital market is among the best regulated markets." Sebi chairman UK Sinha can justifiably feel proud about the comment; the minister's not one to lavish such praise often.

Sinha, born in Gopalganj in the old Saran district, completed a postgraduate course in physics at Patna Science College and then acquired a Bachelors degree in law from Patna University. Taking over as Sebi chairman in February 2011, Sinha brought to the table rich experience in the capital markets. A 1976 batch IAS officer from the Bihar cadre, he had been a joint secretary in charge of capital markets in the ministry of finance before he went on to head UTI Asset Management Co. Ltd. Prior to that, as joint secretary in the banking division of the ministry, Sinha had played a key role in the merger of ICICI Ltd with ICICI Bank Ltd to create India's first universal bank. He had begun his career as a probationary officer in the State Bank of India.

A love for music and Urdu poetry helps Sinha fight the high stress of being the market regulator. "In the mornings, while walking, I listen to music on my iPod. Every day, I enjoy listening to music for an hour after reaching home... Listening to music, while driving to work or back home is very relaxing," Sinha once wrote in a newspaper. "Indoor games like bridge also help me unwind; being good at numbers helps there, I guess. I love analyzing numbers."

Upendra Kumar Sinha

Sinha can flawlessly recite Sahil Ludhianvi's famous work *Taj Mahal* and Ghalib's poems have always been an inspiration for him. Beneath this love for poetry and music is a shrewd regulator who knows his job well. One example of this is the set of changes in the consent order process. Serious offences like insider trading or front-running are no longer part of any consent process. Sebi, under him, also formulated a new takeover code and norms for governing market infrastructure institutions.

Sinha's initial days at Sebi were not easy. There had been a few public interest litigations against his appointment and, on top of that, there was Abraham's whistle blowing letter, alleging that Sebi was under tremendous pressure from the ministry. Sinha handled them well. He refuted Abraham's allegations point by point, and without wasting time on external issues, focused on putting the house in order.

Not a tough job for a seasoned bureaucrat who, early in his career, worked as the district magistrate of Patna for three years under four chief ministers. Later, in the finance ministry in Delhi, Sinha had worked with four different finance ministers – Yashwant Sinha, Jaswant Singh, Pranab Mukherjee and P Chidambaram.

Sinha has always brought innovation to his tasks. As a sub-divisional magistrate at Jamshedpur, his first posting, he established a slag pickers' cooperative society for tribal workers to end their exploitation by contractors.

At Unit Trust of India Asset Management Co., he floated micro-pension schemes in association with the Self

Employed Women's Association in Ahmedabad, the Bihar State Co-operative Milk Producers' Federation, members of the Paradeep Port and Dock Mazdoor Union, and an urban cooperative bank run by women, among other organizations. He also wanted to bring in sex workers from Mumbai's Kamathipura area under the micro-insurance fold, but a pilot project failed.

To his credit, Sinha never lost sight of Sahara or went soft on it. While Abraham, being a whole time member of the Sebi board and head of investigation, took the first call on Sahara and ordered it to repay money to the bondholders with interest, Sinha kept the pressure on and has been trying to move the case to its logical end. Under him, Sebi summoned Roy and other directors of Sahara to get a fix on their assets and even moved the Supreme Court seeking Roy's detention in civil prison and seizure of his passport by the court. In some sense, his job is tougher than Reddy's despite what the latter accomplished in 2008.

Thothala Narayansamy Manoharan

TN Manoharan was the first chartered account in India to receive a Padma Shri, the fourth-highest civilian award, for his contribution to trade and industry. As the president of the Institute of Chartered Accountants of India (ICAI), a statutory body that oversees the regulation of the profession, between March 2006 and February 2007, Manoharan had worked closely with the ministries of corporate affairs, human resources development, and finance. He ran educational programmes for commissioners of service tax on reading balance sheets and financial statements.

He was also among the half-a-dozen experts chosen to rescue Satyam Computers Services Ltd after its promoter Ramalinga Raju in 2009 confessed to a ₹7,136 crore accounting fraud, the largest in India's corporate history.

Manoharan was also associated with Sarva Shiksha Abhiyan, India's flagship programme for achieving universal elementary education. He advised it on tightening internal controls and effective use of funds. During all this, he also built a brand for the profession.

In July 2008, when the RBI first approached him to be on the SIFCL board, Manoharan didn't have much of an idea about the Sahara group. It was followed up by OP Srivastava of Sahara with a formal invitation. The RBI briefed him and two other new members of the soon-to-be reconstituted Sahara board and the next thing Manoharan remembers is the first board meeting at Sahara Star on 13 August 2008. He was made the chairman of the audit committee.

Over the next three years, till October 2011, Manoharan, along with HN Sinor (KD Jadhav, the third board member, did not stay long), kept a close tab on the operations of SIFCL – particularly on the progress of the KYC compliance process for depositors, and on the cash flow through the sale of assets to pay back the depositors, even if that meant at times booking a loss. In fact, for the fiscal year ending March 2011, SIFCL posted a loss of nearly ₹39 crore as it had to

Thothala Narayansamy Manoharan

book losses on the sale of investments.

Manoharan was not an RBI nominee but his appointment as an independent director had the endorsement of the regulator, and in that sense he was answerable to the RBI if anything went wrong.

It was a tough job and needed Manoharan to work on the Sahara assignment with much tact, as Roy is a charmer and extremely generous in hospitality. Manoharan sees in Roy a restless entrepreneur who wants to touch a million lives, but finds himself constrained by regulations. Both Manoharan and Sinor did a superb job managing the winding down of India's largest RNBC and ensuring the group returned money to its depositors.

The Judiciary

The judiciary played a key role in the Sahara saga, both directly and indirectly. Two Supreme Court judges made some crucial comments on the group while a few others made comments on the judicial system, particularly on the Allahabad High Court, and took actions that had a bearing on the outcome of Sahara's fight with the regulators. For the record, Sahara India Pariwar had 131 advocates and legal experts to fight on behalf of the group at the apex court and various high courts.

Markandey Katju

Justice Markandey Katju

Justice Markandey Katju, born into a Kashmiri Pandit family in Lucknow, topped the LLB course at Allahabad University. His courtroom was one of the fastest in the Supreme Court, disposing of at least a hundred cases a week. He is widely known for his unconventional opinions, but one particular comment on the Allahabad High Court stands out.

In a strong indictment of the judge for passing orders on extraneous considerations, Katju asked the Chief Justice of the Allahabad High Court to take action against the judge concerned in the Sahara case and against some other judges facing complaints. A bench of Justices Katju and Gyan Sudha Misra said: "The faith of the common man in the country is shaken to the core by such shocking and outrageous orders as the kind which have been passed by the single judge." Writing the order, Justice Katju said, "'Something is rotten in the State of Denmark', said Shakespeare in *Hamlet*, and it can similarly be said something is rotten in the Allahabad High Court, as this case illustrates."

The Bench said:

> "We are sorry to say but a lot of complaints are coming against certain judges of the Allahabad High Court relating to their integrity. Some judges have their kith and kin practising in the same court, and within a few years of starting practice, the sons or relations of the judge become multi-millionaires, have huge bank balances, luxurious cars, huge houses and are enjoying

a luxurious life. This is a far cry from the days when the sons and other relatives of judges could derive no benefit from their relationship and had to struggle at the Bar like any other lawyer."

In September 2011, at his farewell, Chief Justice of India SH Kapadia said Justice Katju had lost neither the courage to speak the truth nor his concern for the common man. "He will always be remembered for his bold remarks and stern judgments. He always took a tough stand against the social evils. Accepting his own mistakes reveals simplicity and gravity of his personality," Kapadia said.

Sarosh Homi Kapadia

The 36th Chief Justice of India SH Kapadia ruled on several important issues such as the right to education, retrospective tax and the Bellary mines case, but the judiciary will remember him best for his initiative to clean up the judiciary, transferring at least 20 high court judges.

Kapadia together with the Supreme Court collegium of four other senior judges took the initiative in September 2010. It was the largest transfer of high court judges in one go since 1993, when 50 judges were transferred during the tenure of then Chief Justice MN Venkatachaliah.

Kapadia wrote to the 20 judges that the collegium wanted them transferred and asking where they would prefer to be shifted. As reason for the transfers, he only cited "public

Sarosh Homi Kapadia

interest". However, it was clear that the decision was a calculated move to improve the image of the judiciary, which had taken a severe beating following allegations of corruption and misconduct against some judges. It sent a strong signal to the judges who were perceived to be not working in the best interests of the profession. Three judges each from the high courts of Allahabad, Punjab and Haryana and Rajasthan were transferred.

Kapadia was born into a lower middle-class Parsi family – his father was a clerk in a defence establishment – in Mumbai's Khetwadi-Girgaum region. He started his career as a class IV employee and later became a clerk in a lawyer's office in Mumbai – Gagrat & Co. Kapadia joined the Bombay bar at the age of 27 in 1974. He worked as a lawyer in noted labour advocate Firoze Damania's office through the 1980s and was appointed judge of the Bombay High Court in 1991.

Neither Katju nor Kapadia played a direct role in the Sahara saga, but their caustic comments and actions led to a cleanup in Allahabad High Court.

KS Radhakrishnan and Jagdish Singh Khehar

Justice KS Radhakrishnan was born in May 1949 and educated at Cochin. He started his career as an advocate in December 1973 in the Kerala High Court and subordinate civil courts at Ernakulam. He was elevated as judge of the Supreme Court in November 2009.

KS Radhakrishnan

Jagdish Singh Khehar

Jagdish Singh Khehar, three years younger than Radhakrishnan, was a science graduate from the government college in Chandigarh. He began his legal career in 1974.

In August 2011, Radhakrishnan and Khehar told Sahara to refund money to the bond-holders with a 15% interest within three months. The group was also asked to furnish details of investors who had got their money back and Sebi was to check the accuracy of such claims. If Sebi did not find the documents produced by Sahara to be genuine, it would be presumed that the two companies had not refunded any amount, the judgment said. The court also gave Sebi freedom to appoint external agencies and experts to sift through the documents and validate them – all at Sahara's expense.

A sarcastic Radhakrishnan said that if the Sahara group indeed had offered the OFCDs only to persons associated, related or known to it, then it could have furnished details of the bondholders before the fact-finding authorities. Khehar was more biting. To Sahara's explanation to Sebi in May 2010 on why it wasn't able to furnish the details immediately ("In the months of May and June, most of the staff remains on long holidays with their children due to summer holidays of schools/colleges. In our case also the concerned officials are on vacation and gone out of station.") Khehar said, "One wonders whether the appellant companies were running a kindergarten, where their staff was expected to be unavailable during the summer."

A few months later, Radhakrishnan and Khehar pulled up Sahara again for not furnishing details of the depositors to Sebi and reiterated that if the depositors could not be traced, the money would have to be remitted to the central government. "You are not cooperating with Sebi, and you are not obeying our order. You are manipulating the courts. I am surprised at what you are doing," Khehar said. Radhakrishnan added to this, "If your attempt to overreach the orders of this court, it is contempt."

As a Supreme Court judge, Radhakrishnan is known for making interesting observations. In May 2013, in a warning to litigants trying to get relief by hiding facts, a bench of Radhakrishnan and Dipak Misra said, "Court is not a laboratory where children come to play." Around the same time, sentencing one Gurnaib Singh to five years' imprisonment for torturing his wife and driving her to suicide, the same bench said, "A daughter-in-law is to be treated as a member of the family with warmth and affection and not as a stranger... She should not be treated as a housemaid."

Kheher was the first chief justice to disclose his assets and liabilities on the Karnataka High Court's website in 2011 when he was the Chief Justice of the high court.

Part III

9

THE SUBRATA ROY MYTH

Till about the early 2000s, Sahara employees greeted each other with "Good Sahara". That was changed to "Sahara *pranam*" and said with the right hand on the heart, adapting from the Indian salutation that signals a deep respect – a more patriotic version than the anglicized Good Sahara.

The hand-on-the-heart tradition is to Indians what bowing is to the Japanese. Bowing is extremely important in Japan, so much so that companies train their employees on how to execute a bow correctly. Basic bows are performed with the back straight and the hands at the sides (boys and men) or clasped in the lap (girls and women), and with the eyes lowered. Bows originate at the waist. The longer and deeper the bow, the stronger the respect.

Few Indians are as obsessive about their salutations, except, perhaps, at the Sahara group. Junior employees at the group companies notch up their displays of respect, touching the feet of their seniors, saying *asirwad dijiye* (give me your blessing) instead of Sahara *pranam*. At the Sahara Q Shop office in Gurgaon, employees show no reluctance in touching the feet of their boss Romie Dutt. In Mumbai, Vivek Kumar, executive director of Sahara India Pariwar and the youngest CEO in the group, a 1992 post-graduate from Delhi University, heading the group's hospitality property Sahara Star and its Aamby Valley project, is treated with similar reverence. The standard response from the senior executives is a pat on the back with a wish, *khush rahiye* (be happy).

Uttar Pradesh, where Sahara Pariwar is headquartered, has a culture of *charansparsh*, touching the feet of an elder. This is reflected in a big way in the Sahara DNA. In fact, bowing and touching the feet of elders or gurus is more reverential in Indian culture than a *pranam* or a *namaste*.

In Indian politics, it finds place more as a gesture of submission. As a corporate ritual, it naturally draws criticism. To outsiders, the practice smacks of a cult – scores of employees greeting Subrata Roy and other senior executives by bowing to them and touching their feet. The entire Sahara organization soaks in this culture. Many Sahara group employees, though, defend the rituals. For them, these are part of Indian etiquette, transcending language, cast, creed, religion, gender and age.

The theme song of the Pune Warriors team, which was the Sahara franchise in the IPL cricket tournament until the group pulled out in May 2013, revolves around this theme:

Sahara Saharaa, Sahara Sahara Sahara Pranam

Bharat Ki Mitti Mein, Jinki Basti Hai Jaan

Bharat Ki Mitti Mein, Jinki Basti Hai Jaan

Sahara Saharaa, Poorey World Mein Hai Naam

Sahara Saharaa, Poorey World Mein Hai Naam

Sahara Saharaa, Sahara Sahara Sahara Pranam

Sahara Saharaa, Sahara Sahara Sahara Pranam

The ringtone of the mobile phones of all Sahara employees is "*Bharat hai hamara, hum hain Sahara.*"

Roy revels in such efforts at emotional bondage. In the early 2000s, Roy asked some 80 people – friends from school and college in Bihar and UP – to leave their jobs and join his group. It had taken him nearly a year to gather information about them. All 80 joined him. That's quintessential Roy: driven more by emotion and call of the heart than anything else. At least, that's the impression he likes to give.

Amazing Connectivity

I watched his amazing connectivity in January 2013 at Sahara Shaher in Lucknow during his 39th wedding anniversary celebrations. Thousands of employees of the group, as well as many of the others who had come to wish the couple on 18th January, touched his feet. He addressed most of them by their first names. A big photograph of the couple adorned the wall of the octagon-shaped pavilion at Sahara Shaher. Two plasma TVs played Soul Sleigh, a musical dance drama, with two Santa Clauses superimposed with the faces of Roy and his wife Swapna.

For the guests, there were two 50-kg cakes, chocolate and strawberry flavoured. Rows of food stalls in the stadium adjacent offered freshly made samosas, *jelabis* and other snacks as well as milk and buttermilk in pouches. The helpings were liberal. An in-house bakery made the cakes. It also produced Roy'sberry chocolate. On the pack was written "Fruits of Love – Nuts of Surprises. A fine blend of sweet and nutty celebrations."

Guests didn't need to buy flowers to present to the couple. The event managers had placed counters at the entrance to the hall for the guests to pick a rose or a small bouquet to present to Roy and his wife. The arrangement was similar to that outside temples, where stalls sell flowers to be offered to the deities. The only difference at the Sahara event was that no one needed to pay for the flowers.

The couple stood at the centre of the pavilion for hours – Roy, 65, with dyed hair and a *tilak* on his forehead, dressed in a cream tweed jacket; and Swapna, in a pink-yellow-green saree – surrounded by relatives and friends. People touched their feet. Roy put his arms around some, shook hands with others and picked up children for a cuddle.

The ritual ended before noon. Roy took a break to have lunch with the two "queens" of the Sahara empire, his nonagenarian mother and his mother-in-law, both of whom live at his white marble residence, called Chhabi Roy's Swapna Kuti, modeled on the White House. Chhabi is Roy's mother.

In Roy's walled city, there are no restricted zones. "He is our guardian; anyone can walk into his house," the driver told me. We drove into the compound of his residence. The guards watched, but did not stop our car.

Post lunch, we met at his secretariat for an interview for this book. I had chased him for months for this meeting. We had met the previous day in the same room that boasts a big black-and-white photograph of Roy holding the hand of Mother Teresa. "When she held my hand there was something going inside my body; something really difficult to express," Roy says. He had asked me to stay back for the anniversary celebration. It was agreed that we would have an on-record chat in the afternoon.

The Sahara boss appeared to be relaxed. Roy is an inch shy of 6 feet and weighed a trim 79 kg, down from 115 kg a year ago. He said he lost weight by drastically cutting down on carbs and evening snacks. He smoked Davidoff cigarettes, although he had quit the habit for about three years (he used to smoke Benson & Hedges before), but resumed because he "felt like" it. Roy, a staunch believer in astrology, wears precious stones recommended to him by his astrologer Pandit Krishna Murari Mishra of Gorakhpur. He says he draws mental strength from these, but is not dependent on them. I believe him.

Settling for the interview, we had tea and spoke while he munched on homemade *kucho nimki*, a tea-time snack in Bengali households, salty and crunchy.

Roy's key argument in his fight with Sebi is that Sahara, being unlisted, does not come under the purview of the market regulator. Two former chief justices and two additional solicitor generals have given affidavits in favour of Sahara's argument, and former law minister M Veerappa Moily, too, said that the Sahara group was right, Roy stated.

In April 2010, Sebi had forwarded some OFCD investors' complaints to the Registrar of Companies in UP and Maharashtra, saying these Sahara companies were unlisted and had not filed prospectus for raising funds with it. It requested the two Registrar of Companies "for examination (of the complaints) and necessary action," Roy said.

His argument is on the question of whether the OFCD offer to more than 50 people is a public issue. The Supreme Court had recently ruled that they came under Sebi's jurisdiction, but in 2007, Sahara had reported 19.7 million investors for its first issue and none had objected. Moreover, post this disclosure, two Registrar of Companies allowed Sahara to issue fresh OFCDs. "Why is Sebi not initiating actions against the Registrar of Companies?" he asked.

He remains unfazed by Sebi's determination to target the group, because, he said, he was sitting on a massive 36,631-acre land bank, possibly the biggest held by any corporate entity in India. However, Roy doesn't want to sell this land. "We are an unlisted company. We don't need to take care of EPS (earnings per share). Why should we sell?" he asked.

Giving me a feel of the Sahara group, Roy said that turnover wasn't relevant for the group as it had a string of financial and non-financial businesses. Overall, its assets, spread over 4,799 establishments, have a market value of at least ₹1.52 trillion; the group employs over 1.1 million workers.

Our conversation meandered through a range of issues. Here are some edited excerpts:

Author: You look so trim and fit.

Roy: I had put on a lot of weight and started hating myself. I felt breathless while walking at the Delhi airport... I stopped eating carbohydrates; evening snacks.

Author: Is the suit that you wore this morning specially stitched for this occasion?

Roy: No, no... An old one.

Author: Your hair is jet black. Do you dye your hair?

Roy: Yes, I dye my hair.

Author: Do you wear the *tilak* on your forehead every day?

Roy: No. It's for today.

Author: What happened in 2005? You seemed to be terribly unwell. Nobody knew what happened to you.

Roy: There was no health problem. It was created by the media. I had developed (high) blood pressure, which used to shoot (up) and come down in 15 minutes. The fluctuation continued between 200 and 100/110.

The doctors said only a change in lifestyle would help me; overwork for 28 years and little sleep have created the problem. They advised me to follow a routine at least for three months – I was advised to get up in morning, go for a walk, do yoga, stop travelling, etc.

I wanted to consolidate all group activities. That gave me

an opportunity to stay back at home and plan. I was not even aware of the problem till one day, my wife showed me two magazines carrying nasty things about me and my health. I spoke to all (TV) channel owners. I gave one statement.

Author: Why was former RBI governor Reddy after you?

Roy: It was a problem in Delhi – I am 100% sure; beyond that, I cannot say anything.

The RBI first told us that the disputed IT amount could be part of the directed investment – they asked us to give them at least two examples of refund – but later withdrew the directive. We had to bring in ₹1,400 crore – that too in the form of capital, not debt. We could put uponly ₹600 crore.

The RBI first issued a show cause notice, and on the third day, they clamped down a prohibitory order. We had to go to the (Allahabad) High Court; they ran to the Supreme Court. They had to change that order – such a thing never happened in the RBI's history.

They took it with vengeance. We were investing ₹500 crore in the State Bank, but the bank refused (at the instance of the RBI). The RBI threw our directors out.

(HN) Sinor (who was on the SIFCL board) once said if anybody should get a bank licence, Sahara should get it. He was positive. Nobody was willing to hear positive things.

Out of 100% (deposits), if 80% investment are done as per the RBI directive, and there is an RBI inspection, (then) where is the problem? They gave us time till 2015 (to close business); we completed by 2012 – only ₹700–800 crore is (now) left to be paid. We are tracing some depositors... It will take awhile.

Author: Does Sahara make money by forfeiting people's deposits?

Roy: I can only say one thing and you can record it ten times – I have never done one wrong thing in my life. That's how I can fight. People can make all sorts of stories. I call them *chandukhana ki kahani* (tales from the opium house). We read (things) about ourselves which we don't know.

Author: Does Sahara keep politicians' money?

Roy: Never. In fact, a few years back two big politicians – both good friends of mine – came to me and offered (to keep with) me big money. They said they had full faith in me and they wanted to keep ₹10,000–15,000 crore with us.

I told them, I am thankful to you that you have so much trust in me, but I will never keep your money. In 1978–79, when there was question of existence for us, my chartered accountant in Gorakhpur told me if we could just make an entry of ₹10–15 lakh, we can earn a few thousand rupees, but I said no to it.

I told these politicians, if I didn't do it then why should I do it now?

I challenge you to prove (that we keep politicians' money).

Author: We hear that former UP chief minister Vir Bahadur Singh left a pot of money with you and you had started from there...

Roy: I met him twice in my life. Once we took some action against our own people and he called to tell me I should not have done that. We met for the first time for ten minutes.

The second meeting was at a family function of the inspector general of police – I was his tenant. I was introduced to him and I said *namaste*.

Author: Will you join politics?

Roy: No. Everybody offered me Rajya Sabha (seat), but I said no. I will never join politics.

Author: Who is your closest friend? Amar Singh or Mulayam Singh Yadav?

Roy: How can I tell you? I am close to everybody. If you are my friend, you're my friend – I cannot be a *nopungsak* (coward) and disown you – I am not a fair-weather friend.

Author: Is Sahara a vehicle for turning black money white?

Roy: In 34 years, we have not given any unsecured loan to anybody. Not even to our directors. If you keep ₹100 worth of securities, we give you ₹70.

Author: The Supreme Court said you cooked up names like Kalawati and Haridwar as depositors.

Roy: It's a baseless allegation. A newspaper sent its reporters to track them down and they recorded their statement.

I hate to bribe people. They say all this because they have to justify themselves. I will not do it even if somebody wants to kill me. I don't get involved in these things.

Author: There have been allegations that money raised by your group from investors through OFCDs has been partly used to buy the London hotel. This is round-tripping.

Roy: If they find anything wrong, they can hang Sahara. We haven't done anything against the law.

When we bought a guesthouse in Chelsea, somebody suggested some ways to buy the property, but I said we would buy openly – can't we spend $25 million for a guesthouse? We are very strict on law matters.

We vehemently oppose the allegation that the money for the acquisition of Grosvenor House Hotel was remitted from SIRECL (Sahara India Real Estate Corp). The funds were remitted from Aamby Valley (Ltd) to its subsidiary Aamby Valley (Mauritius) (Ltd) which invested in the hotel. SIRECL is a real estate company. As per the objects of the company mentioned in its OFCD prospectus, it made a joint venture investment in some real estate projects with SICCL (Sahara India Commercial Corp.), another group company.

Sebi had not banned SIRECL in any manner whatsoever at the time it made a joint venture investment in SICCL on 20 November 2010.

Thus, at any stage, there has not been a single incident of violation of any regulatory or legal requirement. The flow of funds is very much in accordance with the objects of the respective companies and we have been very open right from the beginning about the entire transaction.

Author: Tell us about your failed aviation venture.

Roy: The reason for getting into aviation was that it would serve the nation. India needed a top-notch airline and Air India was incapable of delivering. Then came the price war as the competition intensified and more players were allowed in.

At that time, I told the concerned ministers, "Look, you should ask us – the existing players – to go for a low price model." I would also like to mention that there is nothing called a low-cost model. It's a low-price model. The cost is the same. We only save on in-flight food and beverages. I even said, don't open the skies; there will be a problem. The minister said, no. So, I said, fine, we will not be in the picture.

We got our money out of it... I am very happy we got out at the right time.

Author: Except for finance, Sahara has not done well in any other areas.

Roy: It's a very wrong impression. Today the asset value of the group is ₹1,52,000 crore. I knew that one would never regret owning land if one purchased the right piece. I have done that continuously. We have 36,000 acres of land. We are not listed; we don't need to maintain EPS. I prefer to save tax and give the money to my workers; spend on social work. Tax savings is not a crime. Had we been listed, you would have seen the profit. Recently, we have adopted 1,100 villages, spending ₹550 crore.

Author: You claimed to have repaid ₹1,70,636 crore to 147 million people. How?

Roy: We started with prize chit schemes in 1978, but that was banned in 1980. Then we went for unincorporated body – Sahara India. When it was disallowed, we shifted to housing finance company. It did not have any ceiling.

When ceiling was imposed (on raising deposits), we went for mutual benefit company. When that too was banned, we went for the RNBC. We were doing very well – we were very happy. Right from the first year, we were making profits. But the RNBC was banned. Then we had to go for the OFCDs.

Now we are into cooperatives. Our 10 million people (agents and employees) were depending on daily accounts. They wanted to start cooperatives. I told them to go ahead. They are the promoters; we are not.

Not a single brilliant young entrepreneur who is not from a very rich family can ever hope to develop a big business in India.

Author: Who is setting up the cooperatives – you or your workers?

Roy: Right now, the workers are doing it, but we have put them in sales of commodity merchandise, housing. We are coming out with typical housing clubs. I have to take care of my 10 million families. It's not a concern of the regulator and the government.

Author: What's your flagship?

Roy: Oh, so many... difficult to say. Housing is a big project. We have the maximum land in the country – 36,631 acres.

Author: You are solid but not liquid – cash flow is a problem for you.

Roy: Not at all. We gave Sebi ₹5,120 crore. We purchased two hotels in the US for thousands of crores. There is no dearth of money.

We are an unlisted company. We don't need to take care of the EPS (earning per share). Why should we sell?

Appreciation of land price is so huge – maybe Sahara is the richest company in the country.

Author: How much more would you need to pay to Sebi?

Roy: We are left with around ₹3,660 crore. When the Supreme Court gave the verdict – they have old figure in their paper. The latest figure is different. They should have reviewed...

Author: Is land your biggest asset?

Roy: No, no... The biggest asset is human asset – it's unmatched. The second is land asset.

Author: What about other businesses?

Roy: Housing is doing well. Aamby Valley (a township project), Sahara Q Shop (the group's retail store) are doing very well. By end of 2013, we should be touching definitely ₹30,000 crore plus sales in Q Shop.

We are helping the manufacturing units. We give them money, enhance the quality of infrastructure. We also procure (goods) from them. The Q Shop has a mixed model: delivery at doorstep, plus we are opening 40,000 outlets in next 15 months. They are all 300–700 sq ft stalls. Now we have around 900 outlets in Delhi, Mumbai, UP, Bihar and Jharkhand.

Author: You spend so much money on sports. Is it love for sports, branding or nationalism?

Roy: A mixture of all these – I have been a sports lover. Right from the beginning, I felt that sports people and Bollywood actors are achievers. The first-generation achievers are good human beings across the world. They have no inhibitions, no false ego. I feel comfortable with them. I get attracted to them. I love them.

Author: How much money do you spend on sports?

Roy: Oh, a lot of money. I don't remember the figure.

Author: You love cricket.

Roy: When Wills (a cigarette brand of ITC Ltd in Kolkata) was going out (as sponsor of the Indian cricket team), they said a new sponsor will come. Mr Jagmohan Dalmia was there (as president of the BCCI). I said, this should not go to any multinational. Cricket has become a religion; call Indian parties, go for an open bid and finalize.

I forgot about this and after a couple of months I heard it was going to IMG (International Management Group-Trans World International – IMG-TWI). It really hurt me. I immediately called up Dalmia and asked him why he did it. I told him that I wanted to take over the sponsorship unconditionally.

He asked me if I would be willing to pay 10% more than what the MNC had offered. I had no idea what the amount was, but I said yes, and that's how we got the sponsorship. It was definitely an emotional decision.

I wanted to discontinue, but my cricketer friends would not allow me to do that.

Author: IPL?

Roy: It came later.

Author: You are also into Formula One. Will you buy out Vijay Mallya's stake?

Roy: Formula One can give the country a very good image. Why should I buy Mallya's stake? He is very much involved.

Author: You have 4,799 establishments. Won't you plan to consolidate?

Roy: This government never gave us the opportunity. They banned one activity after another and we had to jump from one to other... All possible options are banned in India.

We have to expand. I want to see my 10 million people living happily. We did one announcement in the company and everybody's remuneration went up by 50%. I want to do that again. (In 2002, celebrating its 25th year, Sahara group announced a 25–50% hike in gross salaries for all its employees.)

Author: What about stock market listing?

Roy: No more listing in India. Overseas, yes, but it's too early (to say). I am not in favour of listing. It's very costly – we don't need (it). We have virtually no bank loan (on our books). We have taken bank loan only once for buying hotels overseas.

Author: You are not a professional. Your company is run by your relatives.

Roy: I define professionalism as emotionalism. I am appointing 500 MBAs now.

I have four sons. Sushanto and Seemanto are my sons. My elder sister died early and her sons Sudeep and Samrat are also mine. They are all doing well – one of them is always with me.

Author: The Employees' Provident Fund Organization (EPFO) has doubt whether Sahara is paying the statutory dues of its one million employees.

Roy: The EPFO is demanding data on a million employees, but since most of them are piecemeal employees, there is no question of providing them (with) provident fund (PF) benefits. There are about 48,000–50,000 employees on the group's payroll and they are better paid than Union government employees. We give them three benefits - PF, gratuity and pension.

I am a very emotional person – even in my planning, emotion comes first and then I apply my brain. Heart always comes first.

You call it heart, I call it mind. I am very emotional.

I am quite fortunate to have had good friends right from my childhood. Ten years back, I made a list of 80 people – my school and college friends in Bihar, UP and Jharkhand – and asked them to come and join me. It took almost one year to gather information about them. All these 80 people are working with me (today). They left the railways, government departments...

Author: How has Sahara kept away labour trouble?

Roy: When people rise in profession, they get a fat bank

balance, good life; they feel materially secure and then they change. Humans are not born bad... circumstances make them bad. We have taken an oath that nobody can share profit or asset of the company. It's in the true sense an organized cooperative. My personal wealth – including that of my wife, four sons and daughters – will not be more than ₹10–12 crore in 34 years. As a promoter-chairman, I should have hundreds or thousands of crores. But I don't have even ₹15 crore personal wealth... I am happy and content.

I always think about my workers – how my *chaukidar* (watchman) can send his son to a good school, my driver can have a good house. Primarily, I am a teacher. My classes go for 10 hours. I must have taken some 15,000 classes. People in management talk about money motivation, but when I sit with my boys and girls I speak about self-motivation. I love them.

I spoke on this at Harvard University (in March 2011). They invited me to talk on my journey – for three years they were after me. They heard that after Indian Railways, we have given the maximum employment and there is no trade union. No overtime is given. It's like a family.

My pet subject is human psychology – I have written a book on that. [Roy has written two books – *Shanti, Sukh: Santushti* (Peace, Happiness: Satisfaction) and *Maan, Samman: Atmasamman* (Prestige, Dignity: Self-Respect)]

Author: You were very close to Mother Teresa.

Roy: Mother used to just call me and say, send me some clothes. I used to put my boys to collecting clothes and send.

She used to get so happy... Sahara Airline, on a regular basis, used to send food to her charity.

I tell you, I visited her two–three months before her death in Kolkata. She had come back from the hospital; was bedridden. She just took my hand and said, "Hope you are sending food." On her death bed also, she was worried about food for people. I was the only person allowed to touch her feet after her death.

This is why Sahara is in Macedonia, birthplace of the Mother. It is a wonderful democratic country... We are going to do a huge Las Vegas kind of thing there. We are going to develop all facilities for Bollywood and Hollywood shooting. And a dairy project. We have got around 2,000 acres of land on the lakeside at a nominal charge.

Author: Don't you want do such projects in India?

Roy: No, because of regulations.

Author: Will you expand overseas to de-risk your business?

Roy: No. Hotel business is not profitable, but there is capital appreciation, especially for the iconic hotels. We bought the Grosvenor House Hotel in London for $470 million. It was priced at $1.2 billion. Though we are not a company that keeps on selling things if we get big valuation, we may dilute stake (in the hotel).

Author: You are wearing an emerald and sapphire. Do you believe in astrology?

Roy: Astrology, like astronomy, is a science, but 99% of the astrologers are not so knowledgeable. I have got two astrologers who are accurate – one in Lucknow and another in Gorakhpur. These stones help to the extent when there is heavy rain, you should have raincoat and umbrella. These save you from getting drenched, but can't prevent flood. They are just a superficial support, but I found in astrology mental strength.

Author: What is Kartavya Council?

Roy: The council is the body which takes care of justice for 10 million people. Injustice, discrimination should not happen. Sitting here, I cannot ensure that alone. Anybody who has any problem can approach them. Here (at Sahara companies), a director is punished if he misbehaves with his driver. My brother did that once and he was punished severely. When I heard that he had misbehaved with the driver, I asked him why he did this. There is an assembly every Saturday. I told him either he would have to tender an apology to the driver with folded hands or I would take administrative action. He preferred to apologize.

Author: How often does this council meet?

Roy: It does not meet often. All people don't have much time. When I formed the council, almost 20 years ago, they had free time. (TN) Seshan (former chief election commissioner of India) has retired; Amitji (actor Amitabh Bachchan) was not so much loaded then.

Author: Why do you have so many big names on the council?

Roy: We have to take care of human psychology in every aspect – whenever the platform is strong, the faith is more.

Renowned people give them security. Glamour plays a positive role. In the Ramayana and Mahabharata, there is so much glamour. People jump on film actors, they go mad. We believe in glamour.

Author: You give financial support to Kargil war widows.

Roy: When the war was on (in 1999), one day, I was having breakfast with Amitji and reading newspaper. A sepoy at Delhi railway station was asking for a ration card for his family. Abdul Hameed's wife ran from pillar to post for a ration card. (Hameed was a soldier in the 4th Battalion, The Grenadiers, of the Indian Army, who died in the Khem Karan sector during the Indio-Pakistan war of 1965, and was the posthumous recipient of India's highest military decoration, the Param Vir Chakra. His wife Rasoolan Bibi received the award.) I instantly decided to support them.

Till now, every responsibility is ours. We give them double the salary of the person who died and take care of their children's education. They rejected all other offers and accepted only the Sahara help.

Author: You are a patriot.

Roy: We started Bharat Parva – we have glamorized Bharat ma. I love my country. I can die for my country.

Author: What is love?

Roy: Love is giving. I do not believe in saying 'I love chicken'.

Author: How's life beyond work?

Roy: Family, people around me.

We go to London when I am free, for pleasure with work. I have never stayed in my London hotel. I prefer to stay at the guesthouse. When we are free, we say, let's dance. There are good singers in the group.

At times, I sit with my friends. I don't get much chance though. There are so many social obligations. I feel like doing other things, but where is the time? Everything is fine with me, the only problem is time. I am very happy and content. At times, for 72 hours, I don't touch my bed.

I am just like any other human being. I follow the teachings of my father. I was an active NCC (National Cadet Corps) cadet. I even wanted to join the military. I have learnt a lot of things from these.

Author: I repeat again, everyone is curious about your source of money? Where does it come from?

Roy: Sahara India Pariwar commenced its business activities in 1978 and diversified into various businesses like infrastructure and housing, electronic and print media, para-banking, mutual funds, life insurance, hotels, hospitals, sports academy, tourism, dairy products, etc.

The group's activities started with para-banking activities and Sahara India Financial Corp. got registration with the Reserve Bank of India as an RNBC. The company was primarily into accepting deposits from public and making investments as per the RBI directions. Prior to 2004, 80% of the deposits mobilized, including interest, was to be invested in directed securities and the balance 20% or five times of net owned fund as per the discretion of the board. However, from 2004 onwards, the RBI prohibited discretionary investments and the company has had to invest the entire amount in directed securities only.

Sahara India Financial Corp. had invested in certain properties, including hotel Sahara Star, under discretionary investment category, which over the period had seen meteoric rise.

Apart from this, the group through private placement basis had mobilized resources specifically for making investments into the realty sector and several township and commercial projects were created out of the resources. The penetration in the realty sector was further enriched by availing loan and equity contribution from the market. The group has also taken bank loans for funding of several good projects which have resulted in generation of revenue leading to internal accruals like Sahara Estates Lucknow, Sahara Estates Gorakhpur, Sahara Ganj Mall, etc.

Author: How will entrepreneurship flourish in India?

Roy: It's fairly simple. There is nothing hi-tech about entrepreneurship. I believe in team work. I use my time and energy for the development of the team. I teach them, guide them, help them and give them all kind of support. For any successful venture, there has to be a leader and a team – they complement each other.

There is another important thing, particularly for financial intermediaries – we took oath that nobody would take any profit or asset of the company. That's true about my family members also. That has worked well.

The third thing is the chief of any organization should be a guide, a teacher and a guardian. To my last breath, I will be a guardian for them in the true sense of it. I don't believe in bossism.

Author: What's your message for entrepreneurs in India?

Roy: A person can be very successful adhering to rules, regulations, values and ethics, provided in his nature, he is happy and content. Ambition is the biggest enemy in life. I am always content with whatever God has given me.

The situation is not conducive now because an entrepreneur needs to have funds. However promising an entrepreneur is, he has no way to raise funds. If you go to bank for ₹2 crore, you need to have ₹60 lakh as a margin. You cannot enter share market or the debt market.

You cannot raise money from public as all possible options are banned in India. In 1978, Prize Chit and Money Circulation Scheme was banned. Next we saw unincorporated bodies like partnership firms being banned from taking public money. Then mutual benefit scheme was banned. After that housing finance and leasing companies' ability to raise money was curbed. RNBC was banned. And now OFCD is banned from private placement for unlisted companies. How does one raise money?

If I were to start now with ₹2 lakh – equivalent to ₹2,000 in 1978 – I would not be able to cross ₹10 crore turnover in my life. We have faced six bans for raising money. The regulator should regulate and not become an agency to ban business.

Author: You give a sense that you are claustrophobic in regulations. You continuously change regulators.

Roy: I love regulations. This is always good for the company, but it should not be the regulations of Hitler to the Jews. A regulator should not gag you. That's not regulation; that's killing. I was always under regulators, but when regulators ban me, I need to go somewhere else. I have to take care of my lakhs of families. When I asked Mr (YV) Reddy (former RBI governor) and Mr (CB) Bhave (former Sebi chairman), "don't you think of my 10–12 lakh families," they always said that's none of their business.

I never seek any licence... Somebody said Akhilesh (Yadav) has now become the chief minister (of Uttar Pradesh) and I should ask for some land in Noida, which is so expensive, but I will never do that. I knew Akhilesh when he was child. I will not see him being compromised. I am not starving. I am a blessed child of God.

Author: After Subrata Roy who? What is your succession plan?

Roy: Good question. I am very clear about it. We are in the process of setting up a trust that will own all shareholdings. My wife, family members as well as members of the workers will be trustees. Five or six officers also will be there. The trust will take all decisions – no family member can individually take any decision.

Author: Any time frame for setting up the trust?

Roy: I don't think I will die so fast. We are in the process...

Author: Where do we see Sahara ten years down the line?

Roy: Forget ten years; if we cannot do what we want to do in the next five years, we are clearly incompetent. Since we are not listed, you cannot judge us on market cap. In the next five years, in terms of assets and profits, Sahara will be among the top ten companies in the world.

Author: How much of your business will be generated overseas?

Roy: Around 10% from overseas; there will not be any change from the current level.

Author: You are an enigma; you're mysterious and controversial.

Roy: It is very unfortunate if anybody thinks like that. I am probably the most open person; there is no mystery in my life. It's very easy to pass on any statement on anybody (*sic*). I am not controversial. It's a first-generation organization; it has grown big and we are high profile. The conglomerate is unlisted and so people imagine things...

Author: How do you describe yourself?

Roy: You've to tell me that.

After about two hours, we ended our session. Akhilesh Yadav dropped in at Roy's residence towards the evening to wish him. There was *hasya kavi sammelan* (a gathering where poets recite comic verse in Hindi) at the auditorium, where Lucknow's famous *kebab*, *biryani* and other north Indian delicacies and the choicest Scotch were served. I did not see Roy drinking. His favourite drink is Grey Goose, supposedly the world's best-tasting vodka. He prefers a Patiala peg – 120 ml, with an equal portion of orange juice and two ice cubes. He also likes single malt – Glinfiddich, 15 year old – and Singapore Sling, a Southeast Asian cocktail – a tall drink developed in 1915 by Ngiam Tong Boon, a Hainanese bartender at the Long Bar in Singapore's Raffles Hotel - a concoction of dry gin, Dom Benedictine, Cointreau and cherry brandy, shaken up with lime and pineapple juices and a dash of Angostura bitters and Grenadine. Roy is not a regular drinker, but when in the mood, I am told, he can have all three simultaneously.

Sheila Ki Jawani

The UP Wizards team, the Sahara franchise in the Hockey India League, came to the *hasya kavi sammelan* later that evening. The next day, actor Katrina Kaif would come to cheer the team against Delhi Wave Riders at the Lucknow stadium.

There, Roy sat next to the state's young chief minister, Yadav, while Kaif danced to popular Hindi song *Sheila Ki Jawani*, from Farah Khan's 2010 Hindi action comedy *Tees Maar Khan*, starring Akshay Kumar and Kaif. Yadav praised Roy for supporting sports, while Roy explained to him how glamour excited people and cemented bonds. I was not there.

On the morning of 19 January 2013, on a flight to Mumbai, I looked back and found my two days at Sahara Shaher (I stayed in a hotel in Lucknow, but spent most of the time at the gated complex) quite surreal – the setting, the people, the scale of things and an affable Roy, who plays the role of host with much grace. Roy promised to open his heart in the interview, and possibly he did, but I did not get all the answers I was looking for. The mystery surrounding the group only deepened.

Roy and his business conglomerate have acquired a larger-than-life image where the dividing line between myth and reality disappears. The biggest mystery is his source of money. There have been allegations about money laundering by Sahara, but no investigation has been able to prove it. In fact, barring Sebi and the RBI, no agency has seriously investigated this allegation. Is Roy simply lending names of depositors to legitimize money owned by others? Do politicians and big-time businessmen keep their ill-gotten money with Sahara?

Sebi conducted a pilot study to ascertain the genuineness of the investor documents filed by Sahara. Its findings are interesting: about 98.9% of the bondholders were untraceable. Sebi sent redemption notices inviting claims to 21,253 bondholders. It received responses from 233 investors; 7,587 notices could not be delivered; the status of the rest – 13,499 notices – were either not known or were in transit when Sebi furnished this information to the Supreme Court in March 2013. Of the notices undelivered, 47 persons were dead and in 485 cases, there was no such person. Among others, the addresses were incomplete for 3,637 investors.

Roy is aware of the fact that Sebi has sent letters to thousands of investors, but has not got too many replies. "Why would a small investor spend on postage to reply to Sebi when they have already received the payment?" Roy asks. "Sebi is also asking for many documents, but these people do not have such documents and that's why they are keeping quiet."

He, however, admits that there could be some error in data. There are 2,000 such accounts and money involved is around ₹2.65 crore – around 0.01% of the total amount.

Roy wants speeding verification of the identities of investors, but feels the Sebi cannot do it even in years. "No agency can do this as it involves such a large volume of investors and we are suffering for this."

At the same time, Roy says Sahara is ready to produce each and every account holder to authority. "KYC is 'know your customer' and we know our customers – we know each of them through our field workers who introduced them. They are small tea-stall owners on the highway at Gorakhpur, cobblers and rickshaw-pullers."

However, even the income tax department was not convinced about the identities of many depositors in SIFCL and hence used to treat the deposits as income and demand tax on them. In his presentation to the Securities Appellate Tribunal (SAT), Roy claimed he had refunded 90% of the amount raised through OFCDs in cash. His claim and Sebi's findings create more suspense about the identities of the bondholders. How many of them actually exist?

If indeed the money comes from the poorest in India, who do not have access to formal banking channels, why was Roy inhibited about disclosing the names of the subscribers? Why was SIFCL not keen on implementing the KYC norms for its millions of depositors? Roy's argument that vegetable vendors do not have a proper address does not hold water as India's microfinance institutions operate in the same space and they have about 22 million customers with every detail recorded.

Unlike Sahara, microfinance institutions do not accept deposits – under norms, they cannot; these firms give India's poor tiny loans, and so, are particular about the details of their customers' whereabouts. That's why, outside Andhra Pradesh, microfinance institutions have faced only a minuscule percentage of defaults on loan repayments.

In Andhra Pradesh, however, all microfinance institutions suffered massive bad assets as borrowers stopped repaying after the state government promulgated a law in October 2010 to protect borrowers from high interest rates and rouge collection practices; microfinance became a political hot potato.

Even if Roy is a custodian of politicians' money, there is nothing wrong about it and the regulators have no business hounding him, says a seasoned banker in private. He gives a new dimension to the debate, saying that if people can keep their money in Swiss banks and send money to Mauritius to bring it back as foreign investment (India has a bilateral tax avoidance treaty with the Mauritius, a tax haven), what's the problem in keeping money with Sahara?

Of course, these practices aren't exactly legitimate and the Indian government has been trying to end them. "It's not a black box; treat it like a Swiss bank. Period," the banker said in defence of Sahara. I wish I could name this banker!

Forfeiture is, of course, a big source of funds. Most of the depositors are dependent on the agents for meeting their daily, monthly or quarterly commitments, and if the agents lose interest in collecting the money – as the commission is less after the first year – the defaults can rise.

The other source of on-tap money could be Roy's obsession for real estate. He uses money to buy real estate, the value of which appreciates many times more than any other asset and hence, he is always ahead of the curve. However, since Roy does not sell land, it is paper money and cannot be used to invest in other businesses.

Humble Beginning

The son of a sugarcane technologist, Subrata Roy had humble beginnings. Born on 10 June 1948 and nicknamed Chandan, Roy was a poor student who failed thrice but completed a three-year diploma in mechanical engineering from a Gorakhpur college. He was good at mathematics, but Hindi was a nightmare for him. In 1967, at the age of 19, he led a Republic Day contingent and was desperate to join the Indian Air Force, but his mother did not allow him. He then tried his hand at many ventures, including selling handloom sarees and fish, before starting the deposit-taking business.

Beneath the veneer of his emotionalism, Roy is an astute, no-nonsense entrepreneur, though he has not been successful in most of his ventures, except in the financial space, which he knows like a farmer knows his hens.

In early 2011, Roy told Romie Dutt, then head of Sunderbans, an eco-tourism project at Sahara India Pariwar, that he wanted to enter the fast-moving consumer goods (FMCG) segment and that it would be called Q Shops – Q for quality. Dutt, a former general manager, commercial, at Air Sahara, gave shape to the concept in less than a year. Now an executive director of the group and chief executive at Sahara Q Shop, Dutt is one of the few professionals who is not related to Roy but holds a senior position in the group.

Roy's political connections are also a mystery. Sebi insiders say his association with politicians is party-agnostic as leaders of almost every large political party had called the regulator for clearing the proposed IPO of shares by Sahara Prime City, the group's realty firm. But if he indeed is so well-connected, how could he be 'harassed' by Sebi? The regulator summoned him to its headquarters and even sought his detention. Either his relationship with the politicians has become rusty or the regulators are refusing to listen to their political bosses.

People say Roy was against Italy-born Sonia Gandhi becoming India's Prime Minister, and that was the beginning of his fall from grace in political circles. Apparently, in May 2004, when Gandhi was chosen to lead a 15-party coalition government, with the support of the Left parties, Roy tried to intervene. He called Communist leader and then West Bengal chief minister Jyoti Basu to ask him to prevent her from becoming India's Prime Minister.

Roy told Basu that while Gandhi may technically be an Indian citizen, genetically she wasn't. Sonia, the widow of former Prime Minister Rajiv Gandhi, had acquired Indian citizenship in 1983. By 2013, she had emerged the longest-serving president of the Congress party, while never yielding to sycophantic pleas to head the government as well.

At a personal level, Subrata Roy's connectivity remains unmatched. A day before a critical SAT hearing on OFCDs in March 2013, Roy put up a show of strength. At the *annaprashan* (rice-eating ceremony) for his granddaughter Roshna, Sushanto's daughter, which Roy hosted at The Ashok in New Delhi on 22nd March, several celebrities were in attendance.

Politicians came from across parties – Sheila Dikshit, Digvijaya Singh, Ajay Maken and Meira Kumar of the Congress party that was heading the Union government; Arun Jaitley, Sushma Swaraj, Nitin Gadkari, Rajiv Pratap Rudy and Maneka Gandhi of the opposition Bharatiya Janata Party; Mulayam and Akhilesh Singh Yadav of the Samajwadi Party that ruled Uttar Pradesh; Lalu Prasad of the Rashtriya Janata Dal; Sharad Yadav of the Janata Dal United; Praful Patel of the Nationalist Congress Party; and Farooq Abdullah of the Jammu & Kashmir National Conference.

Bollywood was represented by Jaya and Abhishek Bachchan, Sridevi and Boney Kapoor, Hrithik Roshan, Anil Kapoor, Hema Malini, Dia Mirza, Neha Dhupia and Vivek Oberoi. From other film industries, there were Telugu superstar Nagarjuna and Chiranjeevi, also the Union minister of state with independent charge of the tourism ministry.

Among the cricketers at the ceremony were Indian team captain MS Dhoni, vice captain Virat Kohli, Sachin Tendulkar,

Ravindra Jadeja, Suresh Raina, R Ashwin, Shikhar Dhawan, Virender Sehwag, Ashish Nehra and Pragyan Ojha, as well as former Indian players Sunil Gavaskar and Mohammed Azharuddin and the Australian players Michael Clarke and Steven Smith.

Industrialist Vijay Mallya, maverick lawyer Ram Jethmalani, Baba Ramdev – known for his yoga camp and TV shows – former President of India Pratibha Patil, and former Supreme Court judge Markandey Katju, too, blessed Roshna.

On 23 March 2013, *Mumbai Times*, the 'Advertorial, Entertainment Promotional Feature' section of *The Times of India*, carried a two-page photo feature headlined, "This celebration was high on star power," with 68 photographs. This was, in fact, carried in *The Times of India* supplement across 11 editions. The cover page of these supplements carried a photograph of Roy with Dhoni and Australian cricket team captain Clarke.

The two pages would have cost around ₹1 crore, a media buyer said. Incidentally, Sahara One Media and Entertainment Ltd has a so-called private treaty arrangement with Bennett, Coleman and Co. Ltd (BCCL), the publisher of *The Times of India*. Launched in 2004, these treaties translate into BCCL picking up equity stakes in companies in return for promoting those 'partners' through long-term advertising and promotion deals.

The weddings of Roy's sons at Sahara Shaher in Lucknow in February 2004 were grander affairs, with around 11,000 people invited from around the world. Bollywoodshaadis.

com, an online wedding-planning magazine, pegs the cost for the two weddings at ₹552 crore, among the most expensive Indian weddings. However, this is a highly exaggerated figure, say Sahara officials. The actual cost incurred was around ₹28 crore out of which ₹22 crore was spent in building infrastructure at Sahara Shaher, the venue of the wedding.

The late Shiv Sena chief Bal Thackeray stepped out of Mumbai after almost a decade to be a part of this celebration. People still talk about a photograph (though I have not seen it) of Roy in the backseat of a convertible driven by Anil Ambani, the billionaire promoter of Reliance Group. Former Miss Universe Aishwarya Rai was in the back of the convertible with Roy, and superstar Amitabh Bachchan in the front next to Ambani.

Friendship with Roy is very special for many and Bachchan is one of them. Bachchan, who met Roy many years ago through a common friend, Amar Singh, has a very fond relationship with him – almost like family.

"I visited his facility in Lucknow – Sahara Shaher. I saw the work that he does, the people who work for him, and just the general atmosphere. I thought it was all very well organized, and I liked the fact that there was a certain kind of regiment that they followed. There is a certain kind of discipline that has been initiated – and everyone follows it; that is wonderful to see," Bachchan told me at his Juhu bunglow in Mumbai.

When Bachchan's parents passed away, Roy's team organized everything for him: "whether it was taking the ashes to Allahabad, going to the Sangam – it was just like he was a member of the family."

"He has grown from absolute scratch. It's very commendable how he started off on a Lambretta scooter, and he has built this great empire."

Bachchan also spoke about Roy's spirit of patriotism – he's very fond and proud of his country. "Whether it is representing the Indian cricket team or having festivals that honour India, it is all very commendable."

Pomp, Splendour, Loyalty

Roy revels in pomp, splendour and loyalty – ingredients for the success of his financial business. The glitz and glamour attract the poor; they remain glued to Roy, who straddles the world of glamour and the other India that lives in Gorakhpur, Varanasi and Lucknow with consummate ease. His playing field is largely Uttar Pradesh, India's fifth-largest state in size and the most populous. A majority of the state's population lives in the villages and roughly one-fifth of them are from the disadvantaged scheduled castes.

The per-capita income in UP in April 2013, at constant prices, was ₹33,520, the second-lowest among all states, after Bihar ₹26,793; the national average is ₹68,747.[1] Approximately 29.43% of UP's population lived below the poverty line in fiscal year 2012, against the national average of 22% [2]

---

[1] The Ministry of Statistics and Programme Implementation (MoSPI) data.

[2] Planning Commission data.

In absolute numbers, UP, with 59.8 million, has the highest number of poor people in the country, accounting for a little more than a fifth of India's poor, numbering 269.78 million. The Planning Commission fixed the urban poverty line at ₹33.33 per capita daily consumption and rural poverty line at ₹27.2 for calculating the poverty estimates for 2011–12.

Uttar Pradesh is the least penetrated geography when it comes to formal banking. The state has over 11,000 bank branches, but when it comes to mobilizing deposits or giving loans, it lags behind most other states. For instance, UP boasts of 116.26 million deposit accounts but the money kept in these is a mere ₹3.71 trillion. In contrast, Maharashtra's 8,816 bank branches and 85.35 million deposit accounts have mopped up ₹14.53 trillion. UP has 10.7 million loan accounts that have disbursed ₹1.63 trillion, while Maharashtra's 24.54 million loan accounts have disbursed ₹12.07 trillion.[3]

Barring finance, the Sahara group has not excelled in any other business. Even within the finance segment, its mutual fund and life insurance companies are nowhere near the competition. Sahara Airlines introduced the concept of apex or advance purchase fares in India and offered excellent in-flight service, but the loss-making airline had to be sold. Jet Airways (India) Ltd bought it for ₹1,450 crore after protracted negotiations. Originally, the deal was stuck at ₹2,000 crore.

The group's newspaper business and TV channels are also-rans; its land bank generates paper money as it does

---

[3] Basic Statistical Returns of Sechduled Commercial Banks in India, volume 40, March 2011. An annual RBI publication.

not sell; and its real estate business is leagues behind India's listed developers. Aamby Valley is India's first man-made hill station and on a par with the best of luxury resorts the world over (remember Russian tennis sensation Anna Kournikova promoting the project?) but nobody knows how successful it is commercially as the financials are not in the public domain. The group's latest venture Sahara Q Shop is struggling with teething problems as organized retail is not a cakewalk.

Money mobilization is the mainstay of all Sahara operations and to ensure a continuous flow of money, Roy plays three cards with glamor – cricket, compassion and patriotism – all close to the heart of the masses.

Roy is hugely interested in sports in general and cricket in particular, as this, he believes, is the best way to reach the hearts of millions. Sahara was the sponsor of the Indian cricket team for over a decade.[4]

It also sponsored the Pune Warriors of the Indian Premier League and paid Yuvraj Singh, who Roy says is like his third son, $1.8 million for the 2012 season despite his absence. Yuvraj, the hero of India's 2011 ICC World Cup victory, was treated for a rare germ cell cancer in a US hospital and by backing Yuvraj, Roy gets closer to the masses in a cricket-crazy nation.

Roy appears a master of mass psychology. When hockey, India's national sport, was dying due to a fund crunch,

---

[4] Star India Pvt Ltd, the Indian broadcasting arm of Rupert Murdoch's News Corp., replaced Sahara as sponsor to the Indian cricket team from January 2014 onwards.

Roy offered to sponsor the Indian hockey team. He has also backed women's cricket, wrestling, archery, boxing, shooting, athletics and tennis. When the flamboyant Vijay Mallya found buying a Formula One team unaffordable, Roy extended a helping hand.

By supporting the Kargil war widows and the families of the Mumbai police and the National Security Guard commandoes who died in the November 2008 attack on Mumbai by Pakistani terrorists (he offered to pay them five times the gross salaries of the dead heroes, every month, for 10 years), Roy created an enormous amount of goodwill in the constituency that supplies money to his enterprise. He also gave ₹2.51 lakh each to the families of five CRPF jawans who were killed in a Maoist rebels' attack at Dantewada, Chattisgarh in May 2010. All were from Gorakhpur.

Another prop that adds to Roy's popularity are the mass weddings he has been sponsoring every year since 2004 – the first edition coincided with the weddings of Roy's two sons – for 101 poor couples. In addition to taking care of the wedding expenses, he helps the couples set up new homes by giving them TV sets, fridges, cupboards, dressing tables and beds. A roll-on panoramic camera captures the weddings of the 101 Hindu, Muslim, Sikh and Christian couples at Sahara Shaher, the event lending credence to Roy's efforts towards communal harmony.

Every year around Republic Day and Independence Day, the Sahara group hosts a week-long Bharat Parva to celebrate the idea India along with its depositors. And, of course, celebrities who add dollops of glamour. Bharat Mata, seated on a chariot driven by four fierce lions, is the presiding deity of the group. For millions of depositors, Roy's empire is a safe haven to keep their savings.

Master of Human Psychology

Roy clearly knows how to build trust and credibility among the poor, not so much among the regulators. That's probably because he doesn't seem to have faith in regulations – he always shifts from one regulatory regime to another and when one door closes, he finds and opens another in no time. As Roy explained in the interview, he began with prize chits and money circulation schemes in 1978. When these were banned, he set up an un-incorporated body – Sahara India – to raise money from the public, but an amendment to the Banking Regulation Act of 1949 closed that door too. Roy then shifted first to a housing finance company and later to a mutual benefit company or 'Nidhi' company.

To deposit savings in a Nidhi, a person has to first become a member by paying a share subscription. As Nidhis deal with their members and not with the general public, legally, they are not regarded as banks, though in their economic functions they are no different. Nidhis are regulated by the department of company affairs.

When Roy found it difficult to continue with those activities, he took the RNBC route and prospered till RBI's Reddy put an end to that. The next option to tap public money was the OFCD route, until Sebi stopped that.

Amid the fight with Sebi, the Sahara group started running cooperative credit societies. It remains to be seen how he faces the biggest challenge in Sahara's history as India's capital market regulator braces for a fight to the finish.

Once a depositor enters the Sahara fold, all efforts are made to retain him in some form or the other so that his investments remain with the group companies.

Roy says Sahara's field workers try their best to pursue the investors to reinvest the matured amount in some other scheme of the group, but despite that, many redeem their investments. There are others who either reinvest the interest earned or the entire amount. "This is a regular phenomenon and the group does not follow any procedure to make such reinvestments automatic. You will see the same pattern in post office savings and LIC policies where agents are paid commission," he says.

The group runs some 4,799 establishments – many are being continuously set up for regulatory arbitraging. While the main source of money for the group remains a mystery, this is an established fact. The entrepreneur in him feels claustrophobic in regulations and continuously looks for ways to get on top of things. For some time he succeeds, but ultimately he gets trapped. He is smart enough to open another front by that time.

For three-and-a-half decades, he has been playing this game. Come what may, he has money on the tap, be it from the RNBC, through OFCDs, cooperative societies or even the Q Shop. Extending the analogy of cricket, a sport that Roy swears by, a seasoned banker says that Roy loves to play the game without any umpire and boundary line. *Chhookar Mere Man Ko* – a Kishore Kumar song from the 1981 Amitabh Bachchan hit film *Yaranna*, composed by Rajesh Roshan – is very close to Roy's heart. This song is a must-play at every internal celebration of Sahara India Pariwar.

Typically, Roy would listen to the first two lines of the song with rapt attention –

Chhookar mere man ko
Kiya tuney kya ishara

And then sing, tweaking the second couplet from

Badla yeh mausam
Lagey pyaara jag saara

To

Badla yeh mausam
Lagey pyaara yeh Sahara.

At this stage, the entire Sahara clan would join him, singing *yeh Sahara.*

Roy can create mass hysteria. For an outsider, it can look like a theatre of the absurd, but Roy is a master of public theatre – he knows how to reach out to people, excite them and entice them. Even when the Sebi chapter comes to a close, the Sahara show will probably go on.

10

THE ROAD AHEAD

Had the regulators not been after him, Roy would have done wonders in India. First, the RBI forced him to shut down his residuary non-banking company (RNBC) and then Sebi began breathing down his neck about the optionally fully convertible debentures (OFCDs). Each time, Roy tweaked his business, finding new ways to source money. He isn't one to down the shutters or retire to bask in the glory of his accumulated wealth and friendship among the high and mighty.

One option Roy has is to expand overseas to de-risk his business empire. For the record, he says he's against the idea – it won't quite fit in with his jingoistic act – but he has been doing just that. For a start, Roy has bought two hotels in the US – including New York's landmark Plaza Hotel – and one in the UK, the historic Grosvenor House in London.

He plans to overhaul the 420-room London hotel with a spa, a nightclub and more restaurants, including a grand

Indian one, to make it the best weekend spot in Mayfair. The hospitality business may not be hugely profitable, but it offers capital appreciation. At the right price, Roy will sell the hotels.

Another plan is to launch an Indian luxury artisan label, Mastercraft, near Oxford Street in London. Sahara Global Design Studio Ltd, the high-end luxury retail arm of the group, has been established to set up top-of-the-line luxury stores in major cities around the world. Each storey in the flagship Mastercraft store in London will be a museum of sorts – only the exhibits will be available for sale. The group has ambitious plans to scale up its operations with stores at various locations after the flagship's launch in London.

Roy also has big business plans for Macedonia, the birthplace of Mother Teresa, whom Roy adores. He finds Macedonia a democratic nation and plans to make a "Las Vegas kind of thing" there. His idea is to build all that is needed to entice Bollywood and Hollywood to shoot there.

The Macedonian government has given Sahara land on the banks of Lake Ohrid, straddling the mountainous border between southwestern Macedonia and eastern Albania, at a nominal price for the "Las Vegas kind of thing".

The project, Saharayn Makeeduniya, a world-class tourist destination in Europe, will be developed over 593 acres on the shore of the majestic Lake Ohrid. It will offer high-end waterside living with a golf resort, spa and wellness retreat, marina, five-star convention hotel, a retail hub and a casino. Roy presented the master plan to Macedonian

Prime Minister Nikola Gruevski in December 2012 and a government committee is working on it.

Roy has also drawn up a plan for a large dairy project in the European nation spanning over 13,096.6 acres. Building on the concept of grass to glass, Sahara plans to manage an integrated value chain with six million milking cattle and producing 15 million litres of milk every day in the next five years. Sahara Pariwar will spend €4.4 billion for the dairy project.

Roy's rather large shopping bag also has space for oil exploration projects in Jordan, Georgia and Australia and iron ore and bauxite mines in South Africa. There's also a proposal to set up commodities cells in 16 countries.

No Quit India

Roy insists that he's not quitting India. He "loves his country and can die for his country," he told me. His evolving business in India is centered around two growth engines – Sahara Q Shop and the cooperative credit society.

Sahara Q Shop's USP, according to the group, is that it offers a range of unadulterated products.

Sahara Q Shop Unique Products Range Ltd, which runs Sahara Q Shops, was incorporated on 21 June 2011 and registered with the Registrar of Companies in Mumbai. The registered address of the firm is Hotel Sahara Star, Ville Parle, Mumbai.

The shareholders of the company are Subrata Roy, his wife Swapna Roy, sister Kumkum Roy Choudhary, brother-in-law Ashok Roy Choudhary, group director and Roy's deputy OP Srivastava and his brother-in-law Devendra Kumar Srivastava, and Romie Dutt, chief executive of Sahara Q Shops.

At the time of incorporation, the company had an authorized capital of ₹2 crore. Six months later, in December 2011, it rose to ₹10 crore, and by 15 June 2012, its authorized capital had ballooned to ₹4,000 crore. Over that period, in true Sahara tradition, Q Shop spawned 65 subsidiaries and forged partnerships with 74 group companies.

The positioning of the Q Shop is very different from other organized retail ventures. One advertisement showed cricketer Sachin Tendulkar performing the last rites of a family that was at its dining table, Yuvraj Singh digging a grave for a child having a snack in school, and Virat Kohli replacing a shopping trolley with a wheelchair – all trying to portray the ill-effects of adulterated food and Q Shop's commitment to quality. MS Dhoni, Virendra Sehwag, Gautam Gambhir and Suresh Raina also featured in these ads. The tagline read: "*Milawat ke khilaf jung*", which translates to war against adulteration. India's cricket board asked Sahara to pull out the ad but it was still available on YouTube.

Q Shop carried two other ads, these were more temperate, but with similar themes, featuring actors Hrithik Roshan and Priyanka Chopra.

Like with most other things, Sahara goes overboard in rubbing in Q Shop's anti-adulteration focus. The LinkedIn profile of Romie Dutt, executive director and chief executive of Q Shop, reads, "We are Sahara Q Shop, India's largest mega retail and FMCG venture – from Sahara India Pariwar."

Q Shop stocks 895 products and 1,200 items, including soaps, shampoos, packaged drinking water, pressure cookers, mixer-grinders and induction stoves.

In April 2013, the company said it planned to set up 10,000 Q Shop stores by the end of fiscal year 2014. Between its launch on 15 August 2012 and April 2013, the group had set up 550 stores on a franchisee model. Of these, 315 stores were opened in 10 states at 4pm on 1st April, a feat that got the group another entry into the *Guinness Book of World Records*. Ultimately, Roy's plan is to open 40,000 outlets of Sahara Q Shop across 998 cities and towns in India. It will have 10,500 in east zone, 11,500 in north zone, 9,500 in south zone and 8,500 in west zone. Each store will cater to the consumers within a 1.5-km radius.

An average Sahara Q Shop store size ranges from 300 sq ft to 500 sq ft, but along with the small format stores, the metros will have large format 2,000 sq ft stores. A franchisee has to pay ₹1.3–2.75 lakh for a store licence, and some more in advance for the supply of goods. The Sahara group expects to collect between ₹130 crore and ₹275 crore from enrolling 10,000 franchises by April 2014.

At a parallel level, to support its agents, Sahara has created a special business model called 'home franchisee'. Each willing para-banking worker will be asked to serve 500 households of their depositors/investors and supply them consumer merchandise. This will be done by opening 'home *kirana*' outlets. That's about the franchises. Nothing untoward there.

Now comes the money mobilization part.

Under Sahara Q Shop's direct selling plan, the company recruits customers who have to pay ₹12,250 in advance to purchase merchandise from the stores. The advance payment is locked in with the company for five years, and every month 3.5% of the amount a customer spends in the stores will be adjusted against the initial payment. At the end of the fifth year, the company will refund the unadjusted money, if any, without interest.

Another option for customers is to become Sahara sales associates and promote the Q Shop Plan-H. For every new customer or sale made, existing customers earn a "special promotional incentive" of ₹800.

"There are no limits to the number of esteemed customers you can introduce to us and make your gains potentially unlimited. For example, by introducing 16 customers, you earn back your money paid as advance of ₹12,250," the retailer says in a document.

Yet another extension of the Q Shop concept is Q Centres: "a neighbourhood meeting place for families" offering entertainment, hospitality and food, learning and shopping. Sahara plans to set 1,090 such centres across 280 cities with cinemas, study centres and restaurants. Each Q Centre will have between three and six "world class" auditoriums with 55 seats. Sahara Movie Studios will release a 90-minute feature film at such auditoriums every fortnight. Some of the theatres will also have a dance floor.

More than 35 hi-tech food factories will churn out 8.5 lakh meals a day, served in restaurants at the Q Centres. They will also cater to private gatherings, door-step deliveries and even institutional supplies at a later stage.

Going by an internal Sahara document, there will be a pan-Indian transportation network, integrating the supply chain with refrigerated cargo service. The unused food will be taken back to the food factory and distributed for charity.

The group plans to offer employment to 56,000 people in calendar 2014 and four lakh in the next three years through jobs under 12 business verticals including FMCG and retail, dairy, real estate, poultry, food factory and Q Centres and invest ₹32,394 crore.

"The focus of Q Shops in India is not retail, but to add to its visibility among the public through which it gains their trust," says Abraham Koshy, professor of marketing at the Indian Institute of Management, Ahmedabad. "Eventually, the company uses this trust and its image to go to the public for investing in its business ventures."

"While retail continues to offer a very attractive business opportunity, especially retail focussed on relatively small town India and targeted towards the mass market, it is not an easy business," says Arvind Singhal, chairman of the Gurgaon-based retail and consumer products consultancy Technopak Advisors Pvt Ltd. He explains that while retailers need to put in a lot of effort to set up logistics, distribution lines and state-of-art technology, many haven't been successful in India.

India's $455 billion retail market is dominated by the unorganized sector. The organized segment accounts for a mere 8% of the overall retail market in India, according to a study published in February 2013 by Booz & Company India and Retailers Association of India.

Even in 2013, India's fledgeling organized retail market had retailers experimenting with different business models in their search for success.

Reliance Industries Ltd's retail venture has different food and grocery formats: Reliance Fresh, small 2,000-sq-ft stores; Reliance Super, larger 7,500–10,000-sq-ft outlets; and Reliance Mart, big box retail stores. Reliance Retail had built a commendable footprint of 1,000 stores in 86 cities within three years of launching its business in 2006. In 2009, when the world was rocked by the worst credit crunch in history, Reliance Retail imposed a six-month freeze on expansion. At the end of fiscal year 2013, it had 1,466 stores in 129 cities even as the company achieved cash breakeven. In fiscal year 2013, its revenue grew by 42% to ₹10,800 crore from a year ago. On this, the firm recorded earnings before interest, tax, depreciation and amortization of ₹78 crore.

Aditya Birla Retail Ltd, which runs More hyper and super markets, exited from Mumbai in 2012 due to high rental costs.

Among quite a few casualties were companies like Subhikhsha Trading Services Ltd, which aggressively ramped up to double its stores from 650 in March 2007 to 1300 in March 2008, but crashed under the burden of high debts and inventory problems.

However, more experiments are on. Future Retail Ltd (formerly Pantaloon Retail India Ltd), India's largest listed retail company, began piloting franchise models for its Aadhaar Rural Wholesale and KB's Fairprice food and groceries retail chains in November 2012. Future Retail, known for its Big Bazaar and Food Bazaar retail chains, in July 2013 had 50 franchise stores and plans to open close to 1,000 franchise stores by 2015.

Along with the Q Shops, Sahara is also planning to set up high profile lifestyle clubs in major cities of India and redefine the concept of clubbing. Some of these clubs will have five-star hotels attached to them. The field workers of Sahara will be employed for selling memberships (Sahara calls it "citizenship") of these clubs.

Credit Cooperatives

The Sahara group quietly entered another money-raising space that's policed neither by Sebi nor the RBI, nor the ministry of corporate affairs. After being forced to wind down its RNBC business by the RBI and being barred by Sebi from raising money from the public through bonds, Sahara's agents began peddling new investment schemes to raise money on behalf of Sahara Credit Cooperative Society Ltd. Its headquarters and registered office are in Sahara India Bhawan, 1 Kapoorthala Complex, Aliganj, Lucknow – 226024, where most of the Sahara group entities are based. Sahara Credit Cooperative Society has its own Facebook page.

Sahara's official stance is that the cooperative society is run by group workers and the Roys have nothing to do with it. "Our managing worker and three deputy managing workers are not members of the cooperative, which is running some schemes towards financial inclusion of un-bankable people in rural and semi-urban areas who do not go to the bank or are visited by the bank," Abhijit Sarkar, who heads the communication division at the Sahara group among his other responsibilities, told *Business Standard* in 2011.

Strangely then, the cooperative's chairman is Devendra Kumar Srivastava, an executive director of Sahara India Pariwar. A postgraduate from Deen Dayal Upadhyay Gorakhpur University, Srivastava's Facebook page says his personal interests are reading, poetry, ghazals and motivating people. He was on the business revival committee of SIFCL. A wizard in deposit collection, he has been given a private jet by the group to ensure fast travel for money mobilization.

In an interview with this author, Roy said the group had launched a credit cooperative society but was vague on whether it was a venture of the group's employees alone.

The society was set up in October 2009 and registered on 5 March 2010 with a share capital of about ₹2.8 crore. Its plan is to pay up to 15% dividend to its members every year. In a cooperative credit society, individual savings of different people are pooled together to meet the financial requirements of its needy members. But the Sahara Credit Cooperative is yet another money-raising avenue for the group.

Three schemes are the mainstay of deposit mobilization for

the society:

Sahara 'A' Select – A four-year scheme that promises returns of more than 141% of the principal amount. Premature withdrawals are allowed at the end of 24 months. It is similar to the Nirman bonds of a group company, banned by Sebi.

Sahara 'E' Shine – An eight-year scheme that promises returns of at least 226% of the principal amount, very similar to the Abode bonds, banned by Sebi.

Sahara 'U' Golden – A 15-year scheme that offers returns of five times the principal amount.

All three schemes offer loans against deposits and child welfare plans.

In addition, the society offers three schemes – Sahara 'M' Benefit, a five-year recurring deposit scheme; Sahara 'S' Bhavishya, a 15-year recurring deposit scheme; and Sahara 'K' Money, a 10-year plan with monthly interest payments.

While the three mainstay schemes are mirror images of OFCDs banned by Sebi, the rest are very similar to the recurring deposits that SIFCL offered and have been banned by the RBI.

Any disputes related to the deposits are to be settled under the Multi-State Cooperative Societies Act, 2002, according to the application forms for the schemes.

Societies that operate in more than one state are governed by the Central Registrar of Cooperative Societies under the ministry of agriculture and development. The Registrar of Cooperative Societies regulates and supervises cooperative societies that operate within a state.

The Mumbai-based Investors and Consumer Guidance Society in 2012 wrote to the RBI that since Sahara Credit Cooperative Society's capital and reserves exceeded ₹1 lakh and it was mobilizing deposits, the central bank should regulate it; the RBI clarified that it didn't oversee cooperative credit societies.

Under the Banking Regulation Act, 1949, only state cooperative banks, district central cooperative banks and select urban cooperative banks are qualified to be called banks. While the RBI oversees their work, these banks are under part regulation and total supervision of the National Bank for Agriculture and Rural Development (Nabard). This is in addition to the state control of cooperative banks under state laws.

India also has rural credit cooperatives and 93,432 primary agricultural credit societies dealing with individual borrowers as short-term credit cooperatives. District central cooperative banks serve as a link between primary societies and state cooperative banks. They all serve their members.[1]

At the end of March 2013, India had 96,156 credit cooperatives; the money mobilized by them was about 10% of the aggregate banking business.

The credit cooperative society will keep the flow of money going for the Sahara group. This will continue till a regulator

---

[1] *Report of Trends and Progress of Banking in India*, 2011–2012, an annual publication of the RBI

comes forward to block these plans, but by then the group would have mobilized enough to pay off the depositors.

And the cycle goes on.

The Road Ahead

Meanwhile, there is no end in sight for Sahara group's fight with the market regulator. What can Sebi do to get to the bottom of the case, which, according to its counsel Arvind Datar, keeps getting "curiouser and curiouser"?

For one, it can ask Sahara to provide a list of the top 1% or 5% of the investors in the bonds sold by SIRECL and SHICL. Typically, the top 1–5% "creamy layer" of investors account for 20–25% of the money invested. Obtaining this list will make life easier for Sebi as well as for Sahara, as it wouldn't have to send truckloads of documents to the regulator.

Sebi can also look at the concentration of Sahara's investor base. If the regulator can locate five geographical pockets of investor concentration, it would become easier for it to get a fix on the investors as the Unique Identification Authority of India's Aadhaar project can do the rest of the job. Aadhaar, headed by Nandan Nilekani, has so far issued 310 million identity numbers. It plans to cover 600 million in a nation of 1.2 billion by 2014.

Finally, Sebi can ask Roy for details on banks from which he withdrew money to pay the investors. He may have been paying cash but certainly he could not have kept ₹19,000 crore in gunny bags at home or the Sahara offices. In other words, had he indeed paid ₹19,000 crore to the bond investors, he would have had to withdraw the money from banks. Unless, of course, he had raised the money in cash from the cooperative society members and ploughed it back to pay the bondholders.

Sebi has followed the directives of the Supreme Court diligently and never slackened its drive against Sahara even after its fulltime director Dr KM Abraham's term got over. Abraham had alleged that the regulator was under pressure to go soft on quite a few corporate houses, including the Sahara group. But it didn't seem like it. The regulator is not giving a kid-glove treatment to Roy. It froze the bank accounts of Sahara firms and even sought Roy's arrest.

How could Roy find himself in such a situation? The Sahara chief had refused to give information to Sebi and thought he could get away with it, but at a later stage, India's apex court sought the same details from him. Had he provided the information to Sebi in the first instance, he would not have found himself in such a mess.

It may or may not be the end game for Roy, but many lessons can be learnt from the Sebi-Sahara court battle.

First, it is a vindication of the independence of the judiciary. In this case, justice may have been delayed, but definitely not denied. The Supreme Court demonstrated that nobody can be shielded forever.

Second, it's a lesson for the Indian financial system on its loopholes and how a smart entrepreneur can use regulatory arbitraging to his advantage or indulge in regulator shopping.

Third, if Sahara fails to furnish the correct list of investors, the money for which there are no takers will flow into the government's Consolidated Fund for investor education. Failing to provide the list may give credence to the suspicions of many. It may also deal a blow to Roy's business model as he will lose his credibility. Roy may lose his face and the trust of the 'other India' that he cherishes with so much passion, the 'other India' that trusted him enough to keep their small savings with him.

Finally, if indeed the two Sahara group firms had 30 million investors in their bonds, the Indian financial system can learn lessons in financial inclusion from Roy. To put the 30 million in perspective, India's entire micro-finance industry has fewer borrowers and the number of demat account-holders are some 22 million. It would mean indeed that Roy knows better than anybody else how to spread financial inclusion in the world's tenth-largest economy, where about 40% of the adult population still does not have access to formal banking services. The regulators should salute him. And if the RBI chooses to give out only one banking licence, then that should be to Subrata Roy's Sahara group.

For the record, Roy did not apply for a banking licence when the RBI opened its window during the once-in-a-decade ritual to allow new banks to set up shop. The deadline expired on 30 June 2013.

On 21 November, the Supreme Court placed restrictions on the Sahara group's sale of moveable and immoveable property and barred Roy from leaving the country. It came down heavily on the group after finding that it had not complied with the court's October order to file title deeds of properties worth ₹20,000 crore with Sebi.

In subsequent hearings, the country's apex court directed the group to reveal the source of the ₹22,885 crore that has been paid to the OFCD investors, and furnish bank statements and ledger records to show the source of the money paid to investors even as the order restraining Roy from going abroad remained.

A highly anguished Roy says:

"As a law abiding citizen, we are honouring the court's worry by offering group companies' assets as security through nationalized banks' security trustee though it will create hardship for the group as so many assets will remain idle. This will be a big blow to the organization. In past two years, Sahara has lost so much both materially and in terms of respect for absolutely no fault of ours.

Sebi wants to delay and harass us and kill us. We have given ₹5,120 crore to Sebi, but it has disbursed only ₹70 lakh. It will hold on to our ₹20,000 crore worth of assets for as long as possible in the garb of verifying investors. More than 15 months have passed since the court asked Sebi to verify investors but not a single verification has been done.

We provide a livelihood to 1.2 lakh families. We do the maximum CSR work in India. I love my country and can die for the country. The entire world now knows that I am barred from travelling overseas. Sebi is responsible for this. Why has it done so? Am I a defaulter to the banking system? Am I a criminal? Is this justice? Do I deserve this after practising impeccable values and ethics?"

I don't have the answer to his questions. My dear reader, over to you.

Part VI

ANNEXURE I

SHADOW BANKING: A FOUR-LETTER WORD

Both Sahara and Peerless expose the soft underbelly of the Indian financial system – the RNBCs, which were not properly regulated until the Reserve Bank of India (RBI) early this century decided to aggressively address the issue, with YV Reddy at its helm as governor. Reddy found such firms growing too big and too fast and posing a potential threat to the stability of the financial system.

The origin of the name – RNBC – is no less interesting than the animal itself. Sometime in 1967, when the RBI wanted to classify different kinds of non-banking finance companies and arm itself with powers to regulate them by inserting a separate chapter in the RBI Act, 1934 (Chapter III B), DN Ghosh and RK Seshadri, two bureaucrats in the ministry of finance, worked on the project. Based on the nature of assets, certain companies did not conform to any of the established entities such as housing finance firms or chit funds. These companies were raising deposits from people and investing the money in different kinds of assets. In the absence of a better name, Ghosh and Seshadri called such firms residuary non-banking companies, or RNBCs. Seshadri later joined the RBI as an executive director and was elevated to the post of deputy governor in July 1973; Ghosh took over as chairman of the nation's largest lender, the State Bank of India, in 1985.

The government's and RBI's decision to shift from their light-touch and, in some cases, even abstinence from regulation and supervision of non-banking companies was triggered by the failure of Palai Central Bank, headquartered in Kerala, and the mushrooming of non-banks in its aftermath. Founded in 1927, eight years before the RBI was established, Palai emerged as the largest bank in the southern state and the 17th largest in India.

The RBI was set up in 1935 to take over from the government of India functions performed by the Controller of Currency and from the Imperial Bank of India, the management of government accounts and public debt.

Joseph Augusti Kayalackakom, who belonged to a family of agriculturists and traders, set up the bank in Pala, a small town in the central part of the then state of Travancore, which later became part of Kerala. Unhappy with its rapid expansion, the RBI in 1956 stopped the bank from expanding its branch network any further. In August 1960, the RBI moved a winding-up petition in the Kerala High

Court, alleging mismanagement and a rise in bad debts. Justice PT Raman Nair ordered the winding-up on 8 August 1960. Independent India witnessed its first banking crisis that year as a result, with most banks in the southern state facing a 'run' on their deposits as people panicked and began withdrawing their money.

Some banks outside Kerala too were affected, particularly Punjab National Bank in northern India. According to then finance minister Morarji Desai's statement in Parliament, some days after the collapse of Palai Central Bank, withdrawals at the bank had increased steadily from ₹12 lakhs in the week ended 1 July 1960 to ₹17 lakhs in the following week, ₹20 lakhs in the week ended 15th July, and ₹35 lakhs in the week ended 22nd July. Palai's deposits fell by nearly a sixth between 24th June and 8th August. Overall, the total deposits of 94 scheduled commercial banks in India dropped from ₹1,971.97 crore before the crisis to ₹1,741.80 crore in the six months following it.

Then Prime Minister Jawaharlal Nehru, while defending the RBI as "one of the best central banks in the world" with a "high level of efficiency", acknowledged that it may have made a "mistake" in closing Palai Central Bank.[1]

Fraught with appeals, the liquidation proceedings of Palai Central Bank dragged on for nearly three decades, until December 1987.

---

[1] "Appendix C: The Palai Central Bank", History of the Reserve Bank of India, Volume II (1951–1967).

The RBI issued a press statement on 9 August 1960 explaining the reasons for its action. HV Iyengar, the RBI governor then, devoted his presidential address at the annual general meeting of the Indian Institute of Bankers, to put in perspective the roles and responsibilities of the central bank and the managements of commercial bank, in ensuring the soundness of their institutions and the banking system. He said:

> "The Reserve Bank has been given pretty wide powers to inspect, give advice, and issue directives. All this, however, is no substitute for operational responsibility... I do not suppose any one suggests that the Reserve Bank should carry out these responsibilities over nearly 4,000 branches in the country; apart from the sheer physical difficulty, that would be taking over a direct and continuous administrative responsibility which rests on commercial banks. The Reserve Bank's powers are not... a substitute for the efficiency and integrity of the managements themselves... In the final resort, if a management does not listen to advice and chooses to be recalcitrant and it is felt that continued pressure would be useless, the Reserve Bank would have no option but to close down (the bank) in the interests of the depositors. But this decision involves a delicate balancing of several factors, some of them operational, some psychological..."

The failure of Palai Central Bank led the government to give power to the RBI to compulsorily merge weak banks. It also paved the way for the birth of Deposit Insurance and Credit Guarantee Corp. (DICGC) to protect depositors' money – although not the entire amount – in case of a bank failure.

Armed with new power, the RBI merged hundreds of small banks in southern India to protect depositors' interests. As a result, the number of banks in India dropped from around 600 to less than 100, but many of them began setting up non-bank shops hoping to tap people's savings.

First Step to Regulate Shadow Banking

In the wake of the Palai Central Bank collapse, the amendment of the RBI Act – by the Banking Laws (Miscellaneous Provisions) Act, 1963 – and the insertion of a new chapter, III B, on the collection of deposits by non-banking finance companies were the first steps by the banking regulator to bring in a semblance of regulation in the space of shadow banking, which many believe is not a disease but a symptom of a regressive financial system where neither savers nor borrowers have access to formal financial services. The RBI, for the first time, could call for information from the non-banking finance companies.

Roughly 65% of India's adult population does not have any interaction with banks and one needs to view the mushrooming of non-banks including RNBCs (they are very few, though) in this context. However, unlike banks, shadow banks do not have a safety net. Under Indian law, up to ₹1 lakh of deposits kept with a bank is insured, but if a non-bank goes bust, depositors risk losing their entire savings.

Armed with the amendment, in 1966, the RBI issued directions on the maturity period, quantum of deposits and interest rates for non-banking companies, but in 1975 when corporations were allowed to accept public deposits by amending the Companies Act 1956 (Sections 58A and 58B were inserted to frame acceptance of deposit rules), the deposit-taking companies moved into the fold of the government's Department of Company Affairs. Section 58A stipulates that the central government may, in consultation with the RBI, prescribe the limits and the manner and conditions of a company inviting deposits from the public.

The RBI, on its part, started overseeing non-banking finance companies through directives that were shaped by the report of a committee headed by James S Raj, chairman of India's oldest mutual fund Unit Trust of India. Some of the recommendations of the committee, constituted by the RBI in June 1974, were seminal and played a critical role in shaping the non-banking finance industry.

The James Raj committee found that in 1963 India's banking system had a deposit base of ₹2,042.3 crore and non-banking companies ₹153.9 crore, about 7.5% of the bank deposits.[2]

By 1972, bank deposits had grown three-and-a-half times to ₹7,105.9 crore, while non-bank deposits had increased by more than four times – to ₹691.8 crore, or 9.7% of bank deposits. There were 3,155 non-banking companies in

---

[2] *Report of the Study Group on Non-Banking Companies*, headed by JS Raj, Reserve Bank of India, p11

1972, of which 921 were finance companies and 2,234 were non-finance companies.

By 1981, the number of non-banking companies had swelled to 7,063 and, by 1990, to a staggering 24,009, a compounded annual growth rate of 14% over the decade. Again, non-finance companies were more than finance companies.[3]

In 2012, there were 12,348 non-banking finance companies registered with the RBI and 265 of them took deposits.[4]

The total assets of these companies were ₹10.38 trillion, roughly 12.7% of the banking assets. Three hundred and seventy-six of them were large, systematically important non-banking finance companies, and their assets aggregated ₹9.23 trillion, or 11.3% of the banking assets. Forty-two of them had assets more than India's smallest bank and two of them were larger than the smallest public sector bank, Punjab and Sind Bank.

Making a pitch for the RBI to supervise such companies, YH Malegam, noted chartered accountant and a member of the Financial Sector Legislative Reforms Commission, in his dissent note attached to the commission's report in 2013 said the activities of non-banks outside the regulatory environment raised concerns of regulatory arbitrage. Incidentally, Malegam was also a member of the working

---

[3] *Report on the Working Group of Financial Companies*, headed by AC Shah, Reserve Bank of India, p34

[4] *Report of the Financial Sector Legislative Reforms Commission*, headed by Justice BN Srikrishna, p154

group on financial companies in 1992, headed by former Bank of Baroda chairman AC Shah. The working group was set up by the RBI to review the role of various non-banking finance companies and RBI norms for them.

Why the RBI wanted to amend its Act in 1963 and insert Chapter III is evident in the statement of objectives and reasons appended to the Banking Laws (Miscellaneous provisions) Bill, which says:

> "The existing enactments relating to banks do not provide for any control over companies or institutions, which, although they are not treated as banks, accept deposits from the general public or carry on other business which is allied to banking. For ensuring a more effective supervision and management of the monetary and credit system by the Reserve Bank, it is desirable that the Reserve Bank should be enabled to regulate the conditions on which deposits may be accepted... The Reserve Bank should also be empowered to give directions..."

Moving the Bill in the Lok Sabha on 19 December 1963, then minister of state for planning, Bali Ram Bhagat, said:

> "... Deposits which are now received and handled outside the banking system, should be controlled, not only in the interests of the depositors themselves, but also in the general and wider public interest."[5]

In the Rajya Sabha (the upper house of Parliament), on

---

[5] Lok Sabha Debates, Third Series, Volume 24, 16–21 December 1963, pp5681–82

23 December 1963, Bhagat said:

> "As far as the control of non-banking deposits is concerned, this Bill, Sir, contains no provision which, I think, will not be found in the Protection of Depositors' Act, 1963, which was presently brought into force in the United Kingdom. Broadly, what we are aiming at is that apart from individual money lenders, who are governed by the various state enactments relating to money lending, and cooperative societies, which are a class by themselves, all persons or institutions accepting deposits from the public will have the obligation to comply with the regulations, which will be made for this purpose by the Reserve Bank."[6]

Film Production on Public Deposits

Members of the James Raj panel undertook extensive surveys in Ahmedabad, Bangalore, Mumbai, Calcutta and Delhi. In Bangalore, they found finance companies not regulated by the RBI accepting deposits many times their capital or net-owned funds of less than ₹1 lakh, and using the money for film production, construction of hotels and trading.

A bulk of the deposits was used for constructing imposing buildings that also housed the offices of these companies – enough to impress a gullible public.

---

[6] Rajya Sabha Debates, Third Series, Volume 45, 5–23 December 1963, pp4771–72

Such companies borrowed hugely and invested in risky and liquid assets and, hence, if for any reason the business came to a standstill, the depositors would lose their money. The promoters of such finance companies consider the deposits as their money and use and lend it to whosoever they deem fit. So, the James Raj panel suggested that such activities be regulated by putting a ceiling on the borrowing and prescribing how the funds were to be utilized.

The panel submitted its report in 1975, but even in 2013 several companies running so-called collective investment schemes (CIS) in Kolkata were found doing the same thing: treating public deposits as their own money and investing them in whatever caught their fancy – media, real estate or simply a good life.

Till the cookie crumbled in April 2013, large non-banking firms had taken in thousands of crores of rupees from millions of investors in West Bengal. The collapse of the Saradha group – once one of eastern India's biggest deposit-taking companies – marked the first of a wave of such failures in West Bengal. These deposit-taking firms offered significantly higher returns than High Street banks, mostly by inventing businesses that never existed – some claimed to be producing cement, some said they were constructing hotels and resorts, and yet others said they would invest the deposits in exotic financial instruments such as potato bonds to earn super-normal profits.

One company had even raised hundreds of crores of rupees from the public to buy cattle, promising more than double the money in returns by selling ghee made out of milk produced by the cattle. It called the scheme 'Cattles and Ghee'. The company is based in New Delhi and has dairy firms in, among other places, Samalkha town in Panipath district and Ganaur city in Sonipat district, both in Haryana.

Neither the RBI nor Sebi could tackle these companies, citing a lack of teeth. In fact, many of the products these deposit-taking firms sell are so designed that Sebi or the RBI cannot regulate them. While Sebi got into a protracted legal battle with two such companies in West Bengal, MPS Greenery Developers Ltd and Rose Valley Real Estates and Constructions Ltd, to stop them from collecting public deposits under CIS, the RBI pleaded helplessness repeatedly saying that these companies, though they received public deposits, did not come under its jurisdiction.

Sebi's campaign against CIS operators in West Bengal did not have much success because of the intervention of district courts in the state. At least six district courts passed injunctions in 2012 on Sebi's cease-and-desist order against MPS Greenery Developers. Technically, only the Securities Appellate Tribunal, the appellate body of Sebi, has the jurisdiction to review orders passed by the market regulator but that contention was challenged many times in the courts, including at the Calcutta High Court in 2011 by the Rose Valley group. Sebi even moved the Supreme Court against such firms, but could not make much headway.

The scenario is expected to change as Sebi is to get powers to oversee deposit-taking companies collecting ₹100 crore or more from the public barring the chit funds, nidhis and the companies registered with the state governments. President

Pranab Mukherjee promulgated an ordinance on 18 July 2013 empowering Sebi to protect investors.

The mushrooming of deposit-taking firms gained momentum after the RBI asked Peerless General Finance and Investment Co. in 2007 to stop taking fresh deposits after four years. The banking regulator's decision put lakhs of Peerless's field agents out of jobs, and most of them set up or became part of the collection network of deposit-taking companies that flourished in the eastern state.

DN Ghosh, chairman emeritus of rating agency ICRA Ltd, and former non-executive chairman of Peerless General Finance, wrote in May 2013:

> "Regulators must have been aware that several mushroom companies were raising huge sums by way of deposits or similar instruments from poor people in rural and semi-urban areas. Masterminded by a few politically connected unscrupulous persons, these companies were duping poor people of their lifelong savings, luring them with false promises. This is not a new phenomenon in the financial world. If the regulators were not aware of what was happening, they owe an explanation to the citizens of the country. It is their duty to keep their antenna up and tuned." [7]

Indeed, the James Raj panel urged the banking regulator to keep its antenna up and tuned. Since the finance

---

[7] "Are Our Regulators Imaginative?", DN Ghosh, *Economic and Political Weekly* web exclusive, Volume XLVIII, No.21, 25 May 2013.

companies lend the money raised as deposits without being regulated by any one, the panel suggested that lending norms be introduced to ensure the safety of the depositors' money. While it found misuse of public money by non-banking companies in Bangalore, in Delhi it observed that many of these companies were functioning with very little net-owned funds.

A study of 89 companies by the James Raj panel revealed that only two of them had capital more than ₹10 lakh. Six of these firms had capital of ₹5–10 lakh, 52 had capital less than ₹1 lakh and at least seven had less than ₹5,000. The concept of capital adequacy ratio or having capital at a certain percentage of assets did not exist for these non-banks and, as a result, all of them were hugely leveraged.

The committee wanted to link the deposit-taking ability of different types of non-banking companies to their net-owned funds and, at the same time, make them able to meet deposit redemptions at any given time. It suggested that a certain portion of deposits be kept in liquid assets such as bank deposits and government bonds. It also recommended banning loans to the directors of such companies and limiting their investments in other companies.

Finally, the panel said:

> "In view of the substantive nature of the recommendations and also the fact that the deposit acceptance activities of non-financial companies are no longer under the control of the Reserve Bank, we feel that it would be desirable to enact separate

> comprehensive legislation in the place of Chapter III B, of the Reserve Bank of India Act, 1934, for giving effect to the recommendations."[8]

It even suggested that some of the non-banking companies be allowed to convert themselves into commercial or cooperative banks, subject to conditions prescribed by the RBI.

Banning Prize Chit Funds

The James Raj panel also wanted to ban prize chit funds after it found that the capital and reserves of most of these had been wiped out by losses. In such funds, the participants agree that every one of them shall subscribe a certain amount of money by way of periodic instalments over a definite period and that each such subscriber shall, in his or her turn, as determined by lot or by auction or by tender or in any other manner as agreed, be entitled to the prize amount.Running a prize chit fund was akin to running a lottery, an offence under Section 294A of the Indian Penal Code, but since it involved a civil transaction, the offence was a non-cognizable one.

In 1978, Parliament banned prize chit funds, but conventional chits were allowed to remain and four years later, in 1982, the Chit Funds Act was passed by Parliament and many Indian states adopted it.

---

[8] *Report of the Study Group on Non-Banking Companies*, headed by JS Raj, Reserve Bank of India, p120

Since then, in rapid succession, banking and non-banking laws have been changed. For instance, major changes were made in Chapter III B of the RBI Act in February 1984 and a new Chapter III C was introduced to ban unincorporated bodies from taking deposits.

In 1987, the Supreme Court held that the business of companies carrying on camouflaged models of prize chit schemes was not hit by the ban, but empowered the RBI to control and regulate these companies, even if these could not be categorized as prize chits as defined by the Banning Act in 1978.

Instead of regulating these companies under guidelines set for non-banking finance companies, the RBI on 15 May 1987 issued fresh directions exclusively to cover RNBCs, which until then had escaped the regulator's glare. It introduced two critical changes. One, it prohibited the collection of short-term deposits below 12 months and fixed the maximum tenure of deposits at 120 months. Two, it delinked the amount of money that can be raised to the net-owned funds of RNBCs, but the profile of their assets was prescribed.

RNBCs were asked to put in at least 10% of their deposits in fixed deposits of public sector banks and at least 70% of their deposits in government bonds or other securities approved by the regulator. That would leave them with 20% of the deposits raised or ten times their net-owned funds – whichever is less – to invest in other assets.

This wasn't enough to contain the growth of Peerless and Sahara. Ghosh, the former chairman of Peerless, blamed the

RBI for its failure to control the RNBCs. "Why couldn't RBI control them? Why did it allow them to grow to monstrous sizes? Clearly it was a failure of the regulator," he told me at the famed Bengal Club on Russell Street in Kolkata over a Chinese lunch. According to him, the RBI had been lax.

"From late 1970s and 1980s, the RNBCs proliferated and started investing in all kind of assets, but the RBI turned a blind eye. It controlled only liabilities – not assets. It wanted the RNBCs to put money in government bonds, but not entirely as the RNBCs protested. They were asked to put in 80% of the deposits in government bonds and other securities approved by the regulator, but were allowed to use the remaining 20% in any assets they like. This was called discretionary quota. That was a fatal flaw – which was corrected years later by governor Reddy," he says.

Another failure, according to Ghosh, was the RBI's inability to force the promoters of RNBCs to raise capital. All the RNBCs had extremely low capital bases compared to the volume of funds they handled.

If banks could have capital adequacy ratio and tier I and II capital, why couldn't RNBCs, he asked.

"The RBI is responsible for the Peerless and Sahara fiasco. It was a combination of inefficiencies, regulator's indifference and political influence that led to the growth of RNBCs."

Equity and reserves constitute the Tier I capital of banks while Tier II capital has components like long-term debt and revaluation reserves, among others.

The Article that Shook the Regulator

Ghosh is also the author of arguably the best article ever written on RNBCs – "Disciplining RNBCs: A Regulatory Puzzle".[9]

It shook the banking regulator out of its stupor and galvanized it into action against RNBCs. I am tempted to quote extensively from his article, which traces the history of RNBCs since the mid-1960s, when after having brought some semblance of order and discipline among commercial banks, the RBI began taking stock of non-banking deposit-taking entities to develop appropriate regulations. Some of these had distinguished characteristics regarding their deposit liabilities and composition of assets such as hire-purchase firms, nidhis, chit funds and finance companies. But one group of companies did not fit into any of these categories and by a process of elimination they were classified as a "residual" category. They had been functioning for years without any control and competing for deposits by offering attractive rates and flexible repayment terms.

Referring to the RBI's 1987 regulation that allowed RNBCs discretion on 20% of the public deposits collected by them, Ghosh wrote with sarcasm:

> "A very thoughtful relaxation on the part of the RBI; after all, the regulations should not be so tight that it

---

[9] "Disciplining RNBCs: A Regulatory Puzzle", DN Ghosh, *Economic and Political Weekly*, Volume 39, No.18, 1–7 May 2004, pp1766–69.

frustrates the objective of generating good returns that is in the interest of depositors."

How was the flexibility utilized?

"A cursory review shows that these funds have been invested in a wide range of ventures in airlines, shipping, TV channels, hospitals, retail trade, hotels, overseas trade, housing, technology ventures, real estate, construction and others. These investments, generally the pet projects of the promoters, have most often generated little or no return, taking away the very rationale for this discretionary privilege. For the regulatory authority, it would prima facie make eminent sense to do away with such discretionary investments and ensure that these investments are completely delinked from RNBCs...

The obvious question – if... a substantial portion of assets is non-earning, perhaps essentially bad, and a burden, then how is that the business of RNBCs continue to thrive and flourish? What is the secret? To find an answer to this mystery, one needs to go back a little into the past. The pillar of their strength was, till some years ago, the so-called lapsed deposits. What manner of beast is this? It is deposits where the contract stipulates that the depositor makes predefined periodic payments or additional deposits. In the event that the depositor for whatever reason is unable to make good on these terms, the outstanding deposit is credited to the RNBC.... Reportedly such forfeiture was the mainstay of many RNBCs."

Ghosh's article also debunked the belief that RNBCs mostly raised deposits from poor people and unorganized communities in India's villages and small towns, deposits that normally did not flow into the formal banking channel. The prevailing argument then that the RNBCs served a public purpose, he said, should be taken with a "large dose of salt". Ghosh wrote that the deposits mobilized by the RNBCs were not significantly relative to the resources raised by the national financial system, but were significant for sponsoring the pet projects of the promoters of these companies and providing them a springboard to achieve celebrity status.

Finally, Ghosh's article said that the main drivers of growth for these entities were their huge armies of field agents and high pressure sales concentrated mainly among unsuspecting depositors in rural and semi-urban pockets.

> "There is also an impression that many of these institutions are being used as a conduit for collecting funds from persons who would otherwise be hesitant to put through their transactions openly and transparently through banks and other financial institutions. Because of the large distribution network, across the country, through hundreds and thousands of workers, it would seem virtually impossible to enforce the observance of strict requirements regarding the identity of depositors. I would be extremely surprised if the RBI would ever be able to enforce the provision of money laundering and associated Acts on the RNBCs."

These are pages from the diary of an insider who understands the industry like the back of his hand. This article was written in 2004 and many of Ghosh's "findings" were later corroborated by the RBI's inspection of RNBCs. Ghosh wrote this after completing seven years with the Peerless General Finance and Investment Co. Even though he was a non-executive chairman, his mandate was to rescue Peerless from the structural crisis it faced in the mid-1990s that had created a gaping hole in its balance sheet and become a serious threat to its depositors.

He had become chairman of Peerless in August 1996 and continued till 2006, three years after the company achieved a positive net worth. A year after he left, in 2007, the RBI gave Peerless four years to collect fresh deposits, till April 2011, and close shop by 2015. Ghosh had the best of relationships with the promoters of the Peerless group but many in Peerless believe his exposé forced the RBI to tighten the noose around the company first and Sahara later.

ANNEXURE II

EPISTOLARY HISTORY

Pasted below are letters and extracts from letters exchanged between Sahara and the RBI and others. These are not in the public domain and reproduced passages have not be edited.

Subrata Roy wrote many letters to former RBI governor YV Reddy, but Reddy responded to Roy's letter only once.

11 April 2007
Mumbai

Dear Hon'ble Governor,

We have taken a serious note of the concerns of Reserve Bank of India in regard to the growth in deposits of our company. We have ourselves taken a number of steps to moderate the growth like stoppage of both the fixed deposit schemes, direct interface of the company with the depositors (as against earlier through our agent), discontinuing opening of new accounts under RD (recurring deposit) schemes, etc.

We have all along been complying with all the provisions of RBI directions and guidelines issued from time to time. We have made a number of changes in our systems, processes and procedures in deference to the instructions of RBI, either in the form of written communications or oral advices and renew our commitments to RBI for the same in future also. We have always been rendering best of services to the depositors.

I would feel obliged if you permit me to have the benefit of your vision and guidance in speeding up the mitigation of the concerns of our guardian institution. I may kindly be granted an audience with you on any day between April 12 and 17, 2007.

With warm personal regards,
Yours sincerely
Subrata Roy Sahara

---

11 April 2007
Dear Shri Roy,

I have received your kind letter dated April 11, 2007. I am very happy to note that you are having interactive dialogue with our officers. As you are aware, we are totally convergent in terms of our objective to have a strong financial sector in general, and NBFCs sector in particular.

As a large player in the sector, your fullest cooperation will make the task easier for all of us.

I have been briefed by our team led by Shri V Leeladhar, deputy governor, about their periodical discussions with you and I must say that the dialogue has been active even though more intensive efforts may be needed to fully and expeditiously realize our objectives.

I have no personal vision or guidance that could be considered other than what has been articulated in public and also in the series of discussions between us.

With Regards,

Y V Reddy

Reddy put in place the system of holding quarterly meetings with RNBCs to discuss critical issues and build trust. Here are minutes of decisions taken in a typical quarterly meeting with Sahara. The RBI writes to Roy.

16 April 2007

Dear Sir,

Meeting held on March 26, 2007

Please refer to the discussions we had with you on March 26, 2007, regarding the findings of the inspection conducted by the Bank with respect to the financial position of your company as on March 31, 2006. In this connection, we advise you the following.

i) It has been noted that the company has stopped accepting fixed deposits.

ii) As discussed, the company may plan an alternative business model and approach for the regulatory approvals.

iii) The process of transition to the new business model may be completed within a period of three years commencing from April 1, 2007, as conveyed in the above meeting.

iv) The company may plan to scale down its recurring deposit and daily deposit business and gradually reduce the amount accepted under these schemes. The company may also reduce the amount accepted under these schemes. The company may also reduce the tenure of maturity of such deposits in such a manner that the reaching of the desired level of reduction in deposits becomes co-terminus with the time frame set for moving over to alternate business model.

v) The number of points of acceptance of non-fixed deposits may be reduced to gradually compress the geographical coverage.

vi) The company may make adequate provision for repayment of deposits which mature after three years and also for unclaimed/ unpaid deposits held by the company.

vii) Progress made in the implementation of the plan may be intimated to the Bank at quarterly intervals.

2. We shall be glad to have a line of communication from you in this regard at the earliest.

Yours Faithfully,
S Bhatnagar
(General Manager)

---

5 September 2007
Dear Sir,

Review Meeting held on 31.8.2007

We invite your reference to the discussions we had on August 31, 2007.

During the discussion we conveyed our concern in respect of the substantial outstanding income tax refund claims, which have not been admitted by income tax department for a long time now. However, the company continues to recognize in the balance sheet these outstandings as assets. Your explanation that the delays have been on the account of non-availability of officials in the department concerned for processing the cases is not acceptable. It has become necessary that provisions are made in respect of these claims recognized as assets in the balance sheet for the year ending March 2007. The company should also not recognize any income on accrual basis on the outstanding IT claims.

2. There are also large claims on the company by the income tax department. These claims also will have to be treated as contingent liabilities and necessary provision made thereon.

3. We have today advised the statutory auditors of your company about our serious concern in continuing to treat the claims as realizable assets on the balance sheet without making adequate provisions despite no refund being received from the income tax department.

Yours Faithfully,
S Bhatnagar
(General Manager)

First RBI Inspection

5 November 2007

Dear Sir,

Sub: Annual Inspection of Sahara India Financial Corp Ltd-Financial Position as on 31.3.2007.

It has been observed that annual inspection u/s 45N of the RBI Act, 1934, of the company as regard to financial position on 31.3.2007 has been commenced w.e.f. 30.10.2007. As on date, the following service centres of the company have been visited by the RBI officials:

Sl.No	Service Centre	Date of Visit
1	Varchha (Surat)	30.10.2007
2	Azad Nagar (Delhi)	31.10.2007
3	Satna	31.10.2007
4	Bhuvaneshwar	1.11.2007
5	Kankarbagh (Patna)	1.11.2007
6	Shivpur (WB)	1.11.2007
7	Barasat (WB)	1.11.2007
8	Hatia (Ranchi)	2.11.2007
9	Bahrampur (Bhuvaneshwar)	2.11.2007
10	Nagpur	5.11.2007
11	Siliguri (Kolkata)	5.11.2007

You will appreciate that the festival of Deepawali is falling on 9.11.2007 and the employees/staff of the company may take leave, being festival season. For proper security on service centres during these days and also in order to make the availability of the staff at service centres of the company, so that smooth inspection could be carried out by your officials at the proposed service centres, you are requested to kindly make us available the names of those service centres which are proposed to be inspected by RBI.

Thanking you and assuring you of our fullest cooperation at all times.

Yours faithfully,
For SIFCL
Anupam Prakash

This is the first RBI letter on violation of norms after inspection, addressed to Roy.

24 December 2007

Dear Sir,

Compliance with the Bank's instructions — Default

As you are aware, the certificate of registration bearing No 12 000152 issued by the Bank to your company on December 03, 1998, to carry on the business of non-banking financial institution is subject to conditions mentioned therein. One of the conditions subject to which the certificate of registration was issued to the company was that "...company shall be required to comply with all the requirements of the directions, guidelines, instructions, etc.

issued by the Bank and as applicable to it."

2. In this context, we draw your attention to the Bank's letter No. DNBS.CO.ZMD-North(RNBC). No. 8196/04.06.017/2006-07 dated May 28, 2007, wherein the company has been advised that it needs to accept deposits only to meet the outflow on account of maturing deposits ensuring that there is no increase in the current level of deposits. The aggregate liability towards depositors (ALD) of the company as on May 31, 2007 was Rs 18,216.79 crore, and in terms of the above instructions, the ALD should not have increased beyond that level, but the company continued to accept deposits, and the ALD kept on increasing in the subsequent months, which is clearly in violation of the Bank's instructions. Instead, the company vide its letter dated September 03, 2007, informed the Bank that it has unilaterally ascribed a limit of Rs 20,000 crore on its ALD which was in contradiction with our instructions. The matter was also followed up with the company for compliance vide Bank's letter dated September 25, 2007, and November 15, 2007, as also during various meetings held with the company, in which the company was advised to match its inflow of deposits with the outflow to nullify the growth of deposits. But the company has not adhered to the instructions issued by the Bank.

3. We would further like to state that in terms of the provisions of the Residuary Non-banking Companies (Reserve Bank) Directions, 1987, the company is required to maintain a certain percentage of it ALD (RNBCs were advised to invest with effect from April 1, 2006, not less than 95% of their ALD as on December 31, 2005 and 100 per cent of their incremental deposit in approved securities and on and from April 1, 2007, 100% of their ALD in approved securities) as investments in approved securities. However, it is observed that the company has been defaulting in maintenance of required amount of directed investments since the month of April, 2006 (except in June 2006). The company was issued a notice on March 21, 2007, to show cause as to why the Bank should not impose penalty on the company for failing to comply with the provisions of the RNBC (RB) Directions, 1987. Though the company submitted its action plan for rectifying the default, it continued to default in the maintenance of directed Investments. The company's explanation that the shortfall was the result of exclusion of income tax refund claims and current account balances with scheduled commercial banks from directed investments was not acceptable as the company was complying with our directed Investment norms for the quarter ended June 30, 2006, when IT refund claims and current account balances were not allowed under directed investments.

The company was advised by the Bank through a number of letters as also during various meetings conducted with the company to rectify the default and maintain required amount of directed investments and the company is yet to comply with our directed investments norms in spite of allowing sufficient time for compliance with the provisions of the above directions.

4. The company was also advised vide our company circular No 46 dated December 30, 2004, to comply with "know your customers" norms for its depositors by January 31, 2005, compliance of which was followed up through various letters, the latest being our letters dated October 08, November 02, and December 03, 2007, written to the company as also during various meetings held with the company. The norms were further simplified vide Bank's circular DNBS.PD.CC. No.64/03.10.042/2005-06 dated March 07, 2006. However even after a lapse of about three years, the company is yet to furnish its full compliance with the said norms.

5. From the above, it is observed that the company is not complying with the directions/guidelines/instructions issued by the Bank from time to time. We, therefore, advise that the company must initiate necessary steps for scrupulous compliance with the directions/guidelines/instructions and confirm compliance.

Yours faithfully
D Rajagopala Rao
General Manager

Given below are extracts from a note written by Sahara to the RBI on how it collects deposits.

5 November 2007
Sahara India Financial Corp. Ltd

Note on deposit mobiliation activities

Since 1 October 2006, the company is mobilizing its deposits through its own service centres with the help of field forces having direct interface with the company whose detailed KYC is available with the company and identity cards are issued to them by the company. Daily deposit schemes which are being run by the company since its inception are unparalleled and the most liked by the persons of various means and resources, particularly those belonging to the lower strata of the society like the daily wage earners, because they are able to save on daily basis and the company collects deposits from their door steps. The method of deposit mobilization is explained hereunder –

For mobilizing daily deposits, field worker/office staff briefs the prospective depositors on the information about the company, date of incorporation, objects of the company, branches, units, management (board of directors), profitability position of last three years, financial position (brief balance sheet for last two years), details of overdue deposits, rate of interest as regard to deposit scheme and its tenure, pre-maturity conditions, applicability of tax laws, etc. including how the deposit amount shall be fully secured as per RNBC directions.

The field worker/ office staff convinces people about benefits of saving for their future and also help the depositors to select an appropriate deposit scheme, depending upon his capacity and need. The terms and conditions of the deposit scheme which will be part of the contract to be executed between the company and the depositor, once the deposit account is opened, are explained in details.

a) Once the deposit scheme is selected as per the need of the depositors as well as the category (earning members), the field worker provides the deposit application form, gets it properly filled up and signed from the depositors. The general terms and conditions for acceptance of the deposits by the company are as under:

- *The company may at any time alter, vary, add to or delete from these terms and conditions on account of government policy in this regard or as per RBI regulations as applicable from time to time or otherwise by notifying on company's notice board or by publication in the newspapers.*
- *The company reserves the right to settle the account with applicable rate of interest for the completed tenure of the account*

even before the completion of the declared tenure.

- *Deposits are accepted on the understanding that the account holder assumes full responsibility for his source of fund.*

b) Filed workers simultaneously take the KYC documents from the depositors which are annexed with the deposit application form.

c) The field worker has to sign a declaration on the deposit application form, the language of which is reproduced hereunder:

"I have explained everything, in the language, known to the applicant and he/she has given his/her full consent to join the account on terms and condition mentioned above.

I further, hereby declare that all declarations made by the account holder and all the information/personal particulars given here by the account holder are correct and true to the best of my knowledge and belief."

d) Similarly the depositor has to declare on the deposit application form that he has been explained everything properly by the field worker. The exact language on the application form is reproduced hereunder:

"I hereby declare that all the declarations made by me are correct and I have been explained everything related to the above account in the language known to me and also I declare that I am not suffering and have not suffered from any chronic/fatal disease in the last three years. Also I agree to abide by the rules and regulations of the company and I shall never request anything against the terms and conditions of the scheme in letter and spirit. I also certify that all information/ personal particulars given here by me are true to the

best of my knowledge and belief."

e) After the completion of all the formalities at the door of the depositor, field workers/ office staff carry these documents to the service centre of the company.

f) In-charge of the service centre verifies the application forms and KYC documents and opens the account, if the application form is correct in all respect and accepts the deposit amount/instalment.

g) On opening of deposit account, deposit receipt is generated and delivered to the field workers/ office staff along with the pass book for onward delivery to the depositors. Deposit receipt and passbook are generated automatically through computer system. Nothing is manual at service centre level.

h) The field worker is in direct contact with the depositors and company. He collects the money from the depositor and deposits the same with the service centre of the company in most of the cases at daily interval (except in some cases it may be ranging between two and seven days). Every field worker collecting daily deposit is provided with a daily collection sheet which carries the particulars of the depositors from whom he has to collect the instalments. The procedure of daily deposit collection is as under:

(i) Frequency of visit of collector to the service centre is determined and approved at service centre. Frequency in majority of the cases is on daily basis but it may be between two and seven days in some cases.

(ii) The collector comes to the service centre to collect the daily collection sheet (DCS) for the approved number of days.

(iii) The DCS already has the name of the depositors pre-printed.

(iv) On collection of deposits, the collector fills the amount collected and also gets the signature of the depositor on the DCS.

(v) The collector comes to the service centre at the scheduled interval and deposits the sum collected against which he gets a receipt and thereafter collects the next DCS for collections.

(vi) The processing of the DCS at the service centre ensures that the ledger of the account holder is updated automatically by the system on daily/approved intervals.

(vii) A final receipt is generated fortnightly for the depositor which reflects the deposits received date-wise.

(viii) In this process, the deposit amount received by the collector is compulsorily deposited at the branch at the shortest interval, mostly within one day but, as stated earlier, for remote areas, it may vary between two and seven days also.

(ix) The service centres have been instructed to remit surplus funds (retaining funds to the extent of meeting out payments on account of maturity, pre-maturity, secured loan against deposit, etc. for the next fortnight) to the command office on a fortnightly basis and this system is followed by the centres diligently.

(x) The deposit subsidiary ledgers are being updated at the headquarters on daily basis on receipt of data from the service centre.

i) At least two months prior to the date of maturity of the deposit filed worker/office staff carries the maturity intimation letter and delivers it to the depositor to make the depositor informed of the maturity date of the deposit and also impresses on the depositor to make request to the company for taking the maturity amount in time.

j) The depositor calls at the service centre of the company for receiving his maturity payment. The signature of depositor is tallied/verified by the service centre in-charge with the already recorded signature with the company obtained at the time of opening of the account.

k) The depositor produces/submits at the service centre of the company, the original passbook/certificate duly discharged for cancellation and receives the maturity amount.

The first time Sahara wrote to the RBI on alternative business model – migration to banking – was in January 2008. Roy wrote the letter to deputy governor Leeladhar.

19 January 2008

Dear Sir,

Salient measures taken by the company for addressing matter raised by RBI and request for certain forebearances

After the last meeting on August 31, 2007, I had apprised your goodself of our commitments to address the concerns of RBI. I take this opportunity to brief your honour on the progress made by the company in regard to compliance with RBI regulations and instructions in the following paragraphs.

Matching inflow with outflow and Cap on deposits

2. Our company has been informing RBI of various steps taken for moderating the growth in deposits. It may be stated that whatever accretion to ADL is there since March 31, 2007, is mainly because of application of interest on deposits. The company has vide its letter dated 23.12.2007 has assured RBI that the anticipated level of ADL as on 31st December 2007 would be less than the ADL of September, 2007. We wish to confirm that the ADL as on 31st December 2007 at Rs 18,495 crore was less than our ADL of Rs 18,517 crore as on 30st September 2007. We, in our abovesaid letter have also assured that out ADL as on March 31, 2008 shall be at around or even less than the ADL of March 31, 2007.

Provisioning and disclosures in the Balance Sheet

3. As desired by RBI, that the company, on a conservative basis, should not have been accruing interest on refunds due from income tax authorities, and the contingent liabilities as disclosed in the balance sheet should have factored the large outstanding demands from the tax authorities, the company immediately implemented RBI desire and directions in the balance sheet of march 31, 2007 itself.

KYC Compliance

4. As on December 31, 2007, the company has been successful in obtaining KYC compliance from 1.16 lakh depositors out of 1.48 lakh of the total depositors with balance of Rs 50,000 and above. It is learnt from the field staff that some of the depositors are ignoring their plea on the grounds that the post offices are not asking for such documents. The company has already deployed

6,000 mobiles with camera having specific software wherein details of the depositors have been loaded to get their photograph in old accounts. Efforts have been mounted so as to complete the KYC work including obtention (sic) of the photographs from the remaining depositors with deposit balance of Rs 50,000 and above by February 28, 2008. The Company has separately submitted its action plan for other depositors.

5. Although in the past too, proper identification and verification of each depositor was done by the file agent, the company has since issued strict instructions to the service centres that no new deposit account can be opened without obtaining a identity (photograph) and address proof of every new depositor and cautioned the staff against any deficiencies.

Covering gap in Directed Investments

6. The company has been investing the deposits as and when received (incremental deposits) on a regular basis. Further, in order to reduce the gap in investments, the company has divested its other assets and invested the proceeds thereof in the Directed Investments only. The excess of incremental investments in directed securities over incremental ADL since 31st December 2005 has been Rs 1,669 crore. We once again wish to submit that the company is committed to bridge the remaining gap in directed investments, which was Rs.933 crore as on 31st December, 2007 in a time bound manner as already submitted to RBI.

Alternate Business Model

7. We have submitted vide our letters dated September 3 and 11, 2007 that migration of our company from the well established business model of RNBC to any other business model is a very very major issue and also kept RBI informed about the appointment of Ernst & Young, for advising the company in regard to its conversion into a bank. We are confident that E &Y would be able to suggest a way out to move forward in a systematic and methodical manner. Though the management would have to face a number of difficulties in transformation of the Company but it is willing to take steps, which may be required in the larger interest of the depositors, and without adversely affecting the lakhs and lakhs of field workers and employees who are associated with the company and depend on it for their livelihood.

Our Request and Submissions

8. The distinctive feature of our business model is that while the customer goes to the bank, the company goes to the customer at his doorstep by providing tailor made deposit schemes to meet his needs. The company observes that its daily deposit schemes are viable and the company has been running this scheme for two decades successfully. These schemes can also be run under the bank, when permitted. The existing business model, savings products and the target group of depositors, which include persons of small means fulfill the objectives of financial inclusion (from supply side) being vigorously pursued by the government in the recent years. There is a great scope for this type of savings product in the system.

9. In order to meet the challenges of the future the company desires to further strengthen its systems and processes and had accordingly appointed E & Y for an advice to upgrade its systems, controls and procedures. We have also decided to convey the recent observations of the RBI inspection team to them so that the gaps could be addressed in totality. The company would, therefore, need time of about one year for this purpose.

10. We are aware that it would take some time before we are eligible for a bank licence and we assure you that the company would do what may be required. You may kindly appreciate that we have complied with or taken substantive steps to comply with instructions/guidelines/directions of RBI whether issued to RNBCs in general or specifically issued to our company in order to address the concerns of RBI. The company desires to continue to serve the depositors and also continue to provide the livelihood to lakhs of its workers/agents, albeit within the contour of RBI regulations.

11. I as a guardian of Sahara India Pariwar am very much concerned for my lakhs of workers. For their livelihood, I humbly appeal to you that we all need your kind blessings.

Assuring you of our best cooperation at all times
Yours faithfully

---

13 March 2008.

For the first time, Sahara agreed to cap its deposit mobilization in March 2013. The following is an extract from a letter that Subrata Roy wrote to RBI executive director G Gopalakrishna:

i. RBI is already aware that the distinctive feature of our business model is that while the customer goes to a bank, the company goes to the doorstep of the customer. There is a scope for the type of savings schemes being successfully run by the company for the last two decades. The existing business model, saving products and the target group of depositors which includes persons of small means fulfil the objectives of financial inclusion (from supply side) being vigorously pursued by RBI and government in the recent years.

ii. It may be appreciated that the profiles of investors differ, depending on their expectations with respect to the rate of return, risk, liquidity and the servicing aspects. Depending on their preferences, they choose the institutions in whom they wish to invest their savings. In our case, the profile of the depositor requires the company to give utmost priority to the facilitations of small savings and collection of deposits from their doorstep. They are well aware that in the absence of the same, they would never be able to save and accumulate their small savings into larger deposits which will be handy for their rainy days. RBI may appreciate that running of daily deposit schemes is in the interest of small depositors and we are sure that as a regulator, RBI would always support/promote the institutions which are meeting the needs of the depositors.

iii. In view of the directions of RBI, our company has taken several steps despite several challenges and difficulties, inter alia, discontinuation of its high growth schemes of fixed deposits and recurring deposits nature, for moderating the growth in deposits since the beginning of the year 2006 and has been informing RBI about the same. The growth in ALD which was over 30% during the FY04-05 and FY05-06 was brought down to about 16% during the FY06-07 and further to about 2% during the six months ended September 2007. To achieve the above, the company adopted a calibrated approach as to cause minimum disturbance to the environment in which the company functions. It may further be appreciated by RBI that in the normal course, the ALD as on 31st March 2008, could have been above Rs 21,000 crore and would have easily crossed

Rs 25,000 crore by March 2009. It is due to the effective steps taken by the Company, keeping in mind the directions of RBI, that the company now expects its ALD as on 31st March 2008 to be around or even lower than its ALD of 31st March 2007. For further reduction in ALD, it is imperative for the company to consider a number of aspects, some of which are listed below:

a) Our field workers are regular workers and are permanently attached with the company for the last several years. They perform the duty of visiting the doorsteps of depositors everyday to promote the new business/collect money and earn their living. The company is obliged to ensure their livelihood for the future.

b) Ours is a very big organization having more than 1,500 establishments spread throughout the length and breadth of the country. There are lakhs and lakhs of workers who are earning their bread and butter for last 20 years. It is a onerous task to rehabilitate so many lakhs of workers.

c) It is of utmost importance for the company to maintain its efforts to encourage all the field workers to continue their services to the depositors. Any form of discouragement of the workers, including an impression that they would be out of job after some time or there would be substantial reduction in their income level, may adversely affect the quality of service even to the existing depositors and may lead to a highly chaotic condition at the service centres. We firmly believe that it is not the intention of RBI.

d) While for calibrating the earlier steps, the company stopped its high growth fixed deposit and recurring deposit schemes, RBI may also appreciate that any sudden stoppage of the daily deposit scheme or for that matter even abrupt reduction in opening of new accounts (for reduction in ALD/deposits) may create panic among small depositors/workers. In case, the company takes or is forced to take aggressive steps w.r.t reduction in ALD, it will create great amount of insecurity among all the stakeholders and shall become totally unmanageable for the company.

iv. As already informed to RBI, the company has also been exploring the possibility of its conversion into a bank. The company has already engaged Ernst & Young for a detailed study and for advising the company in this regard. The company is also in the process of seeking advice from one more internationally renowned consultancy firm. However, we further wish to submit that in some of our recent meetings with RBI, we were given an impression that before we submit any plan for conversion of the company into a bank, RBI desires that we concentrate and improve on certain of our systems and processes. We have accordingly not only taken several steps ourselves but also have taken the help of a professional agency for assisting us in this regard.

v. The company also proposes to strengthen its knowledge of the banking business and develop its manpower for the new challenges.

vi. In this regard, the company has already established a cell called "New Business Initiative Cell" which is headed by Mr. Ashwani Kumar Sharma, who recently retired as deputy managing director of State Bank of India.

vii. We are of the view that on a banking platform, the workers would not only be able to serve their large number of customers by providing them the daily deposit schemes, but also earn commission on such mobilization/collection as permitted under the banking system. It may be noted here as on 31st December 2007, the company had more than two crore folios under the daily deposit schemes itself. It is expected that under a banking platform, the workers would be able to further strengthen this business.

viii. Apart from seeking an advice for converting into a bank, we shall put the internationally renowned firm, which we propose to appoint, for exploration of other business opportunities which suit our field circumstances for maintaining/enhancing the livelihood of our workers. They shall definitely assess the geographical aspects of our branches and identify the centres which are critical for our proposed businesses.

ix. We are also in dialogue with some firms including a number of international companies with latest technology, to market non-financial products (including consumer durables) through our service centres as virtual shopping. For this purpose, comprehensive surveys and studies would be necessary and the tie up arrangements would take time.

x. All above surveys, studies, possibilities, trainings, other HR requirements, various conclusions, etc. are likely to take about one year's time.

Plan for phased reduction in ALD

At this juncture, we humbly submit that the company has taken and will continue to take all the possible steps to address the concerns of RBI with respect to its certain systems and processes. Further, as already assured, irrespective of the time being taken by IT authorities for refund of the income tax claims, the company would cover the gap in the directed investments in a time bound manner. In the meanwhile, in view of the directions of RBI, we submit that the Company should be able to bring down its ALD as given below:

By March 31, 2008 to less than Rs 18,100 crore

By April 30, 2008 to less than Rs 18,000 crore

By March 31, 2009 to less than Rs 16,800 crore

The Company would continue to monitor the progress of its efforts with respect to addressing all concerns of RBI and also the reduction in its ALD and, depending on all kinds of impact on its depositors/workers, will chalk out its future plan and submit the same to RBI within 12 months from now. We would also seek regulatory approvals from RBI as may be considered necessary so as to ensure that the depositors' interest and livelihood of the workers associated with the company are fully protected.

We have taken 20 years to nurture this company and created a niche for ourselves. The company and its workers request for your patronage and I, as their guardian, am very much concerned about their livelihood. I humbly appeal to you for your kind blessings and support.

Warm regards
Yours sincerely
Subrata Roy Sahara

This is a sample of Roy's desperate letter to Reddy, seeking his intervention in getting more time to put his house in order.

28 April 2008
Hon'ble Sir,

We wish to submit that the company has always made its sincere efforts to comply with the directions of RBI on a continuous basis. The sincere efforts made by the company in the light of several regulatory changes in the recent past have also been evidenced to RBI from time to time.

We had requested RBI to allow us one-year time in order to ensure that the action plan to be submitted by our company is realistic and balanced in the short-term and long-term taking into account all the RBI's point of views, depositors' interest along with the interest of workers.

We hereby once again request you to consider the plea made by us vide our letter dates 13 April 2008 for allowing us one-year time for preparation and submission of the action plan as desired by RBI. We reiterate that we, in the meantime, would make all possible and sincere efforts to address all the concerns of RBI.

With warm regards,
Yours sincerely,
Subrata Roy Sahara
(Managing Worker and Chairman)

This is an extract from a letter Roy wrote to the RBI outlining the company's plan to reduce deposits.

7 May 2008

Action Plan for Reduction in ALD in a phased manner and Alternate Business Model

In view of the rejection of our request for grant of adequate time, we were constrained to review our need for one year's time to prepare the action plan for the reasons explained in paragraph 5 but realize that we have to submit the said plan immediately.

As expected by RBI, we are, enclosing a chart, prepared by us under the given circumstances, showing the phased reduction in ALD in a manner that the outstanding ALD is repaid by March 31, 2015. We submit that the we propose to accept fresh deposits for the next six years in such a way that

(i) in the first year, we would accept fresh deposits for maturity of not more than six years,

(ii) in the second year for maturity of not more than five years,

(iii) in the third year for maturity of not more than four years and so on, and

(iv) in the sixth year, we would accept deposits for one year maturity only.

We are confident that RBI would appreciate that the smooth and orderly reduction in ALD alone may help us to achieve that there is minimal disruption in the market and in the working of the company. We also need to ensure that there is no harm to the depositors' interests or dissatisfaction and unrest amongst the lakhs of workers and employees. We look to RBI to grant its appropriate dispensations, cooperation and guidance for resolution of difficulties, roadblocks and obstacles, if any, as we make progress in implementation of the action plan; consider requisite regulatory approvals for alternative business model as and when we are ready; and for facilitating approvals for promoting other businesses under the jurisdiction of other regulatory bodies.

With warm regards
Yours sincerely

Here is Roy's letter to Reddy assuring him of compliance with all RBI norms, seeking certain relaxations and his blessings on Sahara's way to become a bank.

19 January 2008
Respected Sir,

Salient measures taken by the company for addressing matter raised by RBI and request for certain forebearances

1. I have apprised, in details, Shri V. Leeladhar, hon'ble deputy foverner, RBI of the present status with respect to alternative business model and KYC exercise of old as well as new deposit accounts. We humbly submit that we have complied with or taken substantive steps to comply with the instructions/guidelines/ directions of RBI whether issued to RNBCs in general or specifically issued to our company in order to address the concerns of RBI. With respect to matching of inflow to outflow of deposits as well as cap on deposits, reduction in gap between directed investments actually held and required to be held and provisioning as well as disclosures in balance sheet of March 31, 2007 itself.

2. We have already engaged E&Y for an advice on conversion of our company to a bank. I submit that there is a great scope for daily deposit schemes being run by our company for the past two decades and the existing business model, savings products and the target group of depositors which includes persons of small means fulfill the objectives of financial inclusion (from supply side) being vigorously pursued by the government in the recent years. We can run these schemes, as a bank also when permitted. We assure you that the company would do what is required. In order to eradicate the deficiencies and gaps in totality and to upgrade our systems as may be expected by RBI, we are taking advice of E&Y. The company desires to continue to serve the depositors and also continue to provide the livelihood to lakhs of its workers/agents, albeit within the contours of RBI regulations.

3. I as a guardian of Sahara India Pariwar am very much concerned for my lakhs of workers. For their livelihood, I humbly appeal to you that we all need your kind blessings.

Thanking you and assuring you of our fullest cooperation at all times.

With warm personal regards,
Yours sincerely,
Subrata Roy Sahara

Sahara seeks a year's time to submit its action plan, and the RBI rejects it.

28 April 2008
Dear Sir,

We acknowledge your letter dated April 28, 2008 addressed to the governor seeking one year's time for submission of an action plan by the company to address the RBI's concerns.

2. In this regard we would like to inform you that our earlier communication dated March 31, 2008 conveyed to the company, followed a careful evaluation of all facets of the functioning of the company and the depositors' interest.

3. The bank expresses its inability to grant any further time. We seek company's compliance with the instructions conveyed in our letter No.DBNS.CO.RNBC.No.6798/04.06.001/2007-08 dated March 31, 2008 (copy of which is enclosed for your ready reference).

Please acknowledge the receipt of this communication.

Yours Faithfully,
G. Gopalakrishna

The following extract shows minutes of the crucial 20 May 2008 meeting, which the RBI held after issuing the show cause notice and before clamping down the prohibitory order on SIFCL. Some background:

Pursuant to the action plan submitted by the company on 7 May 2008, the RBI issued to the company a show cause notice dated 9 May 2008. The company felt that while the formal reply to the show cause notice may be sent within the time granted by the RBI, its intentions may not have been appropriately captured in the last letter, and as such there was a need for clarifying:

i) That Sahara would exit from the RNBC business at the end of the plan; and

ii) The reasons as to why the action plan had been submitted for 6+1 year, as against the earlier RBI advice that the action plan should be for three years.

Accordingly, the company vide its letter dated 15th May gave plausible clarifications to the above and also sought a meeting with the hon'ble deputy governor to bridge the gap between the requirements of the RBI and the submissions made by the company. RBI vide its letter dated 15 May 2008 granted the meeting to the company on 20 May 2008 at 3pm.

Minutes of the meeting held at the 15th Floor Conference Room No.1, at the Central Office Building, RBI, Mumbai at 3pm.

Participants:

Reserve Bank of India –
Mr. G. Gopalakrishna Executive Director
Mr. P. Krishnamurthy CGM, DNBS
Mr. G. S. Hegde Legal Advisor,
Mrs Reena Bannerji, Dy. General Manager, DNBS

Sahara India Financial Corp. Ltd –
Hon'ble Saharasri ji (HSS)
Mr. Pallav Kumar Agarwal

Mr. Gopalakrishna (ED, RBI) welcomed Sahara representatives and invited them to make their submissions. HSS conveyed that the as directed by RBI, the company will make its written submissions dealing with all the issues raised by RBI. However, the purpose of seeking this meeting was to bridge the gap between requirements of RBI and the submissions made by the company vide its letter dated 7th May, 2008. (The) ED explained that the meeting has been granted to the company pursuant to show cause notice issued by RBI to the company and the company is free to make its submissions, which will be duly recorded by the RBI.

HSS restated the purpose of seeking this meeting and requested RBI for its guidance in the matter so as to bridge the gap. HSS mentioned that the company has submitted an action plan for 6+1 working years keeping in mind his size of the company and lakhs of worker who are dependent for their livelihood on the company. He mentioned that as compared to the other RNBC, Sahara's size in terms of number of branches and workers is at least 10 times, and in terms of deposits about four to five times. He requested RBI to consider the same while looking at the action plan submitted by the company. HSS mentioned that nevertheless he looks forward to the advice of RBI in the matter. (The) ED mentioned that RBI has no advice to give in the matter and, if any, the same has already been conveyed to the company vide the letters as annexed with the show cause notice. He once again reiterated that RBI will listen to the submissions made by the company and record the same.

Mr. Pallav Kumar Agarwal reiterated that the limited purpose of seeking this meeting was to bridge the gap between the requirements of RBI and the submissions made by the company. He submitted that the company has always complied with the directions/advices of

RBI and has never in the past or in the future with any intentions of defying any of the RBI directions/advices of RBI. He submitted that at times when company has faced difficulties in fulfilling any of the advices/directions, the company has made reasoned representations but if the same have not been acceded to by RBI, the company has made sincere efforts to comply with the same.

He further submitted that the idea behind giving an action plan for 6+1 year was to ensure that while the company achieves the objective of phased reduction, there is minimal disturbance in the environment in which the company functions. Any disturbance in the area of its operations will not only affect the company adversely but will also not be in the interest of depositors. In this background, the company requests RBI to guide it in the matter.

(The) CGM *explained that the meeting has been granted to the company as part of the process so as to give the company an opportunity to supplement what it submits in writing. He explained that whatever submissions are being made by the company, are being recorded and as and when the company makes its written submissions,* RBI *would take a note of the company's oral submissions along with the written submission.* ED *conveyed that since an opportunity has already been given to the company, giving another opportunity may not be possible. He pointed out as mentioned in their letter dated* 15th May, 2008, *any further submissions pursuant to this meeting also have to submitted by the* Company *by* 26th *of* May, 2008 *only.*

HSS *enquired as to whether it was possible to seek the guidance of* RBI *in any manner, may be by seeking another informal meeting,* CGM *replied in the negative and mentioned that any additional meeting at this stage may not be possible.*

Since RBI was not willing to give any guidance on the issue of bridging the gap between requirements of RBI and the submissions made by the company, the meeting concluded at 3.25 PM with HSS conveying his thanks to the RBI team for giving the company the opportunity for the meeting.

A desperate Roy wrote to Prime Minister Manmohan Singh, as a last resort, to stop the RBI from closing Sahara's RNBC business.

The following are some excerpts.

26 May 2008
Dr Manmohan Singh Ji,
Hon'ble Prime Minister
Government of India
New Delhi
Hon'ble Sir,

Request for intervention for protection of interest of lakhs of workers of Sahara India Financial Corp. Ltd – a residuary non-banking company.

Sahara India Financial Corp. Ltd has been functioning since 1987 as a residuary non-banking company, a sub-set of an NBFC, under the regulations of Reserve Bank of India. Sahara has played a significant role for the past two decades in the growth of financial services among the under-banked segments. A majority of company's deposit service centres are located in rural and semi-urban areas. It may be emphasized here that about 97% of the deposit accounts (about 76% in terms of aggregate liabilities to depositors) had deposit balance of less than Rs20,000. Thus, the company is basically serving masses of small means by collection of deposits as less as Re 1 per day at their door steps, for meeting their future needs and economic well-being.

...

In their letter dated May 9, 2008, RBI has served a show cause notice on our company for prohibiting the company from acceptance of deposits. Such an action against the company threatens the interest of lakhs of workers and crores of depositors and may cause a run on the company by seeking preferential repayment of the existing deposits.

...

RBI has asked us to reply to the show cause notice by June 2, 2008. The company shall be submitting a reasoned reply and is hopeful that the show cause notice is satisfied on the merits of the compliances and submissions. However, if RBI proceeds to issue the prohibitory orders against our company, we would be facing a logjam for relief and a very serious problem, and we feel that the same would definitely not be in the interest of the depositors and the workers of the company in particular and for the environment in general. In these circumstances, we are forced to approach your honour and humbly appeal to you for your kind intervention so that RBI may appreciate our submission and may please allow us a reasonable time (we are agreeable for less than 6+1 year also but it can actually be arrived by mutual discussions).

We submit that the company is fully solvent and there has never been any issue related to liquidity of the company or intention of the company to comply with the RBI regulations to the best extent feasible and possible. We may also state that we have never defied any order of the RBI. We are just seeking reasonable time for an orderly and honourable exit from the RNBC business...

Sir, we are sure that you would spare a few moments out of your very busy schedule and grant us a urgent audience.

Yours obediently

Finally, the RBI issued the prohibitory notice on 4 June 2008, trigger a petition in Allahabad High Court by Sahara and a special leave petition by the RBI at the Supreme Court and ultimately closure of the RNBC.

ORDER

... on being satisfied that to protect the interests of depositors and in public interest, it is necessary and expedient so to do, in exercise of the powers vested in RBI under Sections 45K and 45 MB(1) of RBI Act, 1934, RBI hereby passes the following order.

(i) SIFCL is hereby prohibited with immediate effect from accepting any deposit in whatsoever manner including instalments under any running daily deposit or other recurring deposit schemes or otherwise, either from its existing depositors or new depositors whether by way of renewal or otherwise

(ii) SIFCL shall repay the deposits as and when they mature

(iii) SIFCL shall not treat non-payment of instalments under any running daily deposit or other recurring deposit schemes by depositors after the date of this order, as a default by depositor

and SIFCL shall be liable to pay the agreed rate of interest on the amounts actually held by it for the entire term of the deposit as if there was no default.

(iv) SIFCL shall lodge all securities held in its custody with the designated bank for custody

(v) SIFCL subject to (i) (ii) (iii) above shall strictly comply with the requirements of all the applicable provisions of the RBI Act, the directions, guidelines, instructions and circulars issued by RBI there-under from time to time until such time as all the deposits are repaid with interest in full. For repaying the depositors, SIFCL shall first apply its income and investments other than the investments it is required to maintain under paragraph 6 of RNBC Directions. SIFCL shall ensure that the investments directed in paragraph 6 of RNBC Directions are maintained in respect of it aggregate liability to depositors both towards principal and interest.

(vi) SIFCL shall forthwith notify all its agents and employees that is has been prohibited from accepting deposits and shall paste a copy of the operative portion of this Order in a conspicuous place at each of its branches and offices.

(vii) SIFCL shall, without prejudice to the above, be entitled to carry on its other business activities in accordance with law.

A copy of this order be served on SIFCL with instructions to comply with this order. The attention of SIFCL shall be drawn to the provisions of Section 58B and 58C of the RBI Act as to the consequences of not complying with this order.

For the benefit of the members of the depositors and the public, this order shall be given reasonable publicity.

(G. Gopalakrishna)
Executive Director
June 4, 2008

The following is one letter that SK Roy wrote to the Peerless depositors at the height of crisis in Peerless.

Peerless Bhavan
3 Esplanade East
Calcutta- 700 069
MDS-SPL-6/SKR/86 *28 April, 1986*
Dear Shareholder,

You must be aware that in view of the enactment of the Prize Chit & Money Circulation Schemes (Banning) Act 1978, (the 'Act'), the government of West Bengal and others had served a notice on the company in 1979 stating that the business carried on by the company comes under the purview of the Act and directed the company to wind up its business. The company had filed a writ application before the Hon'ble High Court at Calcutta challenging the applicability of the Act. The Hon'ble court was pleased to grant an interim injunction restraining the respondents from giving effect to the impugned notice and from enforcing the said notification till disposal of the rule. The writ application came up for hearing and has been decided against the company by an order passed by the Hon'ble court on 14 March 1986.

The said judgment, however, does not affect the interest of the certificate- holders of the company in any way because the contractual liability of the company to its certificate-holders are fully covered by fixed deposits with nationalised banks and government securities amounting to more than Rs 600 crore.

The company has filed an appeal before the division bench of the said Hon'ble court. The hearing the said appeal has been concluded and the judgment of the bench is awaited.

In this connection, the board of directors regrets to inform you that in view of the said judgment the normal work of the company has been disrupted to a great extent. The board, however, assures you that it will put all-out efforts to restore normalcy depending on the judgment of the appeal.

Thanking you,
Yours faithfully
SK Roy
Whole Time Director

ANNEXURE III

TIME LINE

PEERLESS & RBI – COURT BY COURT

1932: On 25th October, Radhashyam Roy, 33, a school teacher and an insurance agent, along with close friend Kali Kumar Chatterjee and an actuary AT Pal, sets up Peerless Insurance Co. Ltd with a capital of ₹300 in Narayangang, Bangladesh.

1935: Headquarters of Peerless Insurance shifts to Kolkata.

1956: Peerless Insurance is among 245 insurance companies and provident societies that are merged with the state-run Life Insurance Corp. of India.

Peerless General Insurance and Investment Co. Ltd is floated. It starts issuing welfare certificates under Peerless Social Welfare Scheme.

1960: Radhashyam Roy dies; his eldest son Bhudeb Kanti Roy takes over.

1970: Peerless's first office outside Kolkata opens in Siliguri, in northern Bengal.

1972: Peerless starts offering life insurance to depositors without any extra cost.

1974: Peerless General Insurance and Investment Co. Ltd becomes Peerless General Finance and Investment Co. Ltd.

1975: Welfare certificates are sold to non-resident Indians in the UK, the US and Canada.

1978: Industries minister George Fernandes opens the Delhi branch of Peerless at Connaught Place.

Parliament passes the Prize Chit and Money Circulation (Banning Act), which becomes effective from December.

1979: The Reserve Bank of India says Peerless schemes are prize chit schemes and should be closed. In September, Peerless files a writ petition in the Calcutta High Court claiming the Act did not apply to its business. The court rules in favour of Peerless. The RBI moves Supreme Court appealing against the high court judgment.

1982: Peerless celebrates its golden jubilee with 4,00,000 agents and field officers and 17 million customers.

1987: Supreme Court observes that Peerless schemes are outside the ambit of the prize chit law, but allows the RBI to take steps to regulate such schemes "to prevent exploitation of ignorant subscribers".

RBI issues Residuary Non-Banking Companies (Reserve Bank) Directions on 15th May. No RNBC is allowed to take deposits for less than one year and more than ten years and the minimum rate of return is fixed at 10% per annum for ten-year deposits. The RBI makes it clear that no RNBC can forfeit any amount deposited.

Timex General Finance & Investment Co. Ltd files a writ petition in the Calcutta High Court, challenging the RBI's directives.

1990: Peerless gets itself impleaded in the case as a respondent in the Timex writ petition.

A division bench of the Calcutta High Court disposes of this case and tells the RBI to modify its directions. The RBI challenges the high court order at the Supreme Court.

1992: Supreme Court holds that the RBI's directives are legally valid.

1993: The RBI amends its 1987 directions and says no RNBC can levy processing or maintenance charges from any depositor. It, however, allows RNBCs to charge a one-time fee of up to ₹10 towards costs for issuing brochures and application form and servicing depositors' account. The maximum period for deposits is reduced from 120 months to 84 months.

Peerless files a writ petition in the Calcutta High Court challenging these decisions.

1995: The high court upholds the RBI's action on reducing the maximum maturity period of deposits, but does not allow it to cut commissions. The RBI moves the Supreme Court.

1996: Supreme Court dismisses Peerless's writ petition. Peerless recasts the board – DN Ghosh joins as chairman and SM Datta as director. There is ₹1,400 crore in Peerless's balance sheet after it reverse incomes as liabilities. The company has 40 million depositors.

1997: Former State Bank of India chairman Dipankar Basu joins the Peerless board.

2003: Peerless turns the corner, and its networth becomes positive.

2006: Ghosh steps down as chairman and Basu elevated to the post.

2007: The RBI asks Peerless to stop taking fresh deposits from March 2011 onwards and to close its RNBC business by 2015.

SAHARA: RBI – UNFOLDING DRAMA

15 May 1987: The RBI issues Residuary Non-Banking Companies (Reserve Bank) Directions 1987.

7 August 1987: Sahara group incorporates Sahara India Savings & Investment Corp. Ltd.

23 November 1994: The company changes name to Sahara India Financial Corp. Ltd.

3 December 1998: The RBI gives its registration to SIFCL as an RNBC.

6 September 2003: YV Reddy takes over as RBI governor, for five years.

22 June 2004: The RBI issues investment norms for RNBCs, phasing out their discretionary investments completely by June 2006. Till now, RNBCs are permitted to invest not more than 20% of their deposits or ten times the net-owned fund of the company, whichever is less, in any manner they wish to as per the approval of the board.

31 March 2008: The RBI writes to Sahara asking it to reduce its deposit liability from ₹18,045 crore on 31st March to ₹16,800 by 30th April.

28 April 2008: Roy writes to Reddy, seeking one year to submit an action plan on changing Sahara's business model.

The RBI says no to the proposal one more time.

2 May 2008: Roy writes to the RBI saying he will send a status report on compliance by 7th May.

7 May 2008: Roy writes to the RBI saying deposits will come down to ₹16,800 by Novmber-December 2008 and Sahara will exit the RNBC business by 31 March 2015.

9 May 2008: The RBI issues show cause notice to SIFCL. giving it time till 26th May to say why it should not be prohibited from accepting deposits. The show cause note lists some 28 violations by Sahara.

15 May 2008: Roy writes to RBI deputy governor Leeladhar saying Sahara will exit the RNBC activities and not defy any of the directions of the RBI.

RBI decides to give Sahara a personal hearing on 20th May.

20 May 2008: At 3pm, the RBI gives Sahara a hearing.

22 May 2008: Sahara seeks a week's time from 26th May till 2nd June to respond to the show cause notice.

23 May 2008: The RBI gives a week's time to Sahara.

26 May 2008: Roy writes to Prime Minister Manmohan Singh seeking his intervention.

2 June 2008: Sahara responds to the show cause notice; Roy writes to RBI executive director Gopalakrishna imploring him to give a personal hearing and drop the proceedings.

4 June 2008: The RBI issues the prohibitory order, barring Sahara from taking fresh deposits.

Late that evening, the SIFCL board passes a resolution authorizing director Srivastava to take legal action against the regulator's move.

5 June 2008: Sahara moves the vacation court at Lucknow for interim relief. UK Dhaon and Shabihul Hasnain of the bench stay the RBI directive and order to list the petition in the last week of July for hearing.

6 June 2008: The RBI moves a special leave petition at Supreme Court for an urgent order against the Allahabad High Court's stay.

9 June 2008: Arijit Pasayat and PP Naolekar of Supreme Court say the principle of natural justice has been followed and ask the RBI to give another hearing to Sahara.

12 & 16 June 2008: Over two days, the RBI meets Roy.

17 June 2008: An RBI release says Sahara India Financial Corp. Ltd is directed not to accept any new deposit that matures beyond 30 June 2011, and to stop accepting installments of existing deposit accounts from that date.

Sahara also offers to reconstitute the board of directors of SIFCL within 30 days

11 July 2008: Sahara releases a "fact sheet" giving SIFCL's unaudited financial results as of 30 June 2008 – the first time in the group's history. The fact sheet pegs the company's deposit and interest liability in June 2008 at ₹17,513 crore spread over 39.4 million accounts.

13 August 2008: The reconstituted board with 50% independent directors of RBI's choice meets.

31 August 2008: Sahara replaces its existing auditor by an audit firm approved by the RBI at its annual general meeting.

SAHARA: SEBI – THE STORY NOT OVER YET

30 September 2009: Sahara moves Sebi with a draft prospectus for Sahara Prime City Ltd's initial public offering.

25 December 2009: Sebi receives a complaint from Professional Group for Investor Protection, alleging that Sahara India Real Estate Corp. Ltd (SIRECL) was issuing optionally fully convertible bonds (OFCDs) to investors throughout the country for many months and it was not disclosed in the draft prospectus.

12 May 2010: Sebi asks SIRECL and Sahara Housing Investment Corp. Ltd (SHICL) for details of the OFCDs issued by them such as the number of applications received, details of the red herring prospectus filed by them with the Registrar of Companies etc.

24 & 26 May 2010: Sahara responds without providing details sought by Sebi. The firms say the OFCDs were issued in compliance with provisions of the Companies Act and that they were not listed entities and their securities were not traded in any of the stock exchanges in India or abroad.

24 November 2010: Sebi bars two Sahara companies, SIRECL and SHICL, from raising funds from retail investors.

26 November 2010: Sahara publishes advertisements in newspapers, saying it is astonished by Sebi's irresponsible and wrongful ex parte order.

29 November 2010: Sahara moves the Lucknow bench of Allahabad High Court against Sebi order.

13 December 2010: The Lucknow bench of the Allahabad High Court stays Sebi order.

4 January 2011: Sebi moves the Supreme Court against the Allahabad High Court stay order. The apex court asks Sahara to give details of its OFCD investors.

7 January 2011: Sebi issues public notice against two Sahara firms raising money from investors through OFCDs without its approval. The public notice says the investors in SIRECL and SHICL bonds should take investment decisions at their own risk. The Sebi notice says it "will not be able to provide redress to any investor on any complaint" in connection with the securities.

18 January 2011: The RBI too issues advertisements in newspapers, saying it doesn't guarantee repayment of deposits taken by any company in the Sahara group.

18 March 2011: Sahara gives details of OFCD investors to Sebi.

7 April 2011: The Lucknow bench of the Allahabad High Court vacates the stay on Sebi order.

23 June 2011: Sebi orders Sahara to immediately refund ₹4,843 crore raised through OFCDs with 15% interest per annum from the date of receipt of money till the date of such repayment. The order also restrains Subrata Roy, Sahara and directors of the two firms – Vandana Bharrgava, Ravi Shankar Dubey and Ashok Roy Choudhary – from associating "with any listed public company and any public company which intends to raise money from the public" till the repayments are completed.

24 June 2011: Sahara group criticizes Sebi for making an order against two group companies public and accuses the regulator of resorting to "a media trial in a sub judice case".

27 June 2011: Sahara moves the Supreme Court against Sebi order for refund of money to investors.

15 July 2011: The Supreme Court stays Sebi order on refunds to depositors, directs Securities Appellate Tribunal (SAT) to decide the question of OFCDs within three months.

17 August 2011: Sahara moves SAT challenging Sebi's jurisdiction over OFCDs.

30 August 2011: Sahara India Financial Corp. Ltd decides to wind up deposits and pay ₹9,000 crore to its customers by December, about four years before a deadline set by the central bank.

8 September 2011: SAT asks SIRECL and SHICL to file an affidavit, detailing the total money raised through the OFCDs

18 October 2011: SAT upholds Sebi order and directs two Sahara firms to refund ₹24,029 crore within six weeks to 29.6 million investors who had subscribed to its OFCDs.

11 November 2011: Sahara challenges SAT order in the Supreme Court.

9 January 2012: Supreme Court admits Sahara's pleas, stays SAT order.

31 August 2012: The Supreme Court upholds the SAT order, orders refund of ₹24,029 crore to 29.6 million Sahara investors.

5 October 2012: Sahara files a review petition in the Supreme Court. It claims it sent a truckload of documentation to Sebi within the ten-day deadline, but Sebi did not accept it as the documents arrived after office hours on the tenth day.

19 October 2012: Sebi approaches the Supreme Court bench headed by justice KS Radhakrishnan, alleging non-compliance by Sahara in handing over the documents related to about 30 million of OFCD investors. Supreme Court asks

Sebi to take action against the two companies.

24 October 2012: Sebi floats a multi-crore tender, inviting registry and transfer agents, who can handle data processing work for an estimated 300 million application forms of nearly 30 million beneficiaries.

2 November 2012: Sebi files contempt petition against Sahara in the Supreme Court for not following the 31st August order.

27 November 2012: Sahara moves SAT against Sebi's refusal to accept documents.

29 November 2012: SAT dismisses Sahara's appeal against Sebi.

26 November 2012: Sebi asks OFCD investors not to yield to pressure by Sahara agents and shift investments to Sahara Q shop. "Don't be forced, Don't be misguided," and "hold on to the original documents relating to the investments in bonds and to produce the same to sebi when called for," says Sebi advisory.

30 November 2012: The deadline for completion of refunds ends. Sahara approaches the Supreme Court to appeal against the SAT order asking for more time to refund investors.

5 December 2012: A Supreme Court bench, headed by justice Altamas Kabir, grants Sahara time up to February 2013 to make the full repayment in three instalments (₹5,120 crore immediately, ₹10,000 crore by first week of January and the remaining by first week of February).

6 December 2012: Sahara deposits ₹5,120 crore.

8 January 2013: The Supreme Court dismisses Sahara's October review petition on 31st August order.

6 February 2013: The Supreme Court says Sebi is free to freeze the accounts and seize properties of SIRECL and SHICL for defying court orders by not refunding ₹24,000 crore to investors. The apex court was hearing a contempt petition filed by Sebi in November against the two firms.

13 February 2013: Sebi orders banks to freeze accounts of two Sahara firms, their promoters and directors.

22 February 2013: Sebi cautions investors, public against dealings with Sahara in a public notice.

6 March 2013: Roy moves SAT against Sebi's order freezing his bank accounts and attaching his personal assets.

8 March 2013: Sahara moves Allahabad High Court against Sebi's attachment order.

12 March 2013: SAT denies interim relief to Roy; adjourns case hearing to 23rd March.

15 March 2013: Sebi files plea in the Supreme Court for detention of Subrata Roy and two other directors.

17 March 2013: Subrata Roy challenges Sebi chairman UK Sinha to a live debate on a television channel to present his version of the on-going dispute through an advertisement.

22 March 2013: In a show of strength, Roy invites Bollywood stars, politicians and cricketers at his granddaughter's *annaprasanam* ceremony in Delhi.

26 March 2013: Sebi summons Roy and three Sahara directors and asks them to submit details of their assets and financial holdings by 10th April.

10 April 2013: Roy appears before Sebi's fulltime director Prashant Saran.

22 April 2013: The Supreme Court accuses Sahara of "manipulating courts" by approaching different fora for relief in the OFCD case.

2 May 2013: Supreme Court admits Sebi petition seeking to club all the cases related to the two Sahara group firms in the OFCD case.

6 May 2013: Sahara makes it into the *Guinness World Records* as over 100,000 of its employees gathered in a stadium in Lucknow to sing the national anthem.

8 May 2013: The apex court gives Sebi the power to refund money only to genuine bond investors and directs Sebi not to sell properties of Sahara group which have been attached so far.

17 July 2013: The Supreme Court pulls up the Sahara group for not refunding ₹24,000 crore to bond investors. The apex court says it will summon Subrata Roy and other directors of the two Sahara firms if the direction is not complied with.

19 July 2013: Sahara issues an advertisement in national news papers saying Sebi chairman has made an "irresponsible and incorrect" statement on Sahara's OFCD issue and the market regulator's "agenda" is to "harm" Sahara through "media trial". It also puts up on its website legal experts' comments, saying Sebi has no jurisdiction over the OFCDs.

24 July 2013: Supreme Court issues contempt notices to two Sahara firms for not complying with its order of ₹19,000 crore refund to OFCD investors through Sebi.

4 October 2013: Supreme Court asks two Sahara firms – SIRECL and SHICL – whether they are prepared to give a bank guarantee for ₹20,000 crore.

28 October 2013: Supreme Court directs the two Sahara firms to make available to Sebi title deeds of property worth ₹20,000 crore within three weeks. The court says all the alleged offenders, including Subrata Roy and three directors, will be refrained from leaving the country without the court's permission if they fail to obey its latest order.

21 November 2013: Supreme Court places restrictions on the Sahara group's sale of moveable and immoveable property and bars Subrata Roy from leaving the country. It comes down heavily on the group after finding that it has not complied with the court's October order to file title deeds of properties worth ₹20,000 crore with Sebi.

26 November 2013: Sahara publishes an advertisement in national newspapers saying, "...In order to save time and to conclude the matter amicably at the earliest, we would be submitting title deeds relating to... properties of Sahara aggregating ₹20,000 crore, instead of debating any further on the issue raised."

9 January 2014: Supreme Court directs Sahara Group to reveal the source of the ₹22,885 crore that has been paid to the OFCD investors. The apex court warns Sahara of an inquiry by the CBI and the Registrar of Companies in case it fails to reveal the source of funds.

28 January 2014: Supreme Court refuses to relax its order restraining Subrata Roy from going abroad till his company furnishes details of the refund of ₹22,885 crore made to the investors. The apex court also asks the Sahara group to furnish bank statements and ledger records to show the source of the money paid to investors.

1 February 2014: Sahara releases advertisements in national newspapers to hire over 56,000 new employees this year, along with investments to the tune of nearly ₹32,400 crore.

11 February 2014: Supreme Court raises questions on how Sahara transacted thousands of crores in cash with its sister firms for purportedly refunding ₹20,000 crore to its investors after Sebi alleged that no bank statement was furnished by the group to show the money trail. A bench of justices KS Radhakrishnan and JS Khehar asks Sebi to find out whether the Company Law and the RBI guidelines allow cash transactions of such a large amount of money.

20 February 2014: Supreme Court orders the Sahara group chief Subrata Roy to be personally present in court on 26th February for the failure of his group companies to return money to OFCDs. A bench of Justices KS Radhakrishnan and JS Khehar also directs three other directors of Sahara's real estate companies to be present in the court.

26 February 2014: Subrata Roy does not appear at Supreme Court, citing his mother's illness. The court issues a non-bailable warrant against Subrata Roy.

28 February 2014: Subrata Roy arrested in Lucknow after he surrenders to the polics; to be kept in police custody till 4th March.

4 March 2014: Supreme Court sends Roy and two other directors of Sahara Group to Tihar jail as the judges are not convinced about Roy's plans to refund ₹20,000 crore to OFCD investors. Roy is to be kept in judicial custody until 11th March though he can ask for an earlier hearing if he is ready with a concrete proposal to refun the money.

7 March 2014: Sahara submits a new proposal but the apex court rejects it. Roy remains in judicial custody.

LIST OF PEOPLE

A

Abdullah, Farooq
Abraham, KM
Achuthan, A
Achuthan, C
Agarwal, BN
Agarwal, Piyush Kumar
Agarwal, Pallav
Agarwal, Sanjay
Agarwal, Sekhar
Ahmadi, AH
Alexander, PC
Ambani, Anil
Ambani, Dhirubhai
Ambani, Mukesh
Andhyarujina, TR
Ashwin, R
Azharuddin, Mohammed

B

Babbar, Raj
Bachchan, Amitabh
Bachchan, Abhishek
Bachchan, Jaya
Bagchi, Debi Prasad
Bali, NP
Bandurkar, Kalavati
Banerjee, Reena
Basu, Dipankar
Basu, Jyoti
Bhagat, Bali Ram
Bhargava, Ashok K
Bharrgava, Vandana
Bhatnagar, KS
Bhatnagar, Shekhar
Bhave, CB
Bhide, MG
Bhoria, JB
Bhushan, Shanti
Birla Aditya
Biswas, Anil
Boon, Ngiam Tong
Bansali, Chain Roop

C

Chakrabortti, Amal Chandra
Chandrasekhar, KM
Chatterjee, Ajit Kumar
Chatterjee, Kali Kumar
Chatterjee, Somnath
Chaturvedi, BV
Chaudhary, Ashok Roy
Chidambaram, P
Chaudhary, Kumkum Roy
Chandra, Prashant
Chiranjeevi
Chitale, Mukund Manohar
Chopra, Priyanka
Chowdhary, JP
Clarke, Michael

D

Dalmia, Jagmohan
Dasgupta, Asim

LIST OF INSTITUTIONS

A

Aditya Birla More
Aditya Birla Retail Ltd
All India Congress Committee
All India Field Officers Association
Allahabad High Court
Air India
Amarchand & Mangaldas & Suresh A Shroff & Co
Ambuja Realty Group
Ananda Bazar Patrika
Apple Inc.
Asian Development Bank
Athena Legal
Axis Bank Ltd

B

Bahujan Samaj Party
Balaji Telefilms Ltd
Bank of Baroda
Bank of Maharashtra
Barclays PLC
Batra Hospitality Pvt Ltd
Bharat Bhari Udyog Nigam Ltd
Bhartiya Janata Party
Bloomberg
BM Union High School
Board for Financial Supervision
Board of Control for Cricket in India
Booz & Co
BSE Ltd
Burn Standard Co. Ltd
Business Standard

C

Calcutta High Court
Calcutta Stock Exchange
Centaur Airport Hotel
Chaturvedi and Co.
Chloride (India) Ltd
Citigroup
CM Angle Bengali Intermediate College
Cobrapost
Company Law Department
Confederation of Indian Industry
Controller of Insurance
Corporation Bank
CRB Capital Markets Ltd

D

Daiwa Securities SMBC India Pvt Ltd
Delhi Stock Exchange
Delhi Wave Riders
Deloitte
Development Credit Bank Ltd
DS Shukla & Co.

V

W

LIST OF ABBREVIATIONS

A

ALD: Aggregate liability to depositors

B

BCCL: Bennett Coleman and Co. Ltd

BFS: Board for Financial Supervision

BCCI: Board of Control for Cricket in India

C

CGM: Chief general manager

CIS: Collective investment schemes

CVC: Chief Vigilance Commissioner

CEO: Chief Executive Officer

D

DIGC: Deposit Insurance and Credit Guarantee Corp.

DNBS: Department of non banking supervision

DRPH: Draft Red Herring Prospectus

DP: Depository participant

DCS: Daily collection sheet

E

ED: Executive director

EPS: Earnings per share

EPFO: Employees' Provident Fund Organization

E&Y: Ernst & Young

F

FCD: Fully convertible debentures

FDR: Fixed deposit receipts

FII: Foreign institutional investors

FMCG: Fast moving consumer good

FSLRC: Financial Sector Legislative Reforms Commission

FERA: Foreign Exchange Regulation Act

FY: Fiscal year

FSDC: Financial Stability and Development Council

H

HDFC: Housing Development Finance Corp.

I

ICAI: Institute of Chartered Accountants of India

IMG-TWI: International Management Group - Trans World International

IPL: Indian Premier League

IPO: Initial public offer

IAS: Indian Administrative Service

K

KPMG: Klynveld Peat Marvick Goerdeler

KYC: Know your customer

L

LIC: Life Insurance Corporation

M

MCA: Ministry of Corporate Affairs

MGP: Modernising government programme

MTM: Mark to market

N

NABARD: National Bank for Agriculture & Rural Development

NBFC: Non banking finance company

NCC: National Cadet Corp.

NFL: Nagarjuna Finance Ltd

NISM: National Institute of Securities Management

NOC: No objection certificate

NPA: Non-performing assets

NSE: National Stock Exchange

O

OFCD: Optionally fully convertible debenture

P

PR: Public relations

R

RBI: Reserve Bank of India

RNBC: Residuary non-banking company

RTI: Right to Information Act

S

SAT: Securities Appellate Tribunal

SHCIL: Stock Holding Corp. of India Ltd

SLP: Special leave petition

SICCL: Sahara India Commercial Corp. Ltd

SIRECL: Sahara India Real Estate Corp. Ltd

SHICL: Sahara Housing Investment Corp. Ltd

SEBI: Securities and Exchange Board of India

SIFCL: Sahara India Financial Corp. Ltd

SC: Supreme Court

U

UP: Uttar Pradesh

ULIP: Unit linked insurance plan

ABOUT THE AUTHOR

Tamal Bandyopadhyay, a Deputy Managing Editor of *Mint*, is one of the most respected business journalists in India. His weekly column, "Banker's Trust", every Monday in *Mint*, is widely read for its deep insight into the world of finance and its unerring ability to anticipate major policy moves. His frequent blog "Banker's Trust Real Time" analyzes major developments in the financial sector.

Tamal has kept a close watch on the financial sector over one and a half decades and has had a ringside view of the enormous changes in Indian finance and banking over this period.

His first book, *A Bank for the Buck*, released by P Chidambaram in November 2012, has been a non-fiction best seller.

PRAISE FOR TAMAL BANDYOPADHYAY'S PREVIOUS BOOK:

A BANK FOR THE BUCK

In a period of great financial illiteracy, it's refreshing to have a book written by somebody very literate about matters relating to finance.

– Finance Minister P Chidambaram

In terms of writing India's economic, or business, history, this is a relatively new, unexplored and rare genre.

– *Business Standard*

Tamal... has... converted journalistic weakness into strength and told the story of the HDFC Bank in fascinating... detail.

– *The Hindu Business Line*

Bandyopadhyay says the bank is 'doing ordinary things, the extraordinary way'. The same can be said of his narrative as well.

– *Business World*

It isn't everybody who can take the bare bones of a real life situation and people it with events and personalities... Bandyopadhyay manages that... successfully.

– *Business India*

The book will be a must-read for any business school student for their case studies...

– *Outlook Business*

Tamal's book is a great read and refreshing.

– *Business Today*

A Bank for the Buck... celebrates not only Indian enterprise but also the environment that allowed it to flourish .

– *Hindustan Times*

The book has many colourful vignettes that come alive in the engaging style used by Tamal.

– *The Hindu*

Tamal Bandyopadhyay... focuses on HDFC (Bank) as a way of telling India's growth story.

– *India Real Time* (*The Wall Street Journal*, India)

It's a sort of recent oral history of a financial institution. Tamal has set a new trend in the dissemination of knowledge.

– YV Reddy, former governor, Reserve Bank of India

Tamal is regarded for his incisive reasoning and analysis... It is time to welcome the arrival of a new author.

– Deepak Parekh, Chairman, HDFC

A fast-paced story, told in typical Tamal style. Unputdownable. Well-researched, well-written and extremely readable.

– K. V. Kamath, Chairman, ICICI Bank and Infosys

Tamal's sharp reporting instincts as well as eye for detail help him paint a profile that accurately reflects the original.

– T. N. NINAN, Chairman and Editorial Director
Business Standard